The short guide to international development

Nick Sage

First published in Great Britain in 2022 by

Policy Press, an imprint of
Bristol University Press
University of Bristol
1-9 Old Park Hill
Bristol
BS2 8BB
UK
t: +44 (0)117 374 6645
e: bup-info@bristol.ac.uk

Details of international sales and distribution partners are available at
policy.bristoluniversitypress.co.uk

To Mary, Sophie and Jonathan Sage
Thank you for your support

Contents

List of figures and tables

Figures

Tables

Abbreviations and acronyms

AIDS	acquired immunodeficiency syndrome
BRICS	Brazil, Russia, India, China, South Africa
DALY	disability-adjusted life year
EEB	European Environmental Bureau
FAO	Food and Agricultural Organization of the United Nations
FSIN	Food Security Information Network
GBD	Global Burden of Disease
GDI	Gender Development Index
GDP	gross domestic product
GEM	Gender Empowerment Measure
GGGI	Global Gender Gap Index
GHI	Global Hunger Index
GNI	gross national income
GNP	gross national product
HDI	Human Development Index
HIV	human immunodeficiency virus
HPI	Human Poverty Index
ICT	information and communications technology
ICT4D	information and communications technology for development
IDA	International Development Association
IHDI	Inequality-adjusted Human Development Index
IHME	Institute for Health Metrics and Evaluation
ILO	International Labour Organization
IMF	International Monetary Fund
INGO	international non-governmental organisation
IPL	international poverty line

LDC	least developed country
MDGs	Millennium Development Goals
MNC	multinational corporation
MPI	Multidimensional Poverty Index
NAM	non-aligned movement
NCD	noncommunicable disease
NEF	New Economics Foundation
NGO	non-governmental organisation
NIC	newly industrialising country
OECD	Organisation for Economic Co-operation and Development
OPHI	Oxford Poverty and Human Development Initiative
PHC	primary healthcare
PPP	purchasing power parity
PRB	Population Reference Bureau
SAP	structural adjustment programme
SARS	severe acute respiratory syndrome
SDGs	Sustainable Development Goals
SDSN	Sustainable Development Solutions Network (United Nations)
STWR	Share The World's Resources
TNC	transnational corporation
TWN	Third World Network
UNAIDS	Joint United Nations Programme on HIV/AIDS
UNCTAD	United Nations Conference on Trade and Development
UN DESA	United Nations Department of Economic and Social Affairs
UNDP	United Nations Development Programme
UNESCO	United Nations Educational, Scientific and Cultural Organization
UNFCCC	United Nations Framework Convention on Climate Change
UNFPA	United Nations Population Fund (formerly, United Nations Fund for Population Activities)

UNHCR	United Nations High Commissioner for Refugees
UNICEF	United Nations International Children's Emergency Fund
UNWTO	United Nations World Tourism Organization
UUKi	Universities UK International
WCED	World Commission on Environment and Development
WEF	World Economic Forum
WFP	World Food Programme
WHO	World Health Organization
WSIS	World Summit on the Information Society
WTO	World Trade Organization

Part I

Debating development

1

Introduction: international development in the 21st century

International development refers both to the broad processes of economic, social and political change that affect the world around us, and, more specifically, to the policies that are designed to address key development issues, such as global poverty, environmental concerns and global health pandemics. Such issues are often about saving lives, but transforming lives and changing the way we live are also increasingly significant for international development and building a sustainable future.

International development is a very important area of research and practice, which has progressed from the 20th into the 21st centuries. It is a wide-ranging field that has gone through many changes, and as an area of study it is marked by its interdisciplinary nature. Its combination of approaches and perspectives are derived from the social science disciplines of sociology, economics, geography, history, international relations and politics. The practice of international development also involves a variety of different approaches that have changed over time, notably with the rise of globalisation in recent decades. As a result, it is becoming clearer in the 21st century that development is not only about providing support for developing countries, but also about changing the world as a whole. This has become more apparent as globalisation has accelerated and created a more interconnected world that has reshaped the one that existed at the start of the development era in the mid-20th century. The challenges facing the entire world in the 21st century – notably, climate change, conflicts and pandemics – demonstrate the extent to which the developed and developing worlds are increasingly intertwined to the point at which sustainable development is a global necessity. For development to be truly successful, we have to find a way to live together peacefully on a sustainable planet.

In the third decade of the 21st century we live in a world where development issues are everywhere to be seen. On the one hand, a number of 'developing' countries have moved to a new status on the world stage, with some nation-states, notably China, India, Brazil and South Africa now described as 'emerging global powers'. On the other hand, there is strong evidence of continuing poverty and apparent lack of development to be found in many parts of what was once known as the Third World but has now become widely referred to as the Global South, with the poorest countries of the world today located predominantly in Africa (World Atlas, 2020). Issues of climate change have an impact on development, and, again, these have very much come to the fore in the 21st century, together with global health concerns and the consequences of conflict and wars in a number of countries in the developing world, which in turn have implications for the 'developed world' as evidenced by the flow of refugees and migrants across the world.

Why international development?

Contemporary development issues by their very nature tend to attract international attention and to generate international responses. This is one reason why the term 'international development' is particularly appropriate in referring both to the policy initiatives of international agencies in defining and addressing development issues, and to the study of development as an academic field of enquiry in the 21st century. Recent and current issues in development that have hit the news headlines worldwide include concerns about global population growth, global poverty and inequality, global health issues, refugee crises, famine and rising food prices.

World population will be approaching 10 billion by the middle of the century, four times higher than the population of 2.5 billion a century earlier in 1950. The highest rates of population growth are predicted for the developing countries and most of the global increase is attributable to a small number of countries in Asia and Africa, notably China, India and Nigeria. India is expected to surpass China and have the largest population in the world by 2027, while Nigeria's population is the most rapidly growing in the world and is projected to surpass that of the US to become the third largest in the world around the middle of the century (Roser, 2019). Whether or not these global trends are indicative of a world population crisis, or whether there will be a longer-term global fall in the birth rate in the second half of the century, which will stabilise the world population by the start of the 22nd century, as some forecasts suggest, it is clear that the still rapidly growing population in many parts of the developing world interconnects with other development issues, such as poverty, health, food and water security, and environmental change, to create immediate and growing problems.

The issue of poverty and attempts to eradicate extreme poverty and hunger have been at the top of the agenda for many international agencies concerned with development for some considerable time, and there has been remarkable progress in reducing the number people in the world living in extreme or absolute poverty by around one billion since 1982. However, closer inspection of the data produced by the World Bank reveals that while significant progress has been made in a number of areas with some countries, notably China, seeing the most significant reductions in poverty in recent times, other countries with rising populations have very high poverty rates, notably in sub-Saharan Africa which is home to more than half the world's extreme poor, with over 40 per cent of its population living in extreme poverty in 2020. Nigeria is a very striking case, it having one of the most rapidly growing populations in the world with worsening poverty levels posing a serious challenge to its future development. Around 79 million people in Nigeria were living below the poverty line in 2018 – 39 per cent of its population (World Bank, 2020a: 59). The reasons for the high levels of poverty are related to very high rates of population growth, but also to other development issues which have been given a high profile in recent times; notably, climate change and its impact on agricultural production and food prices. Another contributing factor is the displacement of people as a result of internal conflict: around two billion people today are estimated to be living in countries affected by fragility, conflict and violence. The impact on food insecurity and famine has been especially evident in several conflict-riven countries in Africa, with South Sudan experiencing a particularly severe and prolonged famine. Similarly, in the Middle East, the war in Yemen between the Saudi-backed government in exile and the Iranian-backed Houthi rebels who control much of the north of the country has seriously devastated food supplies and has resulted in many millions of people going hungry (UN News, 2020). Unexpected global issues, such as the outbreak of the coronavirus pandemic in 2020, have also undermined the progress that has been made in addressing hunger and poverty in the developing world.

Another related development issue that has received a good deal of international attention in recent years is public health, and in particular the rise of what have become known as global health issues. The worldwide spread of the previously unknown human immunodeficiency virus (HIV) and the HIV/AIDs pandemic which began in the 1980s was the trigger for a rising concern with 'global health' and 'global health security' and the setting up of international institutes to address these concerns. The World Health Organization had been founded in 1948, and later, specific ventures such as the UNAIDS programme were established to address the most prevalent and challenging contemporary health concerns. Despite significant progress in addressing the HIV/AIDs pandemic, 38 million people worldwide, predominantly located in parts of the developing world, notably sub-Saharan Africa, were estimated to be living with HIV in 2020 (UNAIDS, 2021).

Globalisation and the increasing movement of people around the globe resulted in new global health concerns hitting the headlines in the 21st century, particularly in relation to communicable diseases such as SARS (severe acute respiratory syndrome), the Ebola virus and the coronavirus. The outbreak of the coronavirus pandemic in 2020 soon accelerated into a massive global health concern, and also seriously undermined the progress that had been made in addressing hunger and poverty in the developing world. While such communicable diseases pose clear risks to the developing world in particular, other significant threats to health have become globalised less conspicuously. These include the risks posed by rapid industrialisation in parts of the developing world, environmental pollution, global warming, road traffic accidents and the global 'tobacco epidemic', all of which have contributed towards increasing the burden of non-communicable diseases in many developing countries. Continuing poverty, food insecurity, and lack of access to healthcare facilities exacerbate the problems, and for children the perinatal conditions closely associated with poverty, diarrhoeal diseases, pneumonia and other lower respiratory tract conditions have meant that a child born, for example, in Sierra Leone today is about thirty times more likely to die before the age of five than a child born in the UK. At the same time, interventions to promote development and to address health-related issues by national governments and international aid agencies have contributed towards positive improvements in health in many countries and a global rise in life expectancy.

Despite progress in some sectors, international development remains primarily an area of concern with many new issues to be addressed in an increasingly complex and interconnected global world. Towards the turn of the 21st century, David Korten, an international development practitioner, wrote that the world was entering a 'threefold human crisis' of 'deepening poverty', 'social disintegration' and 'environmental destruction' (Korten, 1995: 13). Three decades later we can see many aspects of the crisis playing out, and a fourth area of 'political destabilisation' can also be added as a result of the rise of international terrorism, fragile states, conflict and violence. A further consequence of conflicts such as those in Afghanistan, Yemen, Ethiopia and Libya is the refugee crisis and mass displacement of people that we have seen in recent years, with 2020 recording the highest-ever figures of over 48 million people displaced within their own countries and 34 million taking refuge in other countries. According to the United Nations High Commissioner for Refugees (UNHCR), forced displacement almost doubled between 2010 and 2020, and with at least 100 million people forcibly displaced it was defined as 'the decade of displacement'

(UNHCR, 2020: 4). One in every 113 people on the planet is now a refugee, and around the world someone is displaced every three seconds, forced from their homes by violence, war or persecution (Edmond, 2017). The UNHCR (2020) estimates that the developing regions host 85 per cent of the world's refugees, and the World Bank (2017a) estimates that 99 per cent of all internally displaced persons are located in developing countries. There are strong predictions that international migration is set to increase in the 21st century as a result of climate change in addition to the current factors which have increased the numbers of both refugees and economic migrants, such as war, conflict and poverty, and natural disasters such as tsunamis and hurricanes.

As the above examples illustrate, international development encompasses an ever-changing world in which the descriptive adjective 'international' takes on a particular significance in the contemporary global context.

Agendas, agencies and movements

International agendas and movements to address the kinds of issues described earlier have also become more prominent in recent years. Movements such as Make Poverty History, the Global Justice Movement, People's Climate Movement and the World Social Forum have played an important part in raising the profile of international development issues, while intergovernmental organisations such as the United Nations Development Programme, the International Development Association and the International Bank for Reconstruction and Development are major players in the global development arena. Meanwhile, the UN's Millennium Development Goals and more recently Sustainable Development Goals have served to set the international agenda for policy intervention. International non-governmental organisations such as ActionAid, Climate Action, the Association of Women's Rights in Development, One World, Practical Action, Amnesty International, Oxfam and Greenpeace, to name but a few of the leading international non-governmental organisations (NGOs) connected with development, have also played a significant role in promoting and addressing ongoing development-related issues. The involvement of various kinds of agencies in the development arena, and especially in the field of international aid, has not been without debate and controversy. Recent debates on aid have focused on whether aid actually promotes development in developing countries or rather serves the interests of the donors, and questions have been raised over the continuing provision of aid to emerging industrial counties such as India.

Debates and dilemmas

As the above examples demonstrate, international development is a highly topical area of concern in the increasingly interconnected world of the 21st century, but it is at the same time widely contested. There are many competing views on the specific components of development and debates about the essential type of development that should be pursued. Economic development is often prioritised, based on the assumption that economic growth will 'trickle-down' to benefit all, but this is contested by those who argue for more emphasis to be given to enhancing human wellbeing and promoting sociopolitical change through international development interventions. The complexity and contested nature of development is further accentuated by the fact that all countries are different, with distinctive cultures and histories, and political and geographical contexts that help to shape their particular course of development. Contrasting views on development are often informed by focusing on particular countries or geographical regions, and the various perspectives adopted may reflect the different interests and concerns of the range of actors and agencies involved in international development, including aid agencies, multilateral organisations, international NGOs, government departments and local communities, along with individual workers in the development field, academics and private companies.

This short guide to international development will explore the continuing debates and the changes that have occurred in our understanding of international development since the idea of development first emerged as a key concept on the international agenda in the aftermath of the Second World War. How and why has development, and the policies and related concepts surrounding it, changed over time, and is the idea of development in the 21st century a very different phenomenon from what it was perceived to be in its earlier incarnation? What is clear today is that international development as a field of study and policy arena poses many unresolved questions regarding the aims and objectives of development, while the implementation of strategies designed to bring about development has created many dilemmas regarding the best way forward to achieve their intended goals. For example, the modernisation and industrialisation of agriculture may boost the local economy and provide greater supplies of food for the local population, but it may primarily benefit transnational agricultural corporations and serve the international rather than local market, while at the same time displacing local farmers and communities. By its very nature development is both complex and ambiguous, creating many dilemmas and opening up a series of debates about contested issues.

Summary and looking forward

In many respects, international development has never been more relevant than it is today, with increasing global inequalities as the incomes of the world's rich elite and those living in poverty grow ever wider, growing environmental concerns over resource depletion and global climate change, and continuing issues associated with the impact of international migration and the refugee crisis of recent years. At the same time, with questions being raised about the nature of development and the ways in which the international agenda for development has been constructed from a predominantly Western standpoint, the relevance of international development in today's world may be open to doubt. It is universally recognised that we live in an increasingly globalised and interconnected world, but interpretations of the effects of globalisation on development are often inconsistent, reflecting different paradigms and generalisations based on specific cases. One of the positive outcomes of globalisation, for example, according to its proponents, is the often-cited reduction in global poverty in the 21st century; this, however, is largely an effect of developments in a few countries with very large populations, notably China and India, and overlooks the extent to which poverty has failed to be adequately addressed in many developing countries of the Global South. International development and globalisation have become increasingly linked together in ways that are seen as both positive and negative, but to properly evaluate the different viewpoints and perspectives, clarity in the definition of key ideas and concepts is required.

We begin, therefore, with Chapters 2 and 3 looking at what is meant by 'development', the debate surrounding the concept, how development is mapped and measured, and the scope of the field of enquiry defined as 'international development'. The remainder of Part I considers competing theoretical perspectives on development, the dilemmas of development in the 21st century, and the role of agencies in the international development arena, with reference to a range of contemporary themes and debates. Thus, Part I sets out the framework for exploring the key policy issues in development that are discussed in Part II; these include population, food and famine, poverty and inequality, health and education, the role of digital technologies in the developing world, gender and development, and environmental issues linked to sustainable development. The final chapter concludes by summarising the current state of international development and looking to the future to consider both the prospects for development in the coming decades and the changing academic context for understanding the trajectories of development in the 21st century.

Overview of *The Short Guide to International Development*

- Explores the key themes and issues in international development in contemporary and historical perspectives, with reference to the political as well as the social and economic dimensions of development.
- Considers how far different intellectual traditions and theoretical perspectives have advanced our understanding of international development.

- Highlights the extent to which 'development' is a contested concept, and reveals the many dilemmas of development in practice.
- Examines the multi-faceted nature of international development and the synergistic relations between the social, cultural, political and economic dimensions of development.
- Shows that the study of development should not be confined to the 'developing countries' of the 'Third World' or 'South', but recognise instead that development is a truly global phenomenon and the processes of globalisation are integral to our understanding of international development today.

Note

All monetary values are in US dollars.

2

The challenge of development: from economic to sustainable development

> Development is [...] a far-reaching, continuous and positively evaluated change in the totality of human experience. (Harrison, 1988: xiii)

The idea of development poses many challenges, both as a concept and as a practical means of shaping society. In this chapter we examine the ways in which the idea of development has evolved over time, why the idea has been vigorously contested, and what this means for the understanding and practice of international development today.

What is development?

Defining development is important, not only in the interests of clarity in public and academic debate, but also because it is a value-laden concept which has implications for development agendas and policies. As such it has tended to be a highly contested concept, both in theory and in practice, and definitions have been challenged and changed over time. Development, as Jonathan Crush (1995: 8) stated in *Power of Development*, 'has never been impervious to challenge and resistance'.

To start with a dictionary definition of development, the Oxford Dictionary refers to 'a specified state of growth and advancement'. What is clear from such definitions is that 'development' is different from 'change' in that it implies a move in a positive or more advanced direction whereas change can be in any direction. The concept is often given physiological connotations in that development is seen as unfolding in a given direction, going through various progressive stages of change and growth rather like a living organism. In applying this general definition to the specific field of international development, reference is often made to Robert Chambers' (1997) simple definition of development as 'good change'. However, while there may be agreement on this broad definition, the question of what constitutes 'good change' is very much open to question and highly contested. It also raises the further question of whether 'good change' implies an interconnected process of social, political and economic change that has a positive impact on the human experience, as David Harrison's definition of development at the beginning of this chapter clearly indicates.

Again, while Harrison's definition is a useful one that recognises the all-encompassing nature of development, the question arises of how such change is evaluated and by whom. This in turn brings into play questions of power and vision. If development is to be seen as a valued state, to what extent are those views shared by members of the development community, and who decides which aspects of change take priority? Here we encounter an important distinction that needs to be drawn between intentional and unintentional development. Is development to be seen as a spontaneous process of change over time in which the old order progressively gives way to the new, or as a deliberate sequence of actions designed to achieve developmental goals? Not all academics in the field of international development agree with the idea that development is about 'positively evaluated change'. Gilbert Rist, for example, argues that, due to its positive connotation, the term 'development' is deceptive. In reality, he asserts, development exploits the poor and destroys the natural environment in the interests of wealth creation that benefits the rich. From Rist's (2014) perspective, development is a spurious and misleading concept which conceals its predominantly negative attributes in the global context of a changing and modernising world. For most academics and practitioners in the field, however, the concept of development is one which remains widely used in the affirmative sense of the term referring to 'good change'.

Perspectives on development: the four Ps

To further explore the various meanings of the concept of development, we need to consider the four main perspectives that have been adopted in identifying what development is about. These are referred to here as the 'four Ps': process, project, prospect and participation.

The first of these views development as a **process**. From this perspective, development is essentially an ongoing historical process in which social change takes place over a long period of time as a result of the internal dynamics of the social and economic systems. The historical development of capitalism is generally viewed as the primary engine of change, and this in turn gives rise to a more all-encompassing process of immanent development that has benefits for the whole of society.

Immanent development contrasts with the idea of imminent or intentional development where deliberate actions are taken to promote development. From the imminent development perspective, development is not so much a process as a **project**. Interventions in the name of development are designed to promote change and to bring about transformations for the benefit of society; for example, by addressing poverty and improving health, education, gender equality and environmental security. This has been referred to as 'doing development' (Thomas, 2000: 40).

A third perspective on the concept of development views it as a **prospect**, a forward-looking vision of a desirable state of being. As with the definition of development as 'good change', there is scope for considerable divergence in the visions held by academics, practitioners and development communities. For some, the prospect of economic growth and modernisation may be paramount in their vision of development; for others, social aspects of development such as living harmoniously together and free from social inequalities and conflict may be equally or more important. What is shared, however, is the idea of a positive and tangible vision of the future that is encapsulated in the concept of development.

A fourth view sees development as being essentially about **participation**. The emphasis here is not on historical processes, interventionist projects by governments and the international community, or prospective visions of the future, but on active popular participation by the people concerned. As a popular people-centred movement, development is in the hands of the people who determine its direction, while at the same time their active engagement is itself indicative of development through empowerment. This perspective on development brings into play questions of politics and power, and challenges conventional top-down views of development as being under the control of governments, intergovernmental organisations and international development agencies.

History of development: from escaping the past to facing the future

The four Ps with their different definitions of development as outlined above have been associated with different stages in the history of international development. This section examines the historical sequence of changing approaches to development, marked by changing perceptions over the decades and the shift from viewing development as a way of breaking away from the past to the more recent focus on addressing the concerns of the future.

Post-1945: the era of development begins

The modern 'era of development', as it became known, started after the end of the Second World War and was firmly established in subsequent decades, with the 1960s being declared the 'decade of development' by the United Nations. The origins of this era have been attributed to the need for national reconstruction after the world war, the break-up of former colonial empires and the emergence of newly independent countries in the developing world, and the start of the Cold War between East and West in which both sides sought to influence development in what became known as the 'Third World'. The person to whom the launch of this new era of development is accredited is Harry S. Truman (1949) in his inaugural speech as president of the United States, in which he declared that, as the developed Western world, 'We must embark on a bold new programme for making the benefits of our scientific advances and industrial progress available for the improvement and growth of underdeveloped areas.'

The speech clearly identified a programme designed to escape the old imperialist past and to move forward to a future marked by economic growth and improvement in people's lives. The modern era of development was thus ceremoniously launched, with the aim of achieving development through economic growth, industrial progress and scientific advancement

1950s–1960s: the golden years of development

The 'golden age of capitalism', a period of economic prosperity extending from the end of the Second World War in 1945 to the early 1970s, marked the achievement of high and sustained levels of economic growth and productivity, especially in Western Europe and East Asia, together with low unemployment. It was also associated with the emergence of new international institutions such as the International Monetary Fund (IMF) and the World Bank as part of the Bretton Woods monetary system, and the United Nations Conference on Trade and Development. With the birth of many new nations in the 1950s, and increasingly in the 1960s as a result of decolonisation, there was considerable optimism that the post-war decades would see development flourish throughout the Third World following the model of Western industrialisation and modernisation, and that these would be the 'golden years' of development. Building on the idea of the Marshall Plan for the reconstruction of Western Europe after the Second World War, the United Nations promoted the idea of the West providing assistance to the Third World to stimulate the process of structural transformation and economic growth that would bring the benefits of development to all. In January 1961, the United

Nations unveiled its strategy for the 'first decade of development' to lessen the gap between developed and underdeveloped countries, to speed up the processes of development and alleviate poverty. A key element here was modernisation, 'to accelerate progress towards self-sustaining growth of the economy' (UN General Assembly Resolution, 1961: 17).

Central to the idea of capitalism and development as an **historical process of structural transformation** is that progress requires a transition from 'traditional' to 'modern' society, and this involves a move from simple to more advanced and complex technologies, from human and animal power to machines, from self-sufficiency to market-oriented production, from farms and villages to towns and cities, and from traditional to modern ways of thinking. While it was generally accepted that multilateral organisations such as the International Bank for Reconstruction and Development could play a role in supporting this process, there was a sharp divide between the neoliberal and structuralist approaches. Neoliberals believed the market should be free and left to its own devices, which in turn would stimulate the economy and promote the forms of transition described here, while the structuralist view held that regulation and some degree of intervention by the state was necessary. In the 1950s and 1960s the latter view, influenced by Keynesian economic theory, held sway, and the idea of what would later be termed the 'developmental state' took hold. The kind of active interventions required by the state included actions to stimulate economic activity by investing in public works and infrastructure, to raise productivity and increase exports, and to improve levels of education. Import substitution industrialisation (ISI) was also widely seen as a beneficial form of state intervention.[1] Development in this period was very much about promoting long-term processes of modernisation and industrialisation with both the markets and the state having key roles to play. Promoting economic growth and modernisation would in

---

[1] ISI was a strategy used by developing countries to decrease their dependence on imports from developed countries by introducing import tariffs and creating newly formed and protected domestic industries.

turn eliminate poverty and raise standards of living generally. The new nationalist elites in the developing world largely adopted this view on coming to power, and it also gained currency in the academic field of development and in the new multilateral institutions with development agendas such as the World Bank and the International Monetary Fund (IMF). The emphasis on equating development with economic growth was reflected in the use of economic indicators such as gross domestic product (GDP), and later GDP per capita and gross national income, to measure and compare the levels of development in different countries.

In this very positive view of development, while the more 'developed' countries of the world are held up as models for 'developing' countries to aspire to, there is no end vision as societies are seen as becoming forever more modern as their economies continue to grow. While the first 'development decade' of the 1960s gave some cause for optimism that the historical process of capitalist development would roll out across the world, there were also growing concerns that development was not a smooth process of change bringing benefits to all. Even if progress was inevitable and modernisation would eventually be advantageous for all of society, in the short to medium term there were winners and losers of development. Recognition of the need to move beyond focusing on economic growth and to address the downside of progress resulted in the emergence of attempts to focus on specific issues, such as poverty alleviation, health and education. The United Nations Development Programme was established in 1966 to meet development challenges and develop local capacity, and aimed to address issues such as poverty reduction, environmental concerns and social development. International non-governmental organisations were also growing in number and significance, and together with intergovernmental and multilateral aid agencies shifted the focus from the longer-term historical process of development to shorter- and medium-term goals. The idea of **development as a project** began to take hold with the aim of setting realistic targets for the foreseeable future. By setting the outcomes to be achieved by 'doing development', it would also be possible to measure progress.

1970s: development in crisis: revisioning development

The idea of measuring progress in relation to clearly defined targets became widely accepted in the 1970s, as the limitations of existing approaches to development, and the failure of development programmes to adequately address global poverty in particular, called into question prevailing assumptions about the 'trickle-down' benefits of modernisation and economic growth. Modernisation theory was heavily critiqued and an opposing perspective on development known as dependency theory became prominent and enjoyed its heyday in the 1970s, with its more radical exponents arguing for a radical break with the modern world-system of capitalism (Wallerstein, 1979). For practitioners of international development, however, the introduction of a **basic needs** approach to development provided an alternative way forward by revisioning development to focus on the need to balance economic growth and modernisation with redistribution to those in most need. Satisfying basic needs means enhancing wellbeing and achieving this by meeting key indicators, such as longevity, infant survival, educational attainment, and so on. Objective assessments for measuring wellbeing were crucial in establishing whether the development project was fulfilling its essential purpose.

The basic needs approach focused in particular on addressing 'absolute poverty', defined as the absolute minimum resources necessary for long-term physical wellbeing. Those resources could then be identified, mainly in terms of essential items of consumption, notably food, water, clothing and shelter. The poverty line was then defined as the amount of income required to satisfy those needs. In addition to the minimum requirements of private consumption, the essential services of collective consumption were also identified: for example, sanitation, healthcare, education, public transport, and so on. The basic needs approach was introduced by the International Labour Organization (ILO) at the World Employment Conference in 1976, which proposed the satisfaction of basic human needs as the overriding objective of national and international development policy. The basic needs approach not only became a central organising principle for development work in the ILO but was also widely endorsed by governments and organisations from all over the world, and increasingly influenced the programmes and policies of major international development agencies. The **prospective vision** offered by this approach was one in which there would be a more balanced approach to development; rather than waiting for the benefits of economic growth to trickle-down to poor people, basic needs could be addressed immediately to improve their state of wellbeing.

The late 1970s also saw the establishment of the Independent Commission on International Development Issues, headed by Willy Brandt, the German chancellor. The Commission was designed to address the failures of the global economy and to find ways to reduce the disparities between the developed and the developing parts of the world – or the 'rich North' and the 'developing South' as the Commission referred to them. Its first report, *North–South: A Program for Survival*, gave primary emphasis to the international issues of food and agricultural development, aid, energy, trade, international monetary and financial reform, and global negotiations, with the intention of resolving the divide between North and South. The Brandt Report, as it became known, also sought solutions to other problems common to both North and South, including the environment, the arms race, population growth, and the uncertain prospects of the global economy. Since these problems concerned the survival of all nations, the Brandt Commission's recommendations emphasised the advantages of cooperation and a shared vision for the future, and were presented as a structural programme to address the world's problems collectively. At the same time, the Brandt Report recognised the need for emergency measures to address the immediate needs of those suffering from absolute poverty in the developing countries of the South. In this regard it endorsed the basic needs approach while going well beyond it to emphasise the overarching international context in which North and South needed to work together in a reciprocal relationship. This was a genuinely new vision of development, and one which attracted considerable attention with the Brandt Report becoming the best-selling book to date on international development. However, the proposals in the report were never fully adopted, due in part to the continuing Cold War but also to what has been described as 'a collective lack of political will among world leaders' at the time (STWR, 2006).

1980s: the rise of neoliberalism and the lost decade for development

The views of both the Brandt Commission and the basic needs approach were overshadowed in the 1980s by the revival of neoliberalism, which saw efficient markets as the key mechanism for satisfying needs. Neoliberalism underpinned the structural adjustment programmes (SAPs) of the 1980s, which were imposed on highly indebted developing countries under the auspices of the IMF and World Bank in the wake of the international debt crisis that started at the end of the 1970s. As the debt crisis took hold this was a very difficult decade for developing countries, and it was exacerbated by the rise of neoliberalism in the Western world, which used the IMF and World Bank to pressure those countries to free their markets and reduce the role of the state as part of the imposed SAPs. Rather than perceiving development as an ongoing project, it was now envisaged as the end product of allowing the freedom of the market to provide the necessary conditions for economic growth. Austerity measures and rapid budget adjustments went ahead regardless of the high social and economic costs for development. According to a report by the UN Department of Economic and Social Affairs (UN DESA, 2017), this 'specific development narrative' imposed on developing countries had seriously negative long-term implications: in Latin America and Africa, for example, the economy took more than a decade to recover.

As a result of this failure in many parts of the world, the 1980s became known as the 'lost decade' for development. For people in many countries this was a decade of development going backwards: government spending was cut, and the provision of services to address basic needs (for example, through free healthcare and education), was badly affected. However, this was not true for all regions of the developing world. While East Asian countries varied greatly in their economic policies, they shared a common feature: the central role of the state in leveraging markets to promote development. The revival of the developmental state approach and the successful experience of countries in East Asia provided a marked contrast to the lost decade of development in Latin America and Africa.

The lost decade for development also saw the emergence of a direct critique of the prevailing Western perspective on development: it was seen not as a grand vision of the future for developing countries, as its proponents maintained, but as a **discourse** imposed on those countries by the West, which ignored their own views and ways of life and subordinated them to a Western vision, which, in turn, maintained the control of the West over the rest of the world.

1990s: the challenges of human development

Following the collapse of communism in Eastern Europe and the Soviet Union, and the proclaimed 'end of history' (Fukuyama, 1992), neoliberalism was unrivalled and went through what became known as a 'second wave' in the 1990s. At the same time, however, there was a growing critique of the neoliberal discourse, sometimes referred to as the Washington Consensus, and this found its most radical expression in the idea that the whole Western enterprise of development had done far more harm than good and should be 'consigned to the dustbin of history', as Wolfgang Sachs noted. His was a bluntly profound call for development to be abandoned: 'The idea of development stands like a ruin in the intellectual landscape [...] the hopes and ideas that made the idea fly, are now exhausted: development has grown obsolete' (Sachs, 1992: 1).

Rejecting development meant that a new kind of politics and new strategies for emancipation would need to be found to avoid the imposition of Western ideas of progress on the rest of the world. Those who did not subscribe to this radical departure from the very idea of development were nevertheless motivated by the 'lost decade' to reconceptualise development and move the development agenda in a new direction. This was a move towards a more **people-centred** form of development based on local **participation**, which would result in individual and collective **empowerment**. This became known as 'popular development' (Brohman, 1996). A key contributor to developing this new vision of development was Amartya Sen. His **capabilities** approach envisaged development as multidimensional and about making improvements in people's lives that would expand their capability. Development is not defined as a growth in income, or solely in terms of improvements in areas of basic needs such as health and education, but as an expansion of capabilities. Development is about wellbeing but it also about giving people the freedom to lead a full life and to realise their potential. In his best-known work, *Development as Freedom* (Sen, 1999), he argued that the expansion of freedom is both a primary goal and a principal means of development.

Sen's approach was influential in informing the concept of 'human development' which was adopted by the United Nations Development Programme (UNDP) in the 1990s. The **human development** approach is so-called because it moves beyond the earlier, predominantly economic perspectives on development and focuses on the human experience of life in its fully rounded form. It is a people-centred approach to development which requires participation and empowerment. Following Sen's emphasis on the need to expand human capabilities, human development centred on the idea of widening choices, fulfilling human potential and guaranteeing human rights. The UNDP published its first *Human Development Report* in 1990 and defined human development as 'the process of enlarging people's choices', thereby allowing them to 'lead a long and healthy life, to be educated and to enjoy a decent standard of living'. The UNDP definition also identifies additional choices, which 'include political freedom, other guaranteed human rights, and various ingredients of self-respect'. Human development is therefore viewed as a process of both widening people's choices and raising their level of wellbeing. At the same time, the UNDP (1997: 15) focus on poverty was maintained because 'if human development is about enlarging choices, poverty means that opportunities and choices most basic to human development are denied'.

The emergence of the concept of human development marked an important shift in the perspective adopted by international development agencies and a different approach to 'doing development', one which was reflected in the setting up of the Human Development

Index (HDI) by the UNDP to provide a way of measuring and comparing levels of human development in different countries. The shift in perspective could also be seen in the World Bank (1991) with the publication of its *World Development Report 1991: The Challenge of Development*, which for the first time acknowledged that development should be defined not only as economic development bringing improvements in living standards, but also in a broader sense to include progress towards greater equality of opportunity, and political and civil liberties. The *World Development Report* for the following year was subtitled *Development and the Environment*, and the year after that (1993) *Investing in Health*. This marked a significant change in conceptions of development, away from the more narrowly focused orthodox economic views, as the new century approached.

The 1990s also saw the emergence, alongside the concept of human development, of the related concept of **human security**. This marked the extension of the concept of security from state security to the security of individual human beings, and gained wider recognition and a clear definition in the UNDP (1994) *Human Development Report*. The report's definition highlights the need for conventional security to be supplemented in seven key areas, to include economic security, food security, health security, environmental security, personal security, community security, and finally political security by which was meant honouring basic human rights. This was a further significant evolution in the understanding of what is meant by development, and one which became more influential in the new century.

2000s: moving towards global development

A move towards greater coordination among those 'doing development' became the basis for advancing development projects centred on human development in the early years of the 21st century, and global targets such as the **Millennium Development Goals** (MDGs) were employed to establish a clear vision of development and to emphasise specific short- to medium-term goals for such projects. The MDGs arose out of the United Nations Millennium Summit in the year 2000, and carried forward the idea of human development with eight specific goals that incorporated areas of human security, such as protecting the environment and improving health and wellbeing. The MDGs were also notable for the inclusion of gender equality and the empowerment of women. Specific dates were set for reaching each of the set goals, with 2015 as the final date for all. The MDGs clearly identified development as a project and one that could be shared by international development agencies, governments and non-governmental organisations.

This approach evolved in the second decade of the new millennium, to recognise the growing need to further incorporate human security into development and to widen the scope of the MDGs to include the concept of sustainable development. The idea of **sustainable development** is people-centred and sees the establishment of self-supporting social and economic systems as key elements of a sustainable society. The concept had its origins in the report published by the United Nations World Commission on Environment and Development in 1987, titled *Our Common Future*, which defined sustainable development as the kind of development that 'meets the needs of the present without compromising the ability of future generations to meet their own needs' (Brundtland Commission, 1987: 87). Central to this were environmental concerns, which the United Nations (UN, 1992) Rio Declaration saw as creating a world in which human beings could lead 'a healthy and productive life in harmony with nature'. Based on this understanding of sustainable development, the UNDP introduced the **Sustainable Development Goals** (SDGs) in 2015 to replace the MDGs. The ultimate aim of the SDGs was to end poverty, protect the planet, and create peace and prosperity for all through a revitalised global partnership as part of a new sustainable development agenda with specific targets to be met by 2030. Human security has also been firmly incorporated into the sustainable development agenda. Broadly defined by the United Nations as the right of people to live in freedom and dignity, free from poverty and despair, human security combines both 'freedom from want' and 'freedom from fear'.

The evolving conceptualisation of development, both in theory and in the ways in which the concept is applied in practice by international organisations and development agencies, has resulted in a significant shift in perspective. Increasingly in the 21st century, there has been a move away from seeing development as a way of abandoning traditional society and replacing it with a modern Western version of society, towards viewing it as a way of addressing the complex and different needs of people in different societies. The emphasis on development has therefore tended to move away from 'what the "experts" say development is, to what people seeking "development" want it to be' (Kingsbury et al, 2016: 7). This in turn, together with the rise of environmental concerns in a globalising world, and a greater concern with human security and 'freedom from fear' as well as 'freedom from want', has turned the perspective more towards facing and surviving the future than the earlier view of escaping the past to catch up with the modern present.

There is also greater recognition that the goals of development are universal and are not limited to 'developing countries'. Development has become increasingly global in scope. Not only is there seen to be a need for all countries to work together whatever their level of development to ensure the future of humanity in an increasingly interdependent world, but also the concerns of international development are seen to extend beyond the developing world, with issues such as poverty, inequality, human rights and global environmental change affecting people in every country of the world. In this sense too, contemporary perspectives on development differ from those of the 20th century and the idea of 'global development' has begun to move centre stage.

The 21st century has also seen more attention being given to 'popular' development, a bottom-up rather than top-down approach with visions of development coming from the local communities and grassroots movements for change. In this view, **participation** becomes an essential aspect of development, not just as a means to an end but also as an end in itself, to create a more flexible and meaningful approach that recognises the contextuality of development and the interplay of objective conditions and subjective concerns. This takes the idea of people-centred development a significant step further. Popular conceptions of development and grassroots movements for social change emerged in many developing countries in the last three decades of the 20th century, but gained further impetus in the first decades of the 21st century, notably with the 'pink tide' in Latin America, which saw many movements for social justice – indigenous movements, women's movements and environmental movements – gather strength. Popular movements of this kind have sought to create new forms of participation, often breaking with conventional forms of politics, which would give people greater control over decisions affecting their lives.

The rise of popular grassroots conceptions of development, and the idea that subjective wellbeing should be considered alongside objective wellbeing in many areas, such as health, work and human security, has also influenced the new approaches taken by multilateral development agencies and international NGOs, all of which will have an impact on future development programmes.

Summary and conclusion

As we have seen, development is not a simple or static concept. Different perspectives on 'what is development?' have evolved over the seven decades since the start of the modern era of development, during which the concept has taken on different meanings. Development remains a contested and equivocal idea, but one which is still very widely used. While some reject the idea altogether as reflecting a Western ideological discourse, it remains a key concept for both academics and practitioners in relation to the contemporary themes and issues identified in the Introduction to this book. The evolution of the concept is shown most clearly in the transition from viewing development primarily in economic terms towards a more people-centred notion of human development. At the same time, there has been a shift from viewing development as a way of escaping the past, and instead towards addressing the concerns of the future, particularly as currently expressed in the idea of sustainable development. For development to be sustainable there must be intergenerational equity to meet the needs of both present and future generations, and in today's interdependent world many aspects of sustainable development are international and increasingly global, making global development a key concept for the 21st century.

KEY POINTS SUMMARY

- The concept of 'development' is powerful and widely used, but also complex and contested.
- There are four different perspectives on the concept of development: the four Ps which alternatively view development as an ongoing historical **process**, as a **project** promoting change for the benefit of society, as a **prospect** with positive and tangible views of the future, and as a form of active popular **participation** in development projects.
- The main focus of development has gone through a series of different stages since the start of the modern era of development: from economic and structural transformation to human development and security, and most recently towards meeting the goal of sustainable development.
- Development is not only about finding solutions to present-day problems, but also about looking to the challenges of the future.
- The rise of the concept of sustainable development makes it necessary to look at the world as a whole in the global age of the 21st century.

KEY READING GUIDE

Overviews of the concept of development and the main challenges that the world faces can be found in most core texts on development. Good examples include: Kingsbury et al, *International Development: Issues and Challenges* (2016); McMichael, *Development and Social Change: A Global Perspective* (2016); and Willis, *Theories and Practices of Development* (2021). There is some overlap between the various texts, but also differences in their interpretations of the idea of development and the key issues that need to be addressed. To explore development and related concepts further it is also worth consulting books which take a concept-oriented approach, such as Desai and Potter, *The Companion to Development Studies* (2014), and Sachs, *The Development Dictionary: A Guide to Knowledge and Power* (2019). United Nations organisations and the World Bank have produced many documents and reports, often on an annual basis, related to development, and these reflect a number of the changing trends and issues that have marked the various decades of the development era. These include, for example, the UNDP *Human Development Report*, with its first edition in 1990 addressing the *Concept and Measurement of Human Development*, and the 2020 edition looking towards *The Next Frontier: Human Development and the Anthropocene*. The *World Development Report*, produced annually by the World Bank since 1978, similarly reflects changing concerns and challenges related to development. The 1994 report focused on *Infrastructure for Development*, while the 2010 report addressed *Development and Climate Change*, and the 2021 report addressed the global COVID-19 pandemic: *From Crisis to Green, Resilient and Inclusive Recovery* (2021a). These reports, which are all available online, are important documents for exploring the changing nature of development and the challenges facing the world in the 21st century.

3

From the Third World to the Global South: mapping and measuring development

In this chapter we examine the ways in which development has been visualised and mapped, both literally in the form of geographical maps and metaphorically in the application of labels to refer to different levels of development and their locations. We then move on to consider the various ways in which development has been measured and how the indicators used to measure development have changed over time, just as definitions and approaches to development have been transformed as we saw in Chapter 2.

Where in the world is development?

As with the concept of development, the terms used to describe and identify the people and places that are the focus of the study and practice of international development have also been hotly contested. Changes over time in the labelling of different parts of the world and sections of the world population similarly reflect the evolution of thinking about the nature of development, international relationships, and issues such as world poverty and inequality.

As noted in the previous chapter, the modern concept of development is often associated with President Truman's 1949 inaugural address as US president when he referred to 'underdeveloped areas' of the world, which he identified as those countries in Africa,

Asia and Latin America that had formerly been under European colonial rule. The term continues to be used to this day and juxtaposes 'underdeveloped' states or countries against those that are deemed to be 'developed'. The latter are generally understood to be those that are modern, scientifically advanced and industrialised, thereby providing a universal standard by which the level of development in underdeveloped countries may be measured. Critics of the term argue that it was based on a Western-centric idea which focused on what other countries lacked. Not only did the term have demeaning connotations, but it also gave priority to a particular form of development centred on economic growth to emulate the Western model. Some critics, however, have employed the term to provide a counter-argument that the lack of development in underdeveloped countries was a product of the processes of exploitation by the developed countries – what Andre Gunder Frank (1966) referred to as 'the development of underdevelopment'.

Emergence of the Third World

The 1950s saw the emergence of a new term to describe those areas and countries that had previously been referred to as the underdeveloped areas of the world. In 1952 the French demographer and historian Alfred Sauvy coined the term *tiers monde* (third world) to refer to countries outside the two major power blocs of the time, the capitalist West and the communist East, or the First World and the Second World. Sauvy (1952) saw the Third World as a way of identifying a diverse set of countries that shared in common their exclusion from power and influence in the world (Figure 3.1). The term carried a positive connotation in that it brought together under the banner of the Third World a range of countries with different histories and development trajectories that were striving for a place in the world.

The establishment of the non-aligned movement (NAM) following the Bandung Conference of African and Asian states in 1955 brought a sense of political unity to countries outside the two major power blocs, and the term 'Third World' continued to convey for some years the idea of a positive and forward-looking approach to development.

Figure 3.1: Map of the 'three worlds'

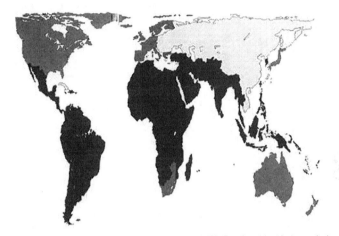

Source: *New Internationalist* magazine (November 1979). Reprinted by kind permission of *New Internationalist*. Copyright New Internationalist. www.newint.org

Julius Nyerere (1979), the first president of Tanzania following independence, was a prominent figure in the NAM, embracing it as a symbol of Third World unity and a way of reshaping the international geopolitical and economic order. Over time, however, the term 'Third World' has taken on rather more negative connotations and has been seen by many as a pejorative and condescending label to apply to particular countries or areas of the world. It is also seen by its critics as implying a hierarchical division of the world in much the same way as the term 'underdeveloped areas' did. An alternative term which played on words and emerged in the 1960s was 'Two-Thirds World'. This refers to the fact that the majority of the world's population live in those areas that are generally seen as denoting the field of international development, but avoids the negative connotations of Third World by defining this part of the world in terms of what it is, rather than what it lacks. However, although it gained some currency, it was never as widely employed as the term it sought to replace.

Although the designation of certain countries and areas of the world as being part of the Third World predominated for many years, this never precluded the use of alternative or related terms to offer a more nuanced classification. The term 'Fourth World', for example, came into existence to supplement and refine the concept of the Third World. It was introduced in the 1970s to refer to the internal colonisation and suppression of the rights of indigenous minorities such as the Aboriginal peoples. Unlike the Third World, the Fourth World is not spatially bounded in the same way, and Fourth World populations can be found in First World countries. However, another use of the term 'Fourth World' later emerged with reference to countries in extreme socioeconomic turmoil as a result of being severely poverty stricken and experiencing acute economic problems or subject to serious internal conflict and political fragility. The term gained traction with the publication of George Manuel's (1974) *The Fourth World: An Indian Reality*.

The continuing relevance of the term 'Third World' was seriously called into question with the fall of the Berlin Wall in 1989 and the beginning of the end of the communist power bloc. The categories of First World and Second World became redundant, but the term 'Third World' continued to be widely used to refer to those areas of the world that were classified as defining the scope of international development in theory and in practice. Evidence of this can be seen, for example, in the continuing existence of the international advocacy agency Third World Network (TWN), and the academic international development journal *Third World Quarterly*. The term has also been retained in the titles of a number of leading books in the field, including Howard Handelman's *The Challenge of Third World Development*, on the grounds that, unlike the terms 'underdeveloped' or 'developing' that refer to the state of specific countries or regions, the term 'Third World' 'makes no value judgment or predictions' about development (Handelman, 2013: 3). Over time, however, the use of the term has gradually reduced, both in academic and practitioner circles, to be replaced by terms which do not refer to a tripartite division of the world and carry rather different connotations. The alternative term 'Majority World' is a good example of the kind of label that has been invented for this purpose. A successor to Two-Thirds World (and later, Three-Fourths World), which reflected the shifting balance of the global population, the label 'Majority World' was more flexible in this regard but continued to highlight the fact that the people included in this category make up the majority of humankind. It also sharply implied that there was a Minority World with disproportionate power over the majority of the world's people. The term 'Majority World' gained currency in the early 1990s and continues to be used in the present day.

The developing world and emerging countries

Many other terms emerged in the 1970s and in subsequent decades to identify the areas of the world that were in need of development or where development was taking off. The label 'less developed country' was often applied in place of Third World country. The growing use of the terms 'developing world' and 'developing countries' implied ongoing progress and moved away from the negative connotations of describing countries as being underdeveloped, but continued to imply a hierarchical split between the developing and the developed worlds. However, the words were never clearly defined. The United Nations and the World Bank both employed these terms but no formal definition of a developing country or the developing world was ever produced.

Measurement of levels of development in different developing countries was initially confined to economic indices such as gross domestic product (GDP) or gross national income (GNI) per capita as introduced by the World Bank, but other indicators of development were incorporated into an index of socioeconomic development introduced by the United Nations in the early 1970s. This resulted in the identification of what the UN Economic and Social Council termed the 'least developed countries' as determined by a combination of their low GNI per capita, scarcity of domestic financial resources, and weak human and institutional capacities as reflected in indicators of nutrition, health, education and literacy. At the other end of the spectrum, terms such as 'emerging markets' and 'emerging countries' came into existence and were employed to describe those countries that were showing positive signs of economic growth and industrial transformation. Some of these were given the title of 'newly industrialising countries', notably the Four Asian Tigers of Hong

Kong, Singapore, South Korea and Taiwan in the early 1970s, and later countries such as Mexico, Brazil, China, India, South Africa, Thailand and Malaysia were added to the list. The use of the term 'emerging' to describe these countries conveyed a sense of optimism for the future that was lacking in the labels 'underdeveloped' and 'Third World' that continued to be applied to many countries.

Critics of the prevailing discourse on development, such as the proponents of dependency theory and world-systems analysis, produced their own terms to describe what were more widely referred to as developed and developing parts of the world. The world-systems approach divided the world into 'core' and 'periphery', but also introduced the idea of a 'semi-periphery' located between the core and periphery of the world-system, thereby acknowledging that countries could move in both directions by moving into and out of the semi-peripheral middle ground. It is therefore possible to see in both the mainstream and radical approaches to development an acceptance of the need to develop terminology that recognises the possibility of transition from one state of development to another. The terms 'developing world' and 'developing countries' continue to be widely used in the international development literature and by international and multilateral organisations including the United Nations and the World Bank. As they have never been precisely defined, there has been no need to formally update their meaning as they can be flexibly used in accordance with changing circumstances and understandings of what is meant by development.

Road to the Global South

The 1980s saw the introduction of a new label to refer to developing countries that emphasised geographical location over other characteristics and therefore did not carry the connotations of other terminology. The new label 'South' appeared to be relatively neutral, although once again it was counterposed to another designated marker, namely 'North'. The terms were given prominence by the publication of *North–South: A Program for Survival*, produced by the International Commission on International Development Issues chaired by the then German chancellor, Willy Brandt (1980). The line on the map running between the North and the South, which became known as the Brandt line, was essentially a line between the northern and southern hemispheres and between the richer countries of the North and the poorer countries of the South, which carefully skirted around Australia and New Zealand in the southern hemisphere (Figure 3.2). It graphically illustrated where in the world development is and where it is most needed.

The use of the term 'South' was taken up more widely in the field of international development, but its limitations became increasingly evident as some of the countries in the South transformed into emerging and newly industrialising countries. China, for example, has undergone a massive transformation in the years since the publication of the Brandt Report, suggesting that the line needs to be redrawn or the label 'South' replaced by one that is less geographically constrained.

In fact, this is exactly what has happened with the appearance of the new term 'Global South', which began to be used widely following the end of the Cold War in the 1990s, and the recognition that the category of Third World was no longer geopolitically relevant with the demise of the communist Second World. Its replacement by the Global South reflected a move towards a more positive designation that moved beyond the simple geographical distinction between northern and southern hemispheres of the Brandt Report, while at the same time avoiding the negative connotations which the term 'Third World' had acquired over time. Just as the designation 'South' was counterposed to the 'North', so too was the Global South contrasted with the Global North in relation to historical and contemporary patterns of wealth and power. The post-Cold War years were marked by the acceleration of globalising trends and an increasing awareness that the major policy challenges of the years ahead would be global, such as addressing climate change, global health concerns, international financial stability, and the threats posed by terrorism and nuclear proliferation. The Global South is a term that acknowledges the increasing interconnection of globalisation and development, and the need for the Global South and the Global North to work together in resolving such issues, but it also recognises the continuing

Figure 3.2: The Brandt line

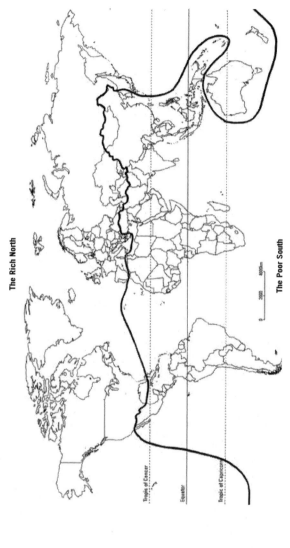

Source: Brandt (1980)

inequalities and power differences between them. Rather like the early usage of the term 'Third World', the idea of the Global South was seen as a way of bringing countries in the southern hemisphere together to work in collaboration on a range of political, economic, social, cultural and environmental issues. This became known as South–South cooperation (Gray and Gills, 2016).

The Global South is generally understood as a socioeconomic and geopolitical term that is not constrained by a strictly geographical definition. It does have a geographical reference to the southern half of the world but the modifying adjective 'global' means that it is not a precise geographical categorisation of the world, which allows it to include areas outside the southern hemisphere that may be classified as belonging to the Global South by virtue of their position within the global economy and the global geopolitical system. It is therefore possible, for example, to identify developing countries in the northern hemisphere, or areas within countries that are part of the Global North, as belonging to the Global South. The flexibility of the term accounts for its growing popularity in the development field. There was been more than ten-fold increase in the number of publications employing the term between 2004 and 2013 (Pagel et al, 2014). The socioeconomic and geopolitical connotations of the term 'Global South' have been welcomed by many as helping to highlight the uneven impact of globalisation in the post-Cold War world. However, the term 'Global South' has also been criticised for being too much of a blanket term, rather like the 'Third World', and for positing a simple binary divide between the dominant Global North and the subordinate Global South in much the same way as earlier categorisations divided the globe into rich world and poor world, and developed and underdeveloped areas of the world.

Where do we go from here?

Many terms have been used to describe the developing world, as shown in Figure 3.3. It is clear that the term 'Global South' is by no means perfect and is open to different interpretations, but it has become very widely used in recent years, replacing the previous

Figure 3.3: The developing world: alternative terminology

- Developing World
- Less Developed World
- Underdeveloped World
- Poor World
- South
- Third World
- Two-Thirds World
- Majority World
- Global South
- Other World

predominance of the Third World both in the literature of international development and in the wider development community. In using this term there is a recognition that global processes and structures make all countries today part of an increasingly interconnected world. It is likely nevertheless that the term 'Global South' will at some stage be replaced. One alternative term that has appeared in the academic literature is the 'Other World' (Weatherby et al, 2018).

Indicators and measurements of development

The earliest indicators to measure levels of development in different 'developing' countries were introduced by the United Nations and the World Bank. These were essentially measures of economic development based on indices such as GDP or GNI per capita. The World Bank uses GNI per capita, translated into US dollars, to measure and compare levels of economic development. On this basis, the World Bank assigns countries to one of four categories: high income, upper middle income, lower middle income and low income. The latter two classifications are referred to by the World Bank as 'developing countries'. The classifications are updated annually to reflect the changes in each country based on factors such as income growth, inflation, exchange rates and population size. The International Monetary Fund uses a looser form of classification to measure development, placing the countries of the world into two categories: the 'advanced economies' and 'emerging markets' or 'developing economies'. The current 37 advanced economies are classified according to GDP valued by purchasing power parity, total exports of goods and services, and population. All other countries are placed in the developing economies category.

Moving beyond strictly economic indicators and classifications opens up a whole new set of possibilities and ways of identifying levels of development in different countries. The United Nations adopted such an approach in the early 1970s when it first published its list of 'least developed countries' (LDCs). The list is still in existence today and updated every three years by its Committee for Development. The LDCs are defined as 'low-income countries confronting severe structural impediments to sustainable development', which are therefore 'highly vulnerable to economic and environmental shocks and have low levels of human assets'. Three indices are used to classify countries as falling into the LDC category: GNI per capita to measure income, a human assets index to measure the level of human capital in relation to health and education, and an economic vulnerability index to measure structural vulnerability to economic and environmental shocks. Using these three indices, 46 countries were listed by the United Nations as LDCs in 2020 (UN DESA, 2020a).

The World Bank has moved from employing strictly economic indicators of development to constructing a wide range of World Development Indicators (WDI), which include six key areas: poverty and shared prosperity, people, environment, economy, states and markets, and global links. The data has been published annually since 1978 and is used to augment the World Bank's annual *World Development Report*. The scope of the data produced and the range of indicators employed have steadily increased over the years, so that the WDI currently includes more than 1,400 indicators covering over 220 countries.

The most significant change in the move towards measures of development that incorporate a more human dimension came with the publication of the first *Human Development Report* by the UN Development Programme (UNDP) in 1990. The report introduced the Human Development Index (HDI) which is based on a measure of average achievement in three key dimensions: a long and healthy life, being knowledgeable, and having a decent standard of living. Appropriate indicators, including life expectancy at birth, expected years of schooling and GNI per capital, are employed to produce three indices which are then aggregated into a composite index using the geometric mean (Figure 3.4).

The HDI uses the composite index to allocate countries to four groupings: very high, high, medium and low human development. Since its inception in 1990 the HDI has been extended to create a further set of measurements related to specific issues, such as poverty and inequality. For example, the Gender Development Index (GDI) and Gender Empowerment Measure (GEM) were introduced in 1995 to supplement the results obtained using the HDI. The GDI focuses on the human development impact of existing gender gaps in the three dimensions of the HDI; rather than just looking at the general level of wellbeing in a particular country the GDI provides

Figure 3.4: Human Development Index (HDI)

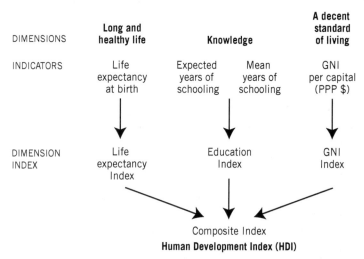

Source: Adapted from the UNDP Human Development Report webpage: http://hdr.undp.org/en/content/human-development-index-hdi

insight into how that is affected by gender differences. In 2010 the UNDP introduced the Gender Inequality Index which went further than the GDI and GEM in identifying areas of gender inequality. It focuses on three key dimensions: health, empowerment and the labour market. The dimension of empowerment, for example, considers the level of female participation in secondary education and the female share of parliamentary seats compared with males as indicators of gender inequality. At the same time, the UNDP also introduced the Inequality-adjusted Human Development Index (IHDI) which combines a country's average achievements in health, education and income with how those achievements are distributed among the population, thereby modifying the HDI scores according to the level of inequality in a given country.

The rollout of these various indexes of development clearly demonstrates the evolution of thinking in the field of international development. The indexes have also been tailored to complement and provide a basis for measuring success in meeting the targets set by the United Nations, first with the eight Millennium Development Goals (MDGs) of 2000 and subsequently with the 17 Sustainable Development Goals (SDGs) set in 2015 to be achieved by 2030 (Figure 3.5). Also commonly referred to as the Global Goals and the 2030 Agenda, the SDGs marked a significant advance on the MDGs and called for action by all countries, at whatever level of development, to promote global prosperity and human development while protecting the planet.

Measuring the achievement of these goals is a complex task that has been taken up by the UN Sustainable Development Solutions Network (SDSN), the World Bank, the OECD, and other international organisations. The SDSN has produced an SDG index based on UN official indicators (Kroll, 2015), and the World Bank (2020c) has published an *Atlas of Sustainable Development Goals* based on the WDIs to quantify progress, highlight the key issues in achieving the SDGs, and identify the gaps that still remain.

Critics of the SDGs have pointed to the breadth and complexity of the goals, especially when compared to the relative simplicity of the MDGs. Additionally, it can be argued that, as with the Human

Figure 3.5: Sustainable Development Goals (SDGs)

Source: UNDP (2015)

Development Index, collecting accurate and reliable data can be highly problematic in developing countries where resources are scarce, especially given the necessity with the SDGs to collect more data covering a wider range of indicators. However, if we accept that development is a complex process of change, then it is inevitable that measurement will be intricate and potentially problematic. Collecting data will continue to be an issue where resources are inadequate, but technological advances in the collation and analysis of data on a global scale have opened up possibilities for measuring progress in the 21st century that were not available in the earlier decades of the modern development era.

Summary and conclusion: onwards to 2030

We have seen in this chapter how things have moved on in relation to mapping and measuring progress in international development. We can expect further changes as we approach the year set for the realisation of the SDGs, and perhaps a new set of UN goals for the middle of the century. We can only speculate on what may happen in the future, but there does appear to be an increasing co-ordination of development initiatives with regard to the 2030 Agenda and a growing consensus on the revisioning of development to focus on its human and sustainable dimensions within a global framework. This has involved a shift in the terminology used to identify development and where it is most needed, and a movement away from geographical mapping towards more symbolic forms of representation as encapsulated in the term 'Global South'. However, while there are signs of a broader consensus on what and where the focus of international development should be as we approach 2030, development itself remains a highly contested concept informed by competing theoretical perspectives, to which we turn our attention in the following chapter.

KEY POINTS SUMMARY

- The identification and labelling of the regions of the world and sections of the population, which are the focus of both the study and practice of international development, have changed over time.
- Most of the concepts that have emerged over time to identify different levels of development across the world have tended to be bilateral, as in the 'developed–underdeveloped' or 'North–South' conceptions of the world, or trilateral, where reference is made to 'First World–Second World–Third World', or 'advanced–emerging–developing' countries and regions.
- The most widely used terms in the international development literature today are 'developed'/'developing' and 'Global North'/'Global South', which have greater flexibility than some of the earlier concepts.
- Indicators and measurements of development have also changed significantly over time, largely in recognition of the multifaceted nature of development, including aspects of human and sustainable development.
- Strictly economic indexes of development have been replaced by a much wider range of indicators, as reflected in the World Bank World Development Indicators and the United Nations Human Development Index.

- Additional indicators have also been added over time as certain issues such as gender inequality have been given more prominence; hence the UNDP Gender Development Index and Gender Empowerment Measure.
- Whatever indicators are used to measure development, the systematic collection of valid data remains problematic, particularly in some developing countries.

KEY READING GUIDE

Not all texts on international development discuss the key concepts and indicators of development in detail, but some provide useful overviews, including Hopper, *Understanding Development* (2018), Haslam et al, *Introduction to International Development* (2017), and Kingsbury et al, *International Development: Issues and Challenges* (2016). More detailed discussion and debate on the rise of the concept of the Global South can be found in a series of articles in Hollington et al, 'Concepts of the Global South' (2015). While some of the authors welcome the advance of the term 'Global South' and see it as having a positive impact, others are more critical and raise concerns about the advance of the concept, including the lack of agreement on exactly which countries are part of the Global South. Official publications by international organisations such as UN DESA and UNDP provide definitions and details of the development indicators that they employ, and updates on their measurements for different countries and regions around the world. This chapter includes reference to UN DESA (2020a *Least Developed Countries*, and several UNDP *Human Development Reports*. The reports are published annually and recognise how new concepts and concerns of development have come to the fore over the years. Sumner and Tribe also explore in some detail the use of different concepts and indicators, and how development research and practice are linked in *International Development Studies* (2008).

4

Theories of development: from modernisation to post-development and beyond

Introduction

> Development studies is necessarily a cross-disciplinary subject.
> (Tribe et al, 2010: 5)

Development is an idea that has long been associated with the rise of the modern world, but it has not produced a single overarching vision or theory of development. There are instead many different and often competing theories of development, which reflect the diverse political positions of their exponents, the time and place where they were formulated, and the range of academic disciplines that have informed development thinking: notably economics, sociology, politics and geography. As we have seen in the preceding chapters, the study of international development by its very nature requires a cross-disciplinary approach combining the insights from a variety of subject areas to provide a meaningful, holistic understanding of development and how it can be best achieved. As the above quotation by Tribe et al (2010) states, the study of development is by its very nature cross-disciplinary. This is clearly evident in the theories of development that will be reviewed in this chapter. These theories seek not only to explain development but also to advocate ways by which effective and desirable societal change can be achieved.

We will explore some of the most influential theories of development to have emerged in the modern era, examining their strengths and weaknesses in the light of experience, and assessing how far they have advanced our understanding and moved the study of international development forward. The chapter begins with the earliest theoretical approaches associated with 'modernisation', which became a key concept in the 1950s and 1960s, before moving on to look at the alternative theoretical perspectives offered by critics of modernisation theory, including 'dependency' and 'world-systems' theories. These in turn were later questioned by 'post-development' and 'alternative' development theories. However, modernisation and dependency theory have experienced revivals in the changing contexts of the late 20th and 21st centuries, and hybrid theories have emerged that highlight the existence of 'multiple modernities' and critical 'reflexive' development. The chapter concludes by considering the current state of development theory in the third decade of the 21st century.

Development economics

The early 'development decades' of the second half of the 20th century saw the emergence of what became known as the specialised field of 'development economics'. It emerged in the political context of ongoing decolonisation of countries in the so-called Third World, the emergence of new independent states, the advent and unfolding of the Cold War between East and West, and the competition between the capitalist West and the communist East to secure the adherence of Third World countries to their opposing political-economic systems. Economic growth, raising national per capita income with the benefits dispersed to everyone through a 'trickle-down' effect, was seen as an effective way of ensuring a process of development that would align Third World countries with the West.

To achieve economic growth and development in the Third World, it was widely recognised that this could not be left entirely to the operation of the free market but required intervention at national and supra-national levels. Just as Europe had been helped to recover and rebuild after the Second World War by the economic assistance provided by the US under the Marshall Plan, so it was necessary to assist Third World countries to achieve economic development. An international conference, held at Bretton Woods in 1944, established the International Monetary Fund to regulate the global economy, and also the World Bank which was set up with several branches, most notably the International Bank for Reconstruction and Development to provide loans to countries in need of reconstruction and development. The first 'development decade' in the 1960s saw Western governments rolling out initiatives to further aid development: for example, the Alliance for Progress, initiated by President Kennedy in 1961, to establish strong economic ties between the US and Latin America. A few years later, in 1964, the new Labour government in the UK set up the Ministry of Overseas Development (ODM) to promote development in Britain's existing and former colonies. The ODM would later become the Department for International Development, founded in 1997. As these economic developments were rolled out, the concept of modernisation came increasingly to the fore.

Modernisation theory

'Modernisation' may be defined simply as moving towards what is considered to be 'up to date' in a particular location at any given time. Modernisation is seen as a progressive process of positively evaluated change whereby society undergoes far-reaching transformation that is ongoing and all-embracing. Modernisation theory views development as a form of sociocultural transformation, a thoroughgoing process of evolutionary change involving cultural values and norms, institutions and structures. These are seen as being interdependent which means that modernisation is a **systematic process** with changes in all areas of society. Second, modernisation is also a **transformative process** in which the structures and values of the old society are totally replaced by modern structures and a new set of values. Third, due to its systematic and transformative nature, modernisation is an **immanent process** which means that change is built into the social system, and once change begins in one area of society it will inevitably lead to changes in other areas too. Through these interconnected processes modernisation has a vast and continuing impact on the societies that undergo this process of transformation, and this in turn leads to a reconfiguration of the world as previously known. Modernisation is therefore broadly viewed as emanating from constructive development. As Richard Peet and Elaine Hartwick (2015: 2) point out, 'Development is a foundational belief underlying modernity.' As a result, modernisation can be seen as a reconstruction of the world, as graphically reflected in Figure 4.1.

Key to the modernisation perspective is the idea that 'becoming modern' involves an historical transition from **traditional** to **modern** society in which modernity replaces traditional ways of life. This is a dichotomous view of the world with a binary distinction between traditional and modern societies. Modernisation theory began to take-off in the 1950s. The theory became closely associated with the US as it reached out to the ex-colonial countries of the Third World with the aim of averting the spread of communism by Westernising the developing world. Modernisation theory found itself caught up in the Cold War politics of the era and can be traced back to what became known as the Truman Doctrine when US President Truman (1949)

Figure 4.1: Modernising the world

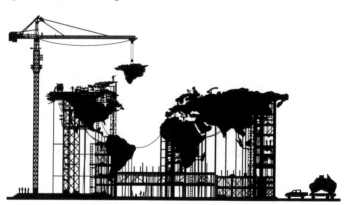

Source: www.istockphoto.com

announced his plan for the West to 'embark on a bold new program for making the benefits of our scientific advances and industrial progress available for the improvement and growth of underdeveloped areas'. The transition from traditional to modern society was therefore seen as a process of giving up traditional systems and ways of life and moving forward to modernity by emulating the West. This process is unidirectional and teleological in the sense that the end point of modernisation and development is already defined by the status of the advanced Western countries of the developed world.

Several academic proponents of modernisation theory were closely associated with the US government, notably W.W. Rostow who was a policy and security adviser in the 1960s to President John F. Kennedy. Rostow's contribution to modernisation theory is one of the best known. In 1960 he published his most famous work, *The Stages of Economic Growth: A Non-Communist Manifesto*, with its clear political alignment embodied in the subtitle. Rostow envisaged the process of development from traditional agricultural to modern industrial society as going through five key stages of economic growth (Figure 4.2).

The final stage is that achieved by the already developed countries in the Western world where a strong manufacturing sector of industry is able to produce consumer goods to meet the needs of a mass population with a growing level of income. To reach this ultimate goal traditional societies must first develop the pre-conditions for economic 'take-off', which include the building of infrastructure to enable the development of industry, the transformation of agriculture to yield

Figure 4.2: Five stages of economic modernisation

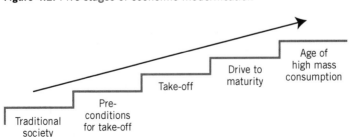

Source: Rostow ([1960] 1990)

higher productivity and release surplus labour to be employed in the industrial sector, the modernisation and expansion of transport facilities to serve industry and markets, the introduction of new technologies, and the development of key ancillary services for industry such as banking. Take-off occurs when there is a doubling in the proportion of national income which is invested in production, and may only take one or two decades, according to Rostow. What follows is the 'drive to maturity' when industrial growth becomes sustained and irreversible with increasingly sophisticated technologies and work processes being introduced. This in turn prepares the economy for the coming age of high mass consumption. The leading countries to have arrived at this point at the time Rostow was writing were those from Europe and North America with some progressing more quickly than others along the path of modernisation, and this is seen as continuing to be the case with later developing countries embarking on take-off such as Argentina, Mexico, China and India. Figure 4.3 clearly illustrates the different stages of economic growth over several centuries across a wide range of countries in the world.

Other proponents of modernisation theory stress that the transition from traditional to modern society can only be achieved with the establishment of a close relationship between the developed and underdeveloped regions of the world. Without such a relationship and models of modernisation to emulate, traditional societies are unable to achieve development on their own. Isolation is therefore seen as being a key cause of underdevelopment and one which can only be overcome by exposure to Western notions of successful development and the sociocultural prerequisites for modernisation. Other modernisation theorists have taken this idea further to explore the ways in which social and cultural changes, the movement of people, the expansion of education, and the dissemination of ideas from the West could all contribute to the process of modernisation and drive forward development across the Third World. David McClelland, a US psychologist, argued that new ways of thinking, or 'other-directedness' as he termed it, would overcome the stagnation of tradition and promote the development of modern ideas and ways of moving forward. McClelland identified those countries that had developed mass media,

Figure 4.3: Stages of economic growth by country

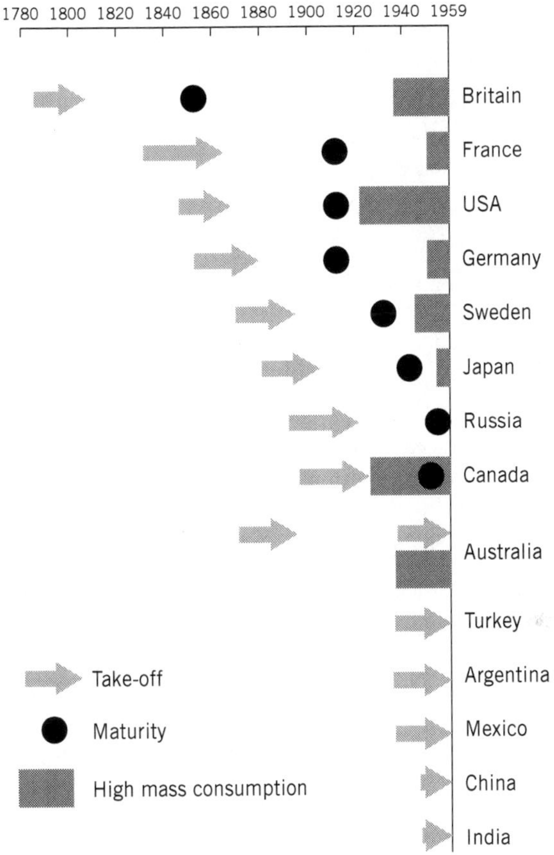

1780 1800 1820 1840 1860 1880 1900 1920 1940 1959

Britain
France
USA
Germany
Sweden
Japan
Russia
Canada
Australia
Turkey
Argentina
Mexico
China
India

Take-off

Maturity

High mass consumption

Source: Rostow ([1960] 1990)

and other means which allowed for the rapid development of public opinion, as achieving much faster rates of economic development. It was these countries that were most successful in creating the psychological motivation, the 'need for achievement', or 'n-Ach' as he also termed it, that would stimulate economic and social development: 'It is the values, motives or psychological forces that determine ultimately the rate of economic and social development (McClelland, 1961: 17).

Daniel Lerner's *The Passing of Traditional Society* is a further example of early modernisation theory in which psychological factors are given prominence. In line with other leading modernisation theorists, he maintains that the rest of the world should follow the Western concept of modernity to achieve development, and again the mass media is seen as playing a crucial role in the modernisation process. Access to the media is facilitated by movement from the countryside to cities, 'from farms to flats, from fields to factories' (Lerner, 1964: 47). Physical mobility accelerates psychological mobility and the transition from a traditional stance towards a more modern perspective. Individual behaviour change and the role of empathy in moving people from a traditional to modern outlook is seen as crucial here, and resonates with a number of other theories of modernisation.

The psychological approach to development and modernisation in which the modern personality is a crucial factor was later followed up by Inkeles and Smith who based their findings on 6,000 interviews in six developing countries in the 1970s: Argentina, Chile, India, Israel, Nigeria and Bangladesh. They concluded that aspects of the 'modern man' were more likely to be located where modern institutions existed; for example, where people were working in factories in cities, and had access to educational facilities and the media, all of which had an impact on their psychology and reduced the obstacles to development: 'We are convinced that *mental barriers* and *psychic factors* are the key obstacles to more effective economic and social development in many countries […] in good part underdevelopment is a *state of mind*' (Inkeles and Smith, 1974: 126, emphasis added).

Sociocultural changes and psychological adaptations as perceived by modernisation theorists facilitate the transition from tradition to modernity. The process of modernisation is evolutionary, replacing traditional with modern forms of living, and it is driven forward by the diffusion of ideas and mechanisms of change from the industrialised West to the 'underdeveloped' world. This can take the form of diffusion through exposure in various ways to the modern world, or more directly through the diffusion of aid from the West, whether in the form of economic assistance or the dissemination of Western ideas and values via media and education. Modernisation is seen as an evolutionary process of Westernisation and industrialisation. The four key characteristics of modernisation are outlined in Figure 4.4.

Figure 4.4: Modernisation: key characteristics

- **Becoming modern**
  Transition from traditional to modern society
  – a dichotomous view

- **Role of values and culture**
  Emphasis on culture, values, empathy and
  individual motivation in development

- **Diffusion**
  Modernisation by exposure to the modern world
  and diffusion from the West to the Third World

- **Evolutionary change**
  Unilinear path to development
  = Westernisation + industrialisation

Critiques of modernisation theory

Modernisation theory was very influential in the 1950s and 1960s, as was evident from the role it played during the Cold War in advancing a Western model of development to the rest of the world. However, it was also subject to a number of strong critiques. First, the view from the West was considered by its critics to be **ethnocentric** and **unidirectional**. Other possible pathways to development were not considered. Second, the **traditional–modern dualism** was criticised for presenting an oversimplified view of different countries in the world by defining them only as traditional or modern. Traditional and modern values are not necessarily mutually exclusive. A third area of criticism of modernisation theory concerns its **ahistorical perspective** or lack of any real grounding in history, including the effects of colonialism and imperialism on countries in the Third World. Finally, the **evolutionism** reflected in the unilinear and teleological view of development offered by modernisation theory presupposes that countries have no alternative way forward. The evolutionary model based on the experience of Western societies is one that Third World countries must follow or else remain trapped forever in underdevelopment. There is therefore no recognition of alternative routes to modernity or different types of economic and social development. China, as we now know, is the leading example of a country that has gone through a very different process of modernisation from that epitomised by the West. The shortcomings of modernisation theory, with its emphasis on a single definition and unilinear route to modernity, means that it lacks the necessary components to make it a viable comprehensive theory of **development**. Modernisation theory is restricted in its interpretation of development in four essential respects, as shown in Figure 4.5.

Alternative perspectives on modernisation were offered by several writers who focused on the **historical sociology of modernisation**. Two of the leading proponents of this approach were Reinhard Bendix and Barrington Moore. Bendix (1964) emphasised the historical specificity of the various experiences of modernisation across the world, and the variety of different routes to modernity which reflected the diversity of cultures and social and political arrangements in different countries.

Moore's famous study, *Social Origins of Dictatorship and Democracy* (1966), identified three clearly distinct routes to the modern world, and significantly each route included a revolution of some kind. The three routes varied according to the nature of the traditional societies from which they emerged, and this is reflected in the subtitle of Moore's work, *Lord and Peasant in the Making of the Modern World*. Historically, the three routes were also sequential. The first of the three

Figure 4.5: Four main limitations of modernisation theory

- ETHNOCENTRISM:
  a view from the West

- TRADITIONAL-MODERN DUALISM:
  an oversimplified view

- AHISTORICAL PERSPECTIVE:
  a failure to consider colonialism and imperialism

- EVOLUTIONISM:
  a unilinear and teleological view

routes was the **democratic route**, which began in England through a process of capitalist industrialisation and bourgeois 'revolution from below' in the 17th century that resulted in the building of a democratic nation. The second route emerged from a different set of social conditions in which the landed aristocracy was much stronger and the emerging bourgeoisie was relatively weak. This led to a 'revolution from above', in the form of fascism in Japan, Germany and Italy, and resulted in an **authoritarian route** to modernity which was capitalist and reactionary. The third route is one in which an agrarian system was dominated by a landed aristocracy with no strongly emerging bourgeoisie to propel change towards a modern commercial economy. In this route, exemplified by China and Russia, the peasantry emerged as the historical agent of social change, and it was through peasant 'revolution from below' that the **communist route** to modernity emerged.

The historical sociology of Bendix and Moore clearly demonstrated that conventional modernisation theory was oversimplified in its view of history, and that a unilinear and teleological approach failed to recognise the different ways in which traditional societies fracture and the different directions that could be taken en route to modernity.

Dependency theory

An alternative theoretical paradigm, focusing on the 'underdeveloped world', emerged shortly after Bendix and Moore published their works, and became one of the most significant and influential critiques of modernisation theory under the name of the 'dependency school' of thought on development, or *dependencia* as it was known in Latin America. The dependency school emerged in Latin America at a time when the modernisation approach and Western aid projects, designed to stimulate economic growth and sociopolitical change to advance democracy, were being widely experienced as failures in that region of the world. The pivotal role in modernisation through aid was being played by the US under the banner of President John F. Kennedy's Alliance for Progress. This was designed to strengthen economic cooperation between the US and Latin America, and to promote economic development and the establishment of democratic governments in Latin American countries. However, the continuing lack of significant economic development and the persistence of high levels of poverty and inequality in many countries in Latin America indicated the failure of this strategy, and there was further concern because of the failure to promote democracy in the region. On the contrary, Latin America saw the rise of many military dictatorships in the 1960s.

Dependency theory derived in part from the work of the 19th-century theorist and socialist revolutionary, Karl Marx, and offered a neo-Marxist critique of contemporary capitalism. It also drew on the earlier research by the Argentine economist Raúl Prebisch, which found that increases in the wealth of the richer nations appeared to be at the expense of the poorer ones, thereby creating a 'centre-periphery' relationship between developed and developing countries. Dependency theory aimed to provide an explanation for the persistent poverty of poorer countries in Latin America and other parts of the Third World. Whereas modernisation theory asserted the need for underdeveloped countries to emulate and eventually catch up with the modern social and economic practices of the developed capitalist world, dependency theory viewed their persistent poverty as a consequence of capitalist exploitation on a global scale. International capitalism is seen as increasing disparities in the levels of development of rich and poor countries because it is based on a set of imperialistic and exploitative relationships between the 'centre' and the 'periphery' which effectively allow the developed countries of the North to extract wealth from the underdeveloped countries of the South.

Development of underdevelopment

One of the leading dependency theorists was Andre Gunder Frank who presented a trenchant critique of modernisation theory and the US-dominated discipline of the sociology of development, attacking it for its inadequate historical perspective and economic illiteracy. Frank described the conventional modernisation approach to development as an exercise in 'comparative statics', and he turned what he perceived as the static concept of a 'backward' or 'underdeveloped' country on its head, arguing that 'underdevelopment' is not a condition but an historical process: the 'development of underdevelopment'. This phrase became a key concept in dependency theory. Economic underdevelopment is therefore to be understood as being actively created and maintained in the dependent societies by the very forces – foreign economic investment, trade and aid – which conventional economic theory holds to be necessary for growth and development. Frank's attack on the modernisation perspective was explicitly stated in what became a famous essay entitled, 'Sociology of development and underdevelopment of sociology' (Frank, 1967a). He denounced the dualism of modernisation theory, challenging the idea that modern societies were once underdeveloped, and that underdevelopment is a condition that characterises so-called traditional societies. Hence, 'The now developed countries were never *under*developed, though they may have been *un*developed [...] Contemporary underdevelopment is in large part the historical product of past and continuing economic and other relations between the satellite underdeveloped and the now developed metropolitan countries' (Frank, 1966: 18, emphasis added).

Underdevelopment is therefore seen as a condition which is created by an unequal relationship with the developed countries of the world, a **metropolis–satellite relationship**. The satellite countries' relationship with the metropolis leads to 'underdeveloped development' (Frank, 1966). Closer ties with the developed countries of the world are therefore not the solution but the problem, perpetuating the underdevelopment of the satellite countries by the metropolitan countries. A series of further metropolis-satellite relationships are created within dependent countries. The capital cities of dependent countries, for example, form sub-metropoles to which the interior regions are satellites, in paradigmatic replication of the dependent relationship which can be seen between developed and underdeveloped countries at the international level. The metropolis-satellite relationships therefore extend from the urban capitalist centres of the developed world through to the rural economic backwaters of the underdeveloped world.

In *Capitalism and Underdevelopment in Latin America* Frank explores these relationships in Chile and Brazil, pointing out that the most remote and underdeveloped satellite regions of these countries today, such as the Northeast of Brazil, were at one time the most closely connected to the capitalist metropolitan centres and therefore experienced the most severe process of underdevelopment leading to their current state. 'Underdevelopment in Brazil, as elsewhere, is the result of capitalist development' (Frank, 1967b: 145). This raises the question of why countries agreed to be drawn into a metropolis–satellite relationship and to participate in a process of surplus appropriation and exploitation. The explanation given for this is the existence of 'comprador' elites in the satellite countries who work with the capitalist metropolitan countries and their multinational corporations to generate dependency and underdevelopment. The 'comprador bourgeoisie' facilitate the development of 'comprador capitalism' from which they also benefit. This ties them into the system. Frank subsequently referred to the comprador bourgeoisie as the 'lumpenbourgeoisie' who were responsible for the stunted, unhealthy status of Latin American economies, a condition he defined as 'lumpendevelopment' (Frank, 1972). Frank's theory of dependency demonstrated that while capital may flow into satellite countries by way of investment, more flows out in the form of profits as a result of their dependent status. The continuing flow of surplus to the metropolitan countries perpetuates the underdevelopment of the satellites. Figure 4.6 graphically illustrates how the world is envisaged from the point-of-view of dependency theory.

Frank maintained that dependency was linked with capitalist development which went back as far as the 16th century, and the only way for dependent countries to experience genuine development was for them to engage in a revolutionary process of change and cut themselves off from the developed capitalist world. It was a simple choice between 'underdevelopment or revolution' (Frank, 1969). Cuba under Fidel Castro was seen as the first prime example of this alternative route to development in Latin America following the Cuban communist revolution of 1959.

Figure 4.6: The world from the viewpoint of dependency theory

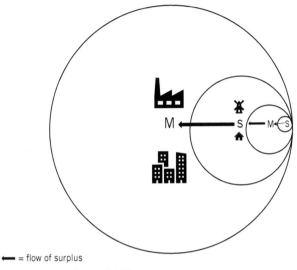

⬅ = flow of surplus

M ⬅ S = Metropolis ⬅ Satellite

Frank's model of underdevelopment

Source: Adapted from Frank (1967b)

Dependencia: *dependent capitalist development*

Frank's dependency theory was, and remains, highly influential, but was challenged on a number of grounds. From a Marxist perspective, the focus on spatial metropolis-satellite relations was seen as downplaying the importance of class relations and the impact of class structures on economic development and underdevelopment (Brenner, 1977). The claim that Latin America was capitalist from the 16th century was repudiated by Ernesto Laclau (1971) as historically inaccurate, as too was the somewhat static notion of 'continuity in change', with several Latin American writers pointing out that it was possible within a relationship of dependency for changes to occur and for some form of development to take place. Fernando Henrique Cardoso and Enzo Faletto were two of the leading figures in *dependencia* theorising in Latin America who reconfigured dependency theory to recognise the possibility of development and dependency occurring together. The original Spanish publication in 1969 of *Dependency and Development in Latin America* by Cardoso and Faletto (1979) was a key moment in recasting dependency theory. Cardoso and Faletto referred to 'dependent development' as a possible, albeit difficult and complex, route out of the periphery. The idea of dependency inevitably leading to the 'development of underdevelopment' was replaced with the concept of 'dependent capitalist development'. Cardoso's claim that dependency and development could be combined was based on the observation that some countries in Latin America had more complex, diversified economies than other countries in the region, and some were witnessing a move away from foreign investment in raw materials and agriculture into new areas of manufacturing and industrial production led by Western multinational corporations (MNCs). Within the dependent countries development was limited to the relatively small modern urban sector, leading to the creation of a 'new type of dualism' in which the 'backward social and economic sectors' of the dependent countries then play the role of 'internal colonies' to the modern urban 'advanced sectors' (Cardoso, 1972: 90).

Dependency theory has therefore proved to be more flexible and nuanced than in its original form, and has itself developed over time. A further development in dependency theory, which moved beyond the idea that capitalism creates a permanent binary division of centre and periphery or metropolis and satellite, was introduced in the 1970s under the title of 'world-systems theory'.

World-systems theory

While building on dependency theory, world-systems analysis introduced a more holistic and global perspective on development. The theory was pioneered by Immanuel Wallerstein, US sociologist and economic historian. The 'modern world system', as he described it, emerged out of the crisis of feudalism in the late 15th and 16th centuries, and was essentially a capitalist system. Wallerstein argues that Europe moved towards the establishment of a capitalist world economy in order to ensure continued economic growth. The development of this modern world system led to the global supremacy of European countries. Unlike the metropolis-satellite dualism of dependency theory, world-systems analysis offered a more open and fluid conception of the spatial and economic divisions of international capitalism, identifying a tripartite world-system comprising three key units: core, periphery and semi-periphery (Figure 4.7). Unlike the dualistic categories of metropolis and satellite, the identification of a 'semi-periphery' recognises the possibility of movement between the different categories as a result of economic development or decline.

World-systems theory thereby recognised the emergence of what became known as the newly industrialising countries in East Asia and Latin America: these were defined as belonging to the semi-periphery. Their rise from the 'periphery' and the fall of some 'core' countries suffering economic decline could result in movement in and out of the different groupings. Wallerstein rejected the concept of a Third World, claiming that there is only one world connected by a complex network of economic exchange relationships within the world-system of capitalism. However, he did recognise the existence of some 'external areas': this referred to the relatively few countries that maintained their own economic systems and remained largely outside the modern world-system of capitalism, the communist Soviet Union being a good example. World-systems analysis therefore advanced a more flexible perspective on development than the earlier theories of dependency while at the same time maintaining that the world system

Figure 4.7: Core, periphery and semi-periphery

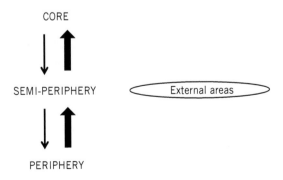

operated as a set of mechanisms that transfer economic surplus from the periphery to the core.

Summary: world-systems theory
- views the world **holistically** and **historically**
- shows how the expansion of **capitalism** created a **modern world system**
- underlines the **inequality** and **unevenness** at the heart of the world system
- demonstrates the possibility of **movement** within the world system

Critiques of world-systems theory: moving towards post-imperialism

World-systems theory became an influential theoretical perspective on development but one which was also subject to a good deal of criticism. Robert Brenner (1977), for example, argued that the overriding focus on a world economic system meant that the role of local class structures and class struggles in moving countries in particular directions was generally overlooked. Theda Skocpol (1977) similarly pointed out that world-systems theory was heavily economistic and therefore failed to give sufficient regard to political and sociocultural considerations. A further critique and alternative theory emerged from what became known as the 'post-imperialism' perspective. According to David Becker, global capitalist imperialism leads, sooner or later, to a nationalist reaction which in turn leads to a strengthening of the regulatory and economic policy-making organs of the state. He also claims that MNCs are less resistant to the unionisation of their workers than are local employees, and this tends ultimately to produce a stronger labour movement with beneficial results for workers. In addition, MNCs are increasingly attracted by the prospect of growing foreign markets for their goods and therefore have an interest in increasing the purchasing power of the population. Becker (1987) also argues that MNCs are indifferent to the type of political regime in the countries in which they invest, and suggests that this opens up the possibility of a move towards democracy: for example, across Latin America where he cites examples of a shift in this direction at the time he was writing in the 1980s. This represented a significant move away from the pessimism of dependency theory towards a much more optimistic outlook, opening up the prospect of greater political freedom and reductions in inequality.

Modernisation theory and dependency theory revisited

The two major and diametrically opposed theories of development were both heavily criticised, as we have seen, and lost the influence they initially had in the field of international development. However, there was a revival of interest in both theories at the end of the 20th century and the beginning of the 21st century.

Modernisation theory enjoyed something of a revival with the fall of the Berlin Wall in 1989, followed by the collapse of communism in the former Soviet Union in the early 1990s and the start of a process of political and economic transformation in the post-Soviet and post-communist countries of Eastern Europe. Famously portrayed as 'the end of history' by Francis Fukuyama (1992), these events were taken to confirm the argument that there was only one genuine path to modernity, that of the Western route of capitalist modernisation. However, developments elsewhere in the world, notably the substantial economic growth of the Asian Tigers – Hong Kong, Singapore, Taiwan and South Korea – and the rapid economic development of China, India, Malaysia and Thailand in the 1990s, suggested that there were also new routes to modernity emerging. Recognition of a plurality of different routes to modernity led to the creation of the concept of 'multiple modernities'. S.N. Eisenstadt (1992) used this concept to refer to the various ways in which modernity spread beyond Europe and how it differed from the process of modernisation that was first launched in European countries. As the world entered the 21st century, globalisation came to the fore and this led to a recognition of the increasingly close relationship between globalisation and modernisation: 'Globalisation is one of the most visible consequences of modernity and has in turn reshaped the project of modernity' (Martinelli, 2005: 101).

Global modernisation has come about because each part of the world is increasingly interdependent with many others. Globalisation is seen as eroding the former sovereignty of the nation-state and fosters the dialectical interplay of different cultural traditions across the world. In this global context the plurality of routes to and through modernity is an inevitable consequence, and creates what has been seen as the new era of **multiple modernities**.

Dependency theory also enjoyed a revival with the emergence of a small group of newly advanced developing countries, classified in 2001 as BRIC (Brazil, Russia, India and China). The advance of the BRICs aligned with dependency and world-systems perspectives by illustrating the uneven nature of development. Most countries in the Global South remained underdeveloped with global economic inequalities between the core and periphery increasing even as a few successful economies entered the semi-periphery. The rapid and extensive development of China with its increasing influence and economic investment in less developed countries in Asia, Africa and Latin America can be seen as evidence of new relations of dependency being established in the opening decades of the 21st century. The BRICs now include South Africa and are referred to as the BRICS (with a capital 'S' for South Africa). A number of recent studies recognise the relevance of dependency theory in analysing the dominance of the BRICS in their relationship with other countries in the Global South, arguing that the BRICS are actually amplifying some of the worst aspects of the global capitalist system by acting as 'sub-imperialist sheriffs' of world imperialism: 'sub-imperialism [is] the highest stage of dependent capitalism' (Bond and Garcia, 2017: 27).

The dependency perspective therefore continues to exert its influence despite losing its earlier prominence. The basic assumptions of dependency theory remain highly relevant in the third decade of the 21st century. There is still considerable evidence to support the notion that there are wide differences in income levels and standards of living between the developed and developing worlds – or between the core and periphery. Similarly, countries in the developing world continue to face challenges that can make them highly dependent on the developed world to provide them with the capital investment and technology needed for development. The continuing economic dependency of most of the developing countries in the world also means that the Western powers continue to exert political and cultural domination over much of the rest of the world.

Post-development theory

What has become known as post-development theory first emerged in the 1980s and 1990s as an overall critique and rejection of development theory and the very concept of development, which was seen as a Western myth imposed on Third World countries (Latouche, 1996). Also referred to as 'anti-development' and 'beyond development', it rejected the developmentalism of modernisation, dependency and world-systems theories. Post-development theory looked to a future era in which development would no longer be the central organising principle of social life. From a mainstream perspective, the idea of development had always been seen as a positive process, one that led to the improvement of life for humankind. By contrast, from the post-development perspective, development is seen as a discourse that closes off alternative ways of thinking and constructs a specific way of looking at the world which reproduces social inequalities and misrepresents the developing world and its people. Development is viewed as Eurocentric, a successor to colonialism and an ideology of the West, which legitimises intervention in the lives of people and countries defined as being in need of development, but essentially serves the interests of the rich and powerful. The Mexican post-development theorist Gustavo Esteva (1985: 78) bluntly declared that for anyone living in a Third World country such as Mexico, 'You must be either rich or numb if you fail to notice that development stinks.'

Arturo Escobar, another prominent figure in post-development thinking, regarded Western support for development as a sham, and argued that the West's apparent 'discovery' of poverty in the Third World allowed it to assert its moral and cultural authority, and impose its own Western agenda, rather than effectively address the problem (Escobar, 1995). The entire development project with its stated aim of universalising the economic growth and way of life of the already developed countries is seen by post-development theorists as having negative consequences for the majority of people in the developing world, leading to incongruous outcomes such as the 'progressive modernisation of poverty' (Esteva, 1985: 79).

Rejection of the whole concept and practice of development, and the theories associated with it, was poignantly stated by Wolfgang Sachs (1992: 1) in his introduction to *The Development Dictionary: A Guide to Knowledge as Power* where he referred to the end of the epoch of development and proclaimed that 'the time is ripe to write its obituary'. The publication of this book, with contributions from 17 authors, marked a significant turn towards post-development thinking, which called not for a better or alternative version of development but for its outright rejection. A number of reasons were given for the need to end development. First, the expansive industrial model of economic development and the spread of the 'developed' way of life across the rest of the world was seen as ecologically unsound; second, the project of development along Western lines was associated with the Cold War, which had now come to an end; third, rather than enabling the developing world to catch up with the developed countries of the world, the gap had widened between rich and poor countries; and, finally, development had proved to be a detrimental enterprise that eliminated cultural diversity through the process of universalising Western ideas and institutions, and would ultimately lead to 'a global monoculture' (Ziai, 2017a: 2548).

Attempts by the Western world to address issues such as the environmental consequences of industrial development have been dismissed by post-development theorists as a form of re-development, which has been tinted green in recent times given the growing concern with climate change and ecological risks. 'Sustainable development' has become part of the mainstream terminology of contemporary development, as reflected in the UN Sustainable Development Goals; however, post-development theory does not see this as a positive initiative but rather as a means 'to sustain development itself, rather than to sustain nature or culture' (Esteva and Prakash, 1998: 281).

This is just one example of how post-development analysis identifies the 'impossibility of development' (Corbridge, 2007). The idea of 'alternative development' is also brushed aside by post-developmentalists as it reflects the same worldview that produced the mainstream concept of development, and replicates the idea that the majority of the world's population is 'underdeveloped' and needs to emulate the West. According to Esteva (1985: 78), alternative development is therefore used as a 'deodorant [...] to cover the stench of "development"'. Instead of alternative development, **alternatives to development** are needed to find a new way forward. Post-development theorists argue that ordinary men and women would be able create their own alternatives to development by abandoning the Western development project and recovering their own definition of needs and autonomous ways of living, thereby reclaiming the commons. Indigenous or traditional concepts and practices would be brought back into play. Empowerment happens when ordinary people can define their lives outside the imprisoning architecture of developmentalism. The alternatives to development are therefore to be found in grassroots movements and in rural and urban local communities.

In discovering these new possibilities for change post-development theorists would point to the success of the new social movements in various parts of the Global South, which have often included marginalised groups such as women and indigenous peoples, as an indication of the way forward. A prominent example is the Zapatista movement in the impoverished Mexican state of Chiapas, which later led to the creation of the international movement Peoples' Global Action. Other striking examples include women's collectives in India and Bangladesh set up to improve their social and economic inclusion and empowerment, the peasant-based Chipko movement in Uttar Pradesh in India, which has resisted deforestation in the area, and the Forest People's Alliance in Brazil, which has united rubber tappers and indigenous groups to resist logging and ranching in the Amazon.

Critiques of post-development theory

A number of exponents of development theory have pointed out that post-development theorists see all economic and technological development as inherently bad, while the alternatives to development they propose are often vague and unsubstantiated. There is an unconditional rejection of modernity and development which disregards some of the significant progress that has been made across the Global South, including, for example, the rise in life expectancy and the decline in child mortality which fell by more than half between 1990 and 2018 (Roser et al, 2019a, 2019b). Outside interventions by international development agencies have played an important role in bringing about such changes, but this is overlooked from the post-development perspective, which advocates the avoidance of international aid as an external imposition of power. This fails to recognise that aid can take a variety of different forms. It is important to distinguish between aid that serves to perpetuate domination over poorer communities, and aid that is more people-centred and involves genuine local participation to manage the process in accordance with the needs of the community.

Critical reviews of post-development theory also point out that there is a tendency to romanticise local cultures by focusing exclusively on 'bottom-up' or 'grassroots' alternatives to development. This approach tends to overlook the role of the state in promoting development, and the broader global tends which have increased the diversity of the Global South with the rise of East Asia and the newly industrialising countries (NICs), the emergence of the BRICS, and the growing inequalities between these and other developing countries. As Nederveen Pieterse points out, the instances cited in post-development literature mainly refer to Africa, Latin America and South Asia, whereas the experiences of East Asia and China and the NICs are 'typically not discussed, even though they are the current trendsetters of development' (Nederveen Pieterse, 2009: 341).

Beyond post-development: reflexive development

Given the substantial criticisms that have been levelled against post-development theory and the serious shortcomings of its 'alternatives to development', it may seem surprising that we have not moved into a 'post-post-development' era in the 21st century. At the turn of the century, Nederveen Pieterse wrote a critique titled, 'After post-development' which, along with many other critical approaches, effectively declared post-development theory to be obsolete (Nederveen Pieterse, 2000). The opening two decades of the new century also saw a revival of conventional development theory and practice. The global advancement of the Millennium Development Goals, and later from 2015 the Sustainable Development Goals, gave a strong impression that 'development' was 'alive and kicking' (Ziai, 2015: 833). Nevertheless, post-development has not only survived as a theoretical perspective but has influenced the whole field of development studies, as can be seen from the more frequent and intensive discussion of post-development in development studies textbooks in the 21st century (Ziai, 2017b). There has been a stronger focus on the meaning of 'development' and the origins of the concept with reference to colonialism and the Cold War era, and a growing recognition of the need to move beyond the conventional Eurocentric perspective on development.

Post-development theory continues to expand on its essential ideas and ways of seeing the world. Notable recent works include *Pluriverse: A Post-Development Dictionary* (Kothari et al, 2019) with essays by over 100 contributors, and Escobar's (2018) *Designs for the Pluriverse*. The concept of the 'pluriverse', defined as 'a world where many worlds fit' (Escobar, 2018: xvi) neatly embodies the key principles of post-development theory: namely, the need to view the world not as a universe or single world-system but as a pluriverse based as a plurality of interconnected worlds. Looking to the future, the pluriverse is designed not to seek modernisation through globalisation, but to move to an ecologically secure future that connects with nature and results in what has been termed 'planetisation'.

The influence of post-development thinking on both mainstream and critical development theory can be seen in a number of areas. For example, the concept of planetisation and connections between the human and natural worlds is particularly appealing at a time when environmental issues such as climate change and pollution from plastic waste have come to the fore, and many development theories have moved to incorporate ecological concerns into their definition and understanding of development. There has also been a move towards greater consideration of human-scale development and acknowledgement of the agency of those living in poverty and the part that can be played by grassroots movements. Alongside this there is a greater recognition of social and cultural diversity, and a move away from the homogenising principles of earlier development thinking. In addition, many development agencies are increasingly moving out from the metropolitan centres and becoming less based on external intervention and more on working in partnership with local organisations, listening to the voice of the people with a view to empowering those who are disempowered and promoting gender awareness. This is a move towards a form of participatory development that Nederveen Pieterse (2012: 373) describes as a shift in development thinking from 'we develop it' to 'we develop'. This approach is referred to as **reflexive development**. The concept of reflexive development refers to an awareness of the need, after the experiences of several development decades in the 20th century, to reflect on and address the many failures and crises of development. It marks a shift away from the grand solutions, grand theories and singular pathways of earlier mainstream approaches to development. By contrast, reflexive development clearly acknowledges the complexity and contextuality of development, and moves towards a much greater concern with human development and a new democratic culture, in which people can voice their concerns about development issues and new ways forward can be found. From this perspective development is becoming more reflexive in a broader social and political sense, as **people's reflexivity** (Nederveen Pieterse, 2010: 160).

Reflexive development, therefore, connects with Brohman's (1996: 352) earlier concept of participatory 'popular development' which 'empowers people to take control of their destinies'. Reflexive development increases awareness not only of the need to respond to the issues facing people in the developing world by focusing on local communities in the Global South and ways to secure their empowerment, but also advocates a shift in focus towards reflexivity and change in the Global North to address the problems of development. In particular, increasing awareness of 'over-development' in the Global North and its social and ecological impacts across the world has triggered reflection on how it might be dealt with. New ideas and concepts have arisen as a result, such as 'de-development' and 'degrowth'. Jason Hickel (2018), for example, argues that there is an increasing awareness that overconsumption is putting our planet at risk, and that what is needed is to focus less on 'developing' poor countries and more on 'de-developing' rich countries. The related concept of 'degrowth' has its origins in the French term *décroissance* from the 1970s, and its later translation into English reflected the rise of the degrowth movement in the 21st century, which argued for the downscaling of production and consumption to help resolve the environmental issues and social inequalities that affect the whole world.

Summary and conclusion

In this chapter we have explored how the major theories of development, both mainstream and alternative, have evolved over the second half of the 20th century and into the opening decades of the 21st century. This has been reflected in the growing number of theoretical perspectives to have emerged during this time, and in the appearance of new concepts that have found their way into development theory and practice such as 'sustainable development', 'human development' and 'popular development'. 'Reflexive development' is a clear sign of what distinguishes current development thinking from earlier times and indicates where development theory appears to be heading. It is post-paradigmatic, in the sense of moving beyond the grand theories of the past and being much more open to reflection and change. There is still of course considerable divergence among different theoretical perspectives in the field of international development, but there has been a significant move towards more open and flexible approaches to understanding development, and generally towards more action-oriented rather than exclusively structuralist approaches. Future directions in development thinking cannot be precisely predicted because much will depend on the impact of future events as the 21st century unfolds, but it is reasonable to conclude at this point that development studies, broadly speaking, has taken a considerable stride forward towards a better understanding of development in theory and in practice. This is illustrated in relation to the decades from the 1950s to 2000s in Figure 4.8.

Figure 4.8: Evolution of development theory over the decades

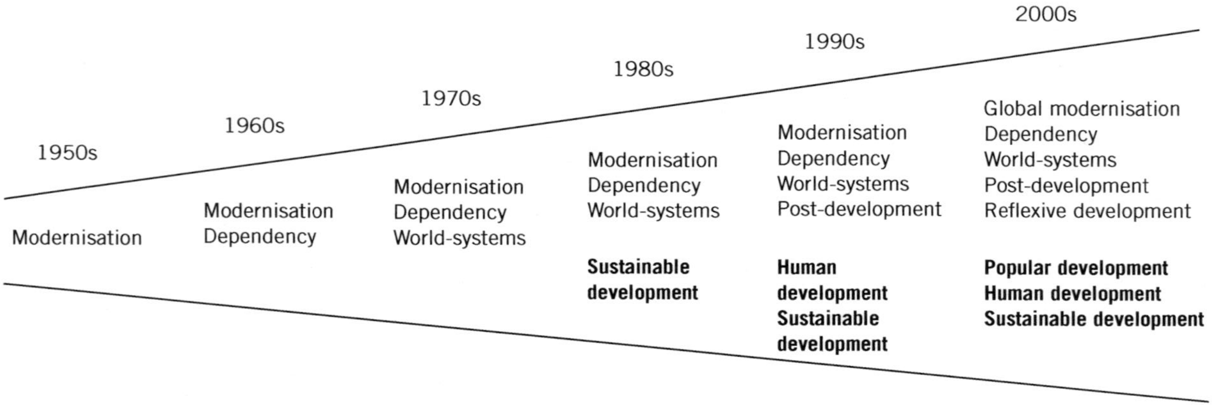

	1950s	1960s	1970s	1980s	1990s	2000s
	Modernisation	Modernisation Dependency	Modernisation Dependency World-systems	Modernisation Dependency World-systems	Modernisation Dependency World-systems Post-development	Global modernisation Dependency World-systems Post-development Reflexive development
				Sustainable development	**Human development** **Sustainable development**	**Popular development** **Human development** **Sustainable development**

KEY POINTS SUMMARY

- From the start of the 'era of development' in the second half of the 20th century, the emphasis was very much on economic growth and a close relationship between the capitalist West and the Third World, enabling a 'trickle-down' effect to promote economic development.
- Development theory has been influenced by 'classical' traditions of social science thinking and has become more diverse over time, with strongly opposing views of development and the best ways forward.
- Modernisation and dependency theories were the main theoretical approaches to development in the 20th century, and while a number of alternatives have appeared in the 21st century, the contrasting paradigmatic perspective of the earlier theories have continued to be influential.
- Later theories, such as global modernisation and world-systems theory, which built on earlier modernisation and dependency theory, have incorporated more recent historical developments such as the rise of globalisation into their theoretical models, but like the earlier theories they have also been subject to strong criticism.
- A radical break with all the earlier theories was incorporated into what became known as post-development theory, which continues to exert influence in the field of development by focusing on grassroots alternatives to conventional development
- Aspects of post-development thinking have been incorporated into what has been described as reflexive development, with its emphasis on addressing the failures of conventional development and embracing the idea of participatory popular development.
- Development theory has clearly moved on in lots of ways, and while there is still considerable divergence between different theoretical perspectives in the field of international development, there is now a more nuanced understanding of development and how it should be addressed, as reflected in the concept of reflexive development.

KEY READING GUIDE

There are number of key texts which have influenced development thinking over time, and it is worth consulting some of these to fully appreciate the different theories of development and their contrasting styles of approach. Examples in relation to modernisation theory include Rostow ([1960] 1990) *The Stages of Economic Growth*, Lerner (1964) *The Passing of Traditional Society*, and McClelland (1961) *The Achieving Society*. Leading exponents of dependency and world systems theory are Frank and Wallerstein, and key texts are Frank (1969) *Latin America: Underdevelopment or Revolution*, and Wallerstein (1974) *The Modern World System*. General texts on theories of development that provide good overviews of different theories include Harrison (1988) *The Sociology of Modernization and Development* on the earlier theories, and Peet and Hartwick (2015) *Theories of Development*, on the full range of theories. A broad view of the various and contrasting theories of development can also be found in Nederveen Pieterse (2010) *Development Theory*, and in Willis (2021) *Theories and Practices of Development*.

5

Globalisation and the dilemmas of development: is globalisation good or bad for the Global South?

Introduction: what in the world is going on?

> The only consensus about globalization is that it is contested.
> (Scholte, 2005: 41)

Globalisation has become one of the key concepts of the contemporary age, and in the world of international development it takes on a huge significance in interpreting and understanding the nature and scope of development across the world. However, as we will see in this chapter, it is also a term which has no universal definition and in many ways it is one of the most imprecise and contested concepts of the 21st century, as the quotation from Jan Aart Scholte (above) illustrates. It is one of the most widely used concepts, but also, as Peter Dicken (2015: 4) points out, 'one of the most misused and one of the most confused terms around today'. There are many different global maps; Figure 5.1 is an example of a cylindrical map devised by Arthur H. Robinson, which is sometimes referred to as the Robinson projection.

In the present age it is impossible to ignore the consequences of what is happening globally and how this affects our daily lives and human development. It is widely felt that the world is changing more rapidly and dramatically in the 21st century than ever before, and the impact of the coronavirus pandemic has significantly accentuated

Figure 5.1: Robinson map (cylindrical projection)

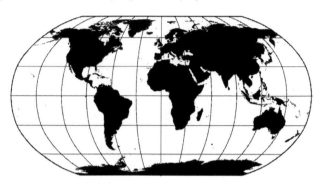

Source: www.freeusandworldmaps.com

global consciousness. There is a growing awareness of planet Earth as a single 'place' where once local events may now take on a global significance. For example, the clearing of trees in Amazonia to make way for 'development' in Latin America has been met with calls throughout the world for international action to preserve the rainforest and the global ecosystem. A further example of the global context in which we now live is the rapid economic growth of newly industrialising countries such as China and India, which deliver vast supplies of clothing and high-tech devices such as smartphones to consumers in the developed countries of Europe and North America. As a final example, in relation to human health there is an increasing awareness that infectious diseases have become more widespread across the world, often spreading from developing to developed countries: examples include HIV, SARS, Ebola and, most recently in 2020, COVID-19. These various examples indicate that global change is happening in many different spheres of human activity: environmental, sociocultural and economic. Furthermore, significant political and technological developments at the end of the last century, such as the ending of the Cold War, the fall of communism, and the transition to more democratic forms of rule in many parts of the world, together with the rapid expansion of global communication networks and the intensification of worldwide patterns of economic, financial, technological and ecological interdependence, suggest that we may be moving towards a 'world society'. However, there is no agreement that this is the direction we are moving in or that it is necessarily a desirable direction in which to move. Anti-globalisation movements and protests across the world are clear evidence of this. We all contribute to the accelerating forces of global interconnectedness, through travel, the use of new media technologies, from mobile phones to the internet, and as consumers of globally produced goods and services. But where is all this leading? Is there evidence of an emerging global culture, a narrowing of social and economic divisions between different parts of the world and a move towards the first truly global civilisation, or are global developments giving rise to growing inequalities, cultural divides, international conflicts, or even a 'clash of civilizations'? The Russian invasion of Ukraine in 2022, for example, created a significant global conflict with potentially serious implications for future development. Is globalisation therefore good or bad for development? Has globalisation effectively overtaken development? We begin by looking at the key features of globalisation.

What is globalisation?

> Globalization is a social process in which the constraints of geography on economic, political, social and cultural arrangements recede, in which people become increasingly aware that they are receding, and in which people act accordingly. (Waters, 2001: 5)

To understand exactly what is going on we need to start with a clear definition of 'globalisation'. The term is used in many different ways and sometimes very loosely now that it has entered the common language. Even in academic circles, there is often disagreement on what globalisation entails, the ways in which and the extent to which it can be said to have changed the world, and where the world is now heading. The above definition by the sociologist Malcolm Waters is therefore a good starting point as it clearly defines globalisation, recognising it both as a social process and as a form of global consciousness. The key features of globalisation are therefore:

- interconnectedness
- the dissolving of boundaries
- the formation of new relationships in which geographical distance is unimportant

Clearly, the definition of globalisation as an intense and accelerated process of interconnectedness of which people are increasingly aware is one which has a significant bearing on how we understand and define development in the current era. In a rapidly globalising world are there more opportunities for developing countries to prosper, or does the new age of the 21st century create greater global divisions and inequalities between different parts of the world?

Evaluating globalisation: alternative perspectives

The debate over globalisation and its impact on development has been marked by optimistic and pessimistic viewpoints. One side takes a 'happy ever after' view of globalisation as improving the quality of life across the world, raising living standards, addressing environmental issues, and bringing people together. The other side, meanwhile, takes a downbeat perspective, viewing globalisation as being out of control, leading to potential ecological disasters, and creating a world dominated by the major political and economic interests of the countries of the Global North with a growing divide between the rich and poor in the Global North and the Global South. George Ritzer (2015: 45) has referred to these contrasting perspectives between those who favour and those who fear globalisation as, respectively, 'globaphilia' and 'globaphobia'. Academic perspectives on globalisation have tended to fall into one of three contrasting schools of thought: hyperglobalist, internationalist and transformationalist.

From the **hyperglobalist** perspective we are entering a new epoch in human history in which accelerating economic forces of globalisation are bringing about a denationalisation of economies across the world through the development of transnational networks of production, trade and finance. This is a world in which nation-states are eroding and fragmenting, and the influence and control that national governments previously held is rapidly diminishing. One of the best-known exponents of this view is Kenichi Ohmae who maintains that the new epoch is one characterised by a 'borderless world', which marks the end of the once powerful nation-state as we enter what he calls 'the next global stage'. The new borderless world offers great opportunities for developing countries to take advantage of the new global conditions, which facilitate growing international trade, increasing financial flows and labour mobility (Ohmae, 2005). Another hyperglobalist is Thomas Friedman who sees dramatic changes in the global economy creating a new scenario in which 'the world is flat'. The flattening of the world displaces the key role previously played by nation-states and government, and creates a level playing field in which all competitors in the global market have an equal opportunity (Friedman, 2007). The hyperglobalist perspective clearly offers a profoundly positive and optimistic assessment of contemporary globalisation, but critics, such as Alberto Martinelli (2005: 105), have pointed out that a borderless or flat world allows the strongest players in the global economy to impose their worldwide domination and create growing inequalities . From this critical viewpoint, globalisation is the problem, not the solution to development.

The **internationalist** perspective is sceptical of the hyperglobalist view of globalisation and rejects the idea of a perfectly integrated global economy as a myth. The idea of the demise of the nation-state is seen as being exaggerated: while globalisation erodes national sovereignty to some extent, nation-states are still very important protagonists in the contemporary world. There are around 200 sovereign nation states today, double the number that existed in the early development era of the 1950s. The intensification and extent of international activity in recent times is seen as reinforcing and even enhancing state powers, rather than reducing them as the hyperglobalists claim. Governments continue to play a very important role in regulating international economic activity, and this means that the advanced economies of the more powerful nation-states continue to have a dominant position in the world. In one of the key internationalist texts, *Globalization in Question*, Paul Hirst et al (2009: 189) acknowledge that the global volume of trade is increasing, but argue that it is mainly between

Europe, North America and East Asia, and is a form of 'supranational regionalization' rather than full-scale globalisation. There is a similar level of scepticism about the idea that we are entering a global civilization when there is also evidence of fragmentation and widening cultural divisions. Geir Lundestad (2010: 288) goes so far as to claim that 'the stronger the globalisation, the stronger the fragmentation'.

The **transformationalist** perspective offers a more flexible and multi-faceted approach to globalisation. It starts from the position that in the 21st century globalisation is the unprecedented driving force behind the rapid social, political and economic changes that are transforming modern societies and the world order. In this respect it diverges from the sceptical internationalist perspective, but at the same time the transformationalist approach takes an open-ended view of the direction in which globalisation is heading, and therefore departs from the unidirectional and positive trajectory of globalisation put forward by the hyperglobalists. Rather than depicting a positive or negative future scenario, the transformationalists 'emphasize globalization as a long-term historical process which is inscribed with contradictions and which is significantly shaped by conjunctural factors' (Held et al, 2001: 7). Globalisation is seen as creating all sorts of new social, political and economic circumstances, which affect the nation-state and transform state power. This is not the end of the nation-state, as the hyperglobalists claim, but part of a process in which new global bodies and multilateral forms of global governance require states to make adjustments and governments to adapt to a changing and more interconnected world. This does not necessarily diminish the sovereignty or power of national governments, but necessitates their accommodation to the growing complexity of processes of governance in a globalising world. This is a process of transnationalisation that goes beyond the internationalist perspective, but challenges the direction advanced by the hyperglobalists, and effectively takes a middle road. The transformationalist perspective therefore offers a more nuanced and open-ended perspective on the relationship between globalisation and development.

The shrinking world

What is clear from all the different perspectives on globalisation is that the world has remarkably and irreversibly changed over time. Globalisation began long before the advent of the concept, and the history of globalisation, from the early empires to the modern age of social and economic development, clearly rested on the principle of linking different parts of the world, extending cultures across the globe, and creating a shared social space that facilitated interconnectivity. At the same time, globalisation has added velocity to this process by speeding up connections across the world, compressing time and space, and creating what has been referred to as 'a shrinking world'. This can be represented graphically, as shown in Figure 5.2, which illustrates the speeding-up of the transportation of people and goods across countries and continents over time.

At the same time, advances in communications systems have also served to shrink the world, from the creation of the printing press in the middle of the 15th century to the invention of the landline telephone in the late 19th century. The most notable communications innovation in the 21st century has been the development of the smartphone and its rapid global spread. This clearly illustrates the extent to which technological developments in communications and media have helped to move the world further towards what Marshall McLuhan (1962: 21) identified in the early 1960s as the 'global village'. It also raises the question of whether a world that is increasingly built around networks is 'chained to globalization' (Farrell and Newman, 2020). The global advance of communications and media developments is outlined in Figure 5.3.

Figure 5.2: The shrinking world

1500–1840   Horse-drawn coaches and sailing ships: average speed 10 mph

1850–1930   Steam locomotives: average speed 65 mph. Steam ships: 36 mph

1950s   Propeller aircraft: average speed 300–400 mph

1960s   Jet passenger aircraft: average speed 500–700 mph

1970s–2000s   Concorde aircraft: average speed 1200–1350 mph

Source: Adapted from Harvey (1989: 241)

Figure 5.3: Communications and media developments

1440   Printing press invented by Johannes Gutenberg

1792   Introduction of first long-distance semaphore telegraph line

1876   Invention of the landline telephone by Alexander Graham Bell

1900   Start of radio broadcasting

1926   Invention of television by John Logie Baird

1947   Start of first full-scale TV broadcasting

1973   First handheld mobile phone, devised by Motorola

1983   Creation of the internet

1990   Second generation mobile phones introduced

1991   Introduction of the World Wide Web by Tim Berners-Lee

2003   Launch of Skype

2007   First touchscreen phone introduced by Apple – iPhone

2019   Introduction of 5G networks for telecommunications

Where are we now?

Much of the recent academic literature demonstrates agreement on the essential elements of globalisation. There is now widespread recognition that globalisation is an ongoing process of growing interconnectedness of the world in many key areas of life, from the economic to the cultural, the technological to the environmental. This is not a simple one-directional process, but rather, as Peter Dicken (2015: 8) points out, 'a complex, indeterminate set of processes operating very unevenly in both time and space'. There is therefore widespread acceptance of the need to take a **multidimensional** approach to globalisation, as distinct from the heavily economistic view of the world taken by world-systems theorists such as Wallerstein. While the techno-economic interconnectedness of the world tends to be emphasised in most of the literature, the sociopolitical and cultural-civilizational dimensions of globalisation are now also more widely acknowledged. Globalisation today depicts a much more complex and fluid social world in an era of increasing time-space compression. This is illustrated, for example, in an exponential increase in the speed of geographic expansion in travel, tourism, terrorism, health-related viruses, commodities, migrants and financial crises. The scope and speed of global flows has increased significantly in recent decades and notably in the 21st century. This marks a **global shift**, which involves more than the stretching and speeding up of social relations and activities across borders, regions and continents, as it also entails new systems and networks of interactions that become increasingly **multi-directional** such that local developments may have global consequences in the same way that global events can have serious local consequences.

The intensity and velocity of contemporary globalisation is also reflected in a growing global consciousness, which recognises and reflects on the consequences of the world becoming a single place. Also referred to as a form of **globality**, this global consciousness has become more pronounced as a result of global developments and incidents in the new millennium, including the rise in global migration, the 9/11 attacks and the spread of international terrorism, the global financial crisis of 2008, and the SARS, Ebola and coronavirus pandemics. Technological advances in communications and media have greatly facilitated the rise of globality, the deepening consciousness of the world as a whole.

Globalisation and global consciousness have clearly moved on in the 21st century to bring us to where we are now. One further direction taken by globalisation is the move towards what has been termed **multipolar globalisation**. This refers to a globalised world that is no longer **bipolar**, divided between the communist East and the capitalist West, nor **unipolar** as it was following the fall of communism, with the US leading the world in a new global age. The rise of the BRICS (Brazil, Russia, India, China, South Africa) in the 21st century, and notably the rise in Asia of China and India, marks an immense global shift in the last two decades. China's economy grew to the point at which it overtook Japan as the world's second largest economy in 2010, and by 2018 it was more than twice as large as Japan's economy. It then overtook the US in the World Bank global rankings of GDP (gross domestic product), measured by PPP (purchasing power parity) to become the world's largest economy in 2020. China has also become a major trading partner to most countries and plays a pivotal role in the success of other markets, acting as a key catalyst for global trade growth. By 2030 it could be joined by India. India's rise would also reflect that of Asia in becoming the dominant economic region of the world by the end of the decade. The top ten rankings in 2020 are presented in Table 5.1.

These global economic changes are also reflected in sociocultural shifts and the emergence of new spheres of influence around the world. China has extended its influence in neighbouring countries, for example, through the Belt and Road Initiative, and by investing in new projects and supply chains in parts of Africa and Latin America. The Belt and Road Initiative replicates in some ways the original Silk Road that was established by the Chinese Han dynasty in the second century BC and continued through to the 18th century. Given the history of globalisation, the return of China to the centre stage of the world suggests that globalisation goes in circles. Today, to quote Nederveen Pieterse's (2018: xi) analogy, 'Like a giant oil tanker, the world is slowly turning.' In the new multipolar world the

Table 5.1: Top 10 GDP PPP rankings, 2020

Ranking	Economy	US$ millions
1	China	24,273,360
2	United States	20,936,600
3	India	8,907,028
4	Japan	5,328,033
5	Germany	4,469,546
6	Russian Federation	4,133,084
7	Indonesia	3,302,377
8	Brazil	3,153,597
9	France	3,115,307
10	United Kingdom	3,019,057

Note: GDP is measured here by PPP.

Source: World Bank (2021b)

emerging economies of Asia and other parts of the Global South mark a significant shift from the period of overwhelming Western dominance and American hegemony. Globalisation today is markedly different from that of the 20th century. North-South relations which were previously dominant and central to development theorising now exist alongside East-South and South-South relations in the current era of multipolar globalisation.

Where is globalisation going? Key dimensions of globalisation and development

Having examined the concept of globalisation and related concepts, and having outlined the history of globalisation and where we are now, it is important to recognise that divergent interpretations of globalisation and its consequences for development prevail in the academic literature. In part this reflects the tendency for different approaches to focus on different aspects of globalisation, from the **techno-economic** to the **sociopolitical** and the **cultural-civilizational** dimensions. In this section, we examine the different ways in which globalisation and its impact on development in each of these key areas has been interpreted. From one viewpoint there is said to be increasing integration and participation in a world moving forward in one direction, which can be classified as a form of **convergence** or **homogenisation**. An opposing viewpoint sees increasing diversity in many areas with divisions and inequalities across the world leading to **divergence** and even global **polarisation**. A third interpretation sees a more complex process of **heterogenisation** taking place, which draws on developments happening both at a global level and at local levels in different parts of the world. The global and the local interact and interplay in various ways, leading to new combinations and mixed outcomes, which can be classified as a form of **hybridisation**.

Techno-economic globalisation

In the **techno-economic** sphere, globalisation can be seen as 'one of the most visible consequences of modernity' (Martinelli, 2005: 101), brought into existence by the growth of economic modernisation across the world and accelerated by the development of new digital technologies and deepening capitalist integration. This transformation of the world has seen the rise of global communications networks and the rapid expansion of transnational corporations (TNCs) operating worldwide with increasing cross-border flexibility. From this perspective, the new global age has supplanted the earlier age of modernity and multinational corporations and created an integrated global economy that challenges national sovereignty and is becoming increasingly homogeneous. Globalisation is seen as creating a one-dimensional world. The process of homogenisation across the world is described by George Ritzer (2019) as 'McDonaldization', a reference to the model typified by the American fast-food chain McDonald's. This concept could be seen as referring to the Americanization of the world, but Ritzer argues that the key to the concept of McDonaldization is the way in which it describes a process whereby the practices, values and institutional arrangements of different countries and their economies are converging across the globe. The process of economic homogenisation is one in which there are no limits to global capitalist expansion of the world's largest and most powerful corporations, facilitated by constantly advancing new technologies. Rapid techno-economic convergence across the world is seen by the hyperglobalists as beneficial to all, whereas for its critics the idea that 'one size fits all' is seen as unrealistic, and the advancing global economy is seen as essentially benefiting TNCs at the expense of the vast majority of the world's population, thereby accentuating uneven development between different countries.

A widely held critical view is that economic globalisation has generated a 'race to the bottom' in which developing countries have had to compete with each other to attract foreign investment by offering cheaper facilities and lower wages for workers than other countries. TNCs in particular are seen as taking advantage of this race to the bottom. Rather than creating convergence and homogenisation across the world, there is increasing divergence and inequity. Dani Rodrik (2016: 3) notes that, while global markets may appear to be good for poor countries, the global rules according to which they are being asked to play, are often not. Globalisation has not lived up to expectations, leading to serious discontents, as the former chief economist of the World Bank, Joseph Stiglitz (2017), has pointed out. The global economy has created both winners and losers.

A more nuanced view is that globalisation is a more complex phenomenon than the hyperglobalists and their critics recognise, and has created various mixed outcomes that can be seen across the world today. Rather than straightforward homogenisation or polarisation of the global economy, we are seeing a process of hybridisation. New sets of relationships, such as those between the strongly emerging economies of the eastern hemisphere, notably China and India, and the developing countries of Asia, Africa and Latin America, have led to the growth of new regional trading blocs across the world, and have helped to boost economic development. Some of the most successful developing countries have followed what has become known as the 'Goldilocks principle', based on the idea of avoiding extremes and following a balanced hybrid path to development. A very good example is India, which has become a significant player in the global economy but has avoided being taken over by global megatrends. It has done this by following a strategy that balances its economy in such a way that it draws in foreign finance and exports many of the goods it produces to other countries around the world, while at the same time taking care not to rely too much on foreign finance or on exports, and has simultaneously employed strategies to develop the local economy. Jan Nederveen Pieterse (2018: 198) goes so far as to claim that we now live in 'a new development era' which is markedly different from the past in that the new industrialising countries of the Global South have become increasingly important drivers of the world economy and have shaped 21st century globalisation.

New technologies can have a negative impact on developing countries, as evidenced by the rise of automation and the decline of the industrial workforce, and may exacerbate inequality, but at the same time new digital technologies may have a positive effect where used appropriately and effectively; for example, in creating a global service economy with employees increasingly located in developing countries such as India. Both automation and the use of digital technologies are likely to speed up in the coming years, driven by new innovations and socioeconomic trends, but also by the impact of global crises such as the COVID-19 pandemic. The economic changes and shifts in employment in the 21st century can already be seen in most developing economies where the share of manufacturing jobs has tended to level off at relatively low levels as labour has shifted from agriculture to services, mainly bypassing the manufacturing sector. However, this structural change and shift to the service sector has generally been growth-enhancing for developing countries, according to the IMF's (2018) *World Economic Outlook*, and has helped to raise economy-wide productivity. At the same time, in some countries, notably China, Indonesia, Malaysia and Thailand, the share of manufacturing jobs in their economies has continued to rise. For example, many of the products sold by leading US technology companies, such as the Apple iPhone, are designed in the US but have parts manufactured in various countries and assembled in China. This once again supports the view that economic globalisation and the new global technologies straddling the world are having different consequences for economic development in different countries and regions. Rather than producing homogenisation across the world, globalisation can be seen as leading to heterogenisation, with the interpenetration of the global and the local in developing countries resulting in what has been termed 'glocalisation'.

Trade, travel and tourism

Techno-economic globalisation and the growth of global trade have clearly brought both benefits and losses to the countries of the Global South. A good example is the rise of global tourism and its impact on developing countries. International tourism has grown on a huge scale since the start of the development era in the second half of the 20th century. For many it is seen as playing an increasing role in economic development around the world, and is a key driver of globalisation in the 21st century. The rise of global tourism is clearly depicted in Figure 5.4.

As the growth of international tourism has accelerated, this in turn has further propelled globalisation with the rise of the tourist industry and the escalating movement of people and ideas across continents. This raises the question of whether travel and tourism present a high-speed route to development. The rapid expansion of travel, the tourist experience and the tourist industry, can be very clearly seen in the rising number of international tourist arrivals, and the shift in tourist destinations from Europe and North America to other regions of the world, including many parts of the developing world. Global tourism

Figure 5.4: The global tourist world

Source: www.shutterstock.com

has grown exponentially since the start of the first development era in the second half of the 20th century. In 1950 the number of international tourist arrivals was just over 25 million, a figure that subsequently rose sharply, particularly in the 1980s and 1990s, to 682 million in the year 2000. That figure has continued to rise and by the end of the second decade of the 21st century had more than doubled to almost 1.5 billion. According to UNWTO (2019a: 2), the spectacular growth in the number of international arrivals confirms tourism as a leading and resilient economic sector to the extent that 'international tourist arrivals and receipts continue to outpace the global economy and both emerging and advanced economies are benefitting from rising tourist income'. The exponential rise in international tourism is represented graphically in Figure 5.5.

Economically, tourism offers developing countries the opportunity to take advantage of their land, environment, culture and heritage, to construct an economic sector that does not require the same level of infrastructure and investment as many other industrial sectors (for example, manufacturing). It is therefore more cost-effective as an economic platform for development. Tourism helps to boost employment in a number of different areas, including jobs related to landscape and heritage site maintenance, tour guiding, work in local hotels and guesthouses, restaurants and souvenir shops, and so

Figure 5.5: International tourist arrivals, 2000–19

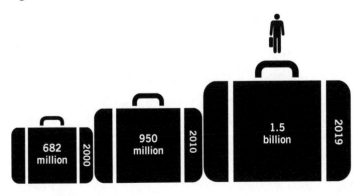

Source: UNWTO (2022)

on. Agricultural and fishing sectors also tend to be stimulated by tourism, together with local construction enterprises and handicraft production. Profits earned from tourism can be reinvested into the country to enable the construction of better travel and communication networks, improve health and educational facilities, and provide funding for conservation efforts where necessary. This is turn can benefit the tourism industry and make the country more attractive for visitors, thereby creating a positive economic development cycle.

On the other side of the coin, however, tourism may not bring so many economic advantages and positive multiplier effects to developing countries. For example, multinational corporations (MNCs) from the developed world are involved in both the construction and the running of hotel chains and restaurants, and the supply of various goods and services. To take just one example, Marriott International is a US hospitality company that owns over seven thousand hotels in 131 countries across the world. As a result of such multinational ownership, the vast majority of the profits from tourism do not remain in the tourist country but are taken away by the MNCs. This is referred to as a process of economic 'leakage' and it has a very serious impact with estimates indicating that up to 75 per cent of revenues from tourism leak away from developing countries as a result of foreign ownership of services, imported resources and foreign tour operators. In some of the more remote and least developed countries as little as 10 to 20 per cent of the money spent by tourists remains in the country of destination. According to the United Nations Conference on Tourism and Development (UNCTAD), leakage is the most serious economic challenge that many developing countries face, particularly LDCs (least developed countries) and those with limited economic diversification that rely heavily on the tourism sector, including small island developing states. In Africa, tourism created 21 million jobs between 2011 and 2014, and it is estimated that a further 32 million jobs will be created between 2020 and 2030; UNCTAD (2017: 3) points out, however, that the high financial leakage of up to 85 per cent of the total profits from tourism means that countries in Africa cannot rely on tourism as the main avenue out of poverty or the pathway to sustainable economic development.

Economic leakage is a serious concern for developing countries, as Figure 5.6 illustrates.

From an economic viewpoint, tourism may therefore have both advantages and disadvantages for developing countries: on the one hand, by creating employment and bringing investment into the tourist-related enterprises; but on the other hand, repatriating most of the revenues from the tourist sector to the developed countries where the MNCs are based. Global inequalities are therefore more likely to be accentuated rather than reduced by the worldwide expansion of the tourism. However, one of the positive impacts of tourism on local populations has been the creation of new employment opportunities. While many new jobs created in the tourist sectors of the economy tend to be relatively low skilled with few opportunities for promotion, the growth of the tourism sector has contributed to a significant rise in the number of female employees. While the overall percentage of women in the global workforce was 39 per cent in

Figure 5.6: Economic leakage from the tourist sector

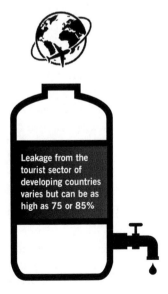

Source: UNCTAD (2017)

2019, in the tourist sector the figure was much higher at 54 per cent (UNWTO, 2019b: 9). Tourism offers more opportunities for female employees, especially in the accommodation and food services sectors in developing countries, and has been widely seen as contributing to the empowerment of women by increasing their self-confidence and community involvement as well as creating new leadership roles. Women living in rural communities are seen as having the most to gain from the new job opportunities created by tourism, as it provides a new source of income and allows domestic skills such as cooking and handicraft making to be deployed in a formal occupational setting. However, there is a significant gender pay gap in the tourist sector with women earning around 10 to 15 per cent less than men. Tourism therefore 'offers both incredible opportunities and huge challenges for gender equality' (Rinaldi and Salerno, 2020: 1466).

The growth of international tourism can accelerate aspects of development, but at the same time it can accentuate global inequalities and also poses risks for the attainment of the Sustainable Development Goals (SDGs) with the significant rise of international travel and the environmental impact of flights across the world, notably as a result of the carbon footprint created by aircraft. Non-governmental organisations (NGOs) such as Tourism Concern have claimed that tourism is being overdeveloped with many parts of the developing world now suffering from 'over-tourism'. While the expansion of tourism across the developing world has brought a number of benefits, it has also created problems and accentuated economic inequalities, which has led to calls for greater equality and sustainable tourism, sometimes referred to as 'ecotourism'.

Sociopolitical globalisation

Developments in the **sociopolitical** sphere have also been interpreted as having both positive and negative consequences for the Global South. From one perspective, a new global order has emerged in which global governance has largely taken over from the role previously played by sovereign nation-states. Global institutions such as the World Bank, the IMF, the World Economic Forum and the World Trade Organization

(WTO) have assumed a more powerful governing role in response to economic globalisation; new global regulatory systems have become the driving force of what has been described as the 'globalisation project', which has replaced the earlier 'development project' with its emphasis on national economic growth under individual state supervision (McMichael, 2016: 13). Global governance, to the extent that it has created rules and regulations for nation-states to follow, can be seen as helping to foster homogenisation. This may be seen as beneficial for development as the same rules apply for both developed and developing countries. However, critics have pointed out that the countries that have been most successful in developing their emerging economies are those which have found ways to avoid being subject to global regulations. Some critics have gone further and argued that globalisation has created a new 'global ruling class', which serves the interests of global corporations rather than creating a level playing field for development. Noreena Hertz (2001) has referred to this as 'the silent takeover' of politics by global corporations, and Susan George (2015: 18) argues that TNCs increasingly exert power at national, regional and supranational levels, such that global corporations are now effectively eclipsing nation-states and seizing power as 'shadow sovereigns'. Or, in the words of John Pilger (2002), they are now 'the new rulers of the world'. Opposition to globalisation and the growing power of global corporations has led to the creation of movements such as the World Social Forum, which was set up in opposition to the World Economic Forum.

An alternative, more nuanced, perspective on recent sociopolitical developments at the global level suggests that nation-states continue to play a significant role in an era of accelerating globalisation, and that there are emerging multilateral forms of global governance that challenge the idea of a universal takeover of politics by global corporations. Nick Bisley, for example, argues that while globalisation enhances the influence of non-state actors at the global level and has produced a shift in the nature of international relations, states have not lost all their power to institutions and global corporations are not 'the new masters of the global universe'. Rather, nation-states have increasingly come to recognise that non-state actors, such as NGOs,

TNCs and international institutions play an important role on the global stage, and states are therefore 'looking to a wide range of means through which they can seek to influence their increasingly complex environment' (Bisley, 2007: 222–3).

A concept that has been used to define the new political environment, in which nation-states and international institutions have become increasingly interconnected, is 'empire'. The new empire of the 21st century, as envisaged by Hardt and Negri, is one which is more pluralistic and in which no nation-state is able to take on a hegemonic role. Developing countries are clearly far less influential within this new empire than the more powerful countries in the world, but may benefit from the replacement of global hegemony by a multipolar global economy and multilateral forms of global governance (Hardt and Negri, 2019).

Finally, in relation to the popular political movements that have emerged in response to globalisation across the world, it is clear that they do not all fall into the same category, but have adopted a variety of different approaches. Rather than viewing all these movements as being essentially 'anti-globalisation', a new concept has emerged in recognition of the fact that while certain aspects of globalisation are rejected, others are accepted. This is known as 'alter-globalisation' and refers to the idea of not abolishing globalisation per se but rather creating new, alternative forms of globalisation which draw on its potentially positive attributes while eradicating its negative aspects. Alter-globalisation movements have therefore opposed aspects of economic globalisation, notably the neoliberalisation of the world economy and the negative impact it has had on developing countries, accentuated by an unequal balance of power between rich and poor member countries of organisations such as the WTO. At the same time, however, they have supported the globalisation of global justice, global communications, global health safeguards and global environmental protection. Once again, globalisation can be seen to be creating a mixed response in a world where 'it is possible for states, the civil society, local communities and citizens to become actors in the global age' (Pleyers, 2011: 263).

Cultural-civilizational globalisation

One of the most striking features of globalisation as experienced by people across the globe is the extent to which the development of new communications systems and digital technologies has increasingly connected people who may never meet face-to-face. Interconnectedness, the dissolving of boundaries, and the formation of new relationships in which geographical distance is unimportant, have ushered in a new era. The new world in which we now live can be interpreted in a variety of ways, from the creation of a 'global village' and cultural convergence to a world in which different cultures are more likely to clash and create deepening divisions and divergence. A widely held view is that modernisation across the world in the form of Westernisation has spread Western culture to countries of the Global South. The debate about Westernisation has continued in the 21st century, with some applauding it as a progressive process of homogenisation, and others viewing it as a form of cultural imperialism and the triumph of Western supremacy over the rest of the world (Bessis, 2003).

A diametrically opposed view of cultural globalisation sees it not as leading to convergence and uniformity, but rather as serving to create serious divisions and the polarisation of the world. The argument here is that, as a result of new technologies and the world becoming a smaller place, awareness of differences between cultures and civilizations increases. Samuel Huntington argued that, following the end of the Cold War in the 1990s and the end of the East-West ideological division of the world, future conflicts would not be between countries but between different cultures, leading to what he described as 'the clash of civilizations'. Different civilizations exist around the world, according to Huntington, based on history, language, culture, tradition and, most importantly, religion, with one of the most significant divides being that between Islamic and Western civilizations (Huntington, 2002). The terrorist attacks by the Islamic group al-Qaeda against the US on 11 September 2001, now widely referred to as 9/11, were seen as a prime example of the clash of civilizations. Ongoing conflicts in the 21st century in the

Middle East and Asia are also seen as stemming from cultural and religious divisions.

Another perspective on the increasing divisions and polarisation of the world, as put forward by Benjamin Barber (2003: xvi), views it not as a clash of civilizations but rather as 'a dialectical expression of tensions built into a single globalization', creating 'not a war between civilizations but a war within civilization' that undermines democracy and the nation-state. This is defined as 'Jihad vs. McWorld'. McWorld refers to the new global world created by the spread of American consumer capitalism, as typified by McDonaldization, which is rapidly dissolving the social and economic barriers between nations. Jihad, on the other hand, refers to the ethnic, religious and racial hatreds that have emerged within this globalised McWorld, creating the predominant conflict of our times: consumerist capitalism versus religious and tribal fundamentalism.

A far more positive and less divisive and disruptive view of globalisation focuses not on the clash of cultures and civilizations but on how it has created new forms of interconnectivity between different local cultures. Ulf Hannerz (2001: 102) saw this emerging at the turn of the 21st century as a 'world culture'. This refers not to the homogenisation of culture, but rather to its interconnected diversity. The world has become one network of social relationships, and between its different regions there is a flow of culture as well of people and goods. This leads to various forms of cultural blending, also known as 'creolization'. Aspects of Western culture, for example, may be blended with different local cultures in the countries of the Global South, resulting in a process of indigenisation or 'glocalism', a merger of the global and the local. From an optimistic viewpoint leads to greater cultural openness and acceptance of new values, ways of life and mores. In addition, it also produces 'reverse cultural flows' whereby the earlier one-way flow of culture, from the North to the South or from the West to the rest of the world, is being replaced by flows in the opposite direction, from the developing to the developed world. Examples include music, literature, religion, cuisine, health and lifestyle. Indian food and yoga, African and Latin American music and dance, Asian alternative medicines and health and fitness practices, are just a few illustrative cases of 'reverse cultural flows' in a globalising world.

Cultural globalisation can therefore be seen as creating a new world, but one that does not destroy localities. Rather, new forms of hybrid cultures and multiple identities are created. This raises the possibility of a progressively interconnected world in the 21st century, combining local and global characteristics to the point at which there is an increasing awareness and understanding of cultural multiplicity, which opens up the prospect of a globally shared collective future and cosmopolitan way of life. In this positive future scenario people from different locations and cultures around the world form relationships of mutual respect with each other, and come together as citizens of the world.

Summary and conclusion: is globalisation good or bad for development?

It is clear from the foregoing discussion in this chapter that not only is globalisation a contested concept, but also that there are many different interpretations of the impacts of globalisation on development. In the complex and fluid social world of the 21st century, globalisation manifests itself in many different ways and in many different areas, including the economy, politics and culture, and can be viewed from a number of perspectives with contrasting assessments of whether globalisation is good or bad for development. Some analyses remain very positive, emphasising the extent to which an increasingly interconnected world has enabled a number of countries in the Global South to develop rapidly and become important players in the global economy, while also extending their political and cultural influence in an increasingly multipolar world. From a more pessimistic perspective, as globalisation has advanced greater concerns have been expressed about the extent to which many countries in the Global South have been left behind and remain underdeveloped in an increasingly unequal world. In recent times there has also been a growing awareness of the broader impact of development on the environment and human life in general. We have seen this in relation to the rising concern to manage the planet in such a way that it is possible to have sustainable development, and also in the new perception of globalisation that has arisen as a result of its acceleration and the increasing interdependency and interconnectedness of the world.

This has raised growing concerns about human security and health which reached new and unprecedented levels with the outbreak of the COVID-19 pandemic in early 2020. Globalisation can therefore be seen both as a great opportunity for development and also as the source of new systemic risks that affect us all. With many countries retreating from global connectivity and moving more towards self-sufficiency as a result of the spread of coronavirus across the world, this raised the question, 'Has COVID-19 killed globalisation?' (*The Economist*, 2020). There may be a partial retreat from globalisation, but it is unlikely to disappear, and its impact on development around the world will continue to be felt, both positively and negatively, depending on the perspective one takes. Some of the key changes brought about by 21st-century globalisation are unlikely to disappear. These include the switch from Western domination to a more multi-polar world with the rise of developing countries such as China and India, the growth of more regional trading blocs and new international institutions, and technical advances that facilitate global communications and cultural flows.

The changes brought about through globalisation have undoubtedly altered our perceptions of the world, and regions that were once peripheralised from a Western viewpoint have taken on a new significance. This raises the question of whether our graphical representations of the world will also change to reflect more accurately the actual size of the different countries and regions of the world rather than the distortions of the Mercator projection which has predominated since the 16th century. Maps based on this projection have depicted countries and regions in the northern hemisphere as being larger than they really are relative to those in the southern hemisphere. Are we now approaching a point in the process of globalisation where an alternative map, such as that based on the Peters projection of the early 1970s (Figure 5.7), which more accurately reflects the true size of the countries and regions of the Global South,

Figure 5.7: Peters projection map, 1973

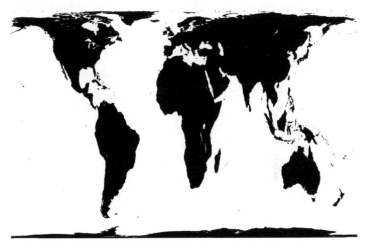

Source: https://commons.wikimedia.org

will seriously challenge the dominant graphical view of the world that has prevailed for several centuries? By using this projection, Peters argued that the less developed, less powerful nations of the world could be restored to their rightful proportions.

The later chapters of this book will all make reference to globalisation and its impact on development in different areas such as poverty and inequality, human security and human rights, health and wellbeing, environment and climate change, gender inequalities, and the advent of new technologies and digital communications. In all of these areas the question arises as to whether globalisation has gone too far, or not far enough. Globalisation has created many dilemmas for development, bringing both advantages and disadvantages for the Global South.

KEY POINTS SUMMARY

- As with 'development', 'globalisation' is a widely used but complex and contested concept.

- Views on globalisation are diverse: from the hyperglobalist, to sceptical internationalist, and the more flexible transformationalist perspectives.
- The key features of globalisation are interconnectedness, the dissolving of boundaries and the formation of new relationships in which geographical distance becomes less important – a 'shrinking world'.
- Globalisation has a long history but the concept really took off in the late 20th century, and has accelerated since then and into the 21st century, especially with the development of new ICTs which have facilitated the interconnectedness of the world.
- A number of important terms have emerged in relation to globalisation, including 'global shift' and 'globality', and growing recognition of what has been termed 'multipolar globalisation'.
- To identify where globalisation is going, it is necessary to look at three key areas: the techno-economic, sociopolitical and cultural-civilizational dimensions of globalisation, and to recognise that in some respects the world may be moving in one direction, but in other ways the world may be diverging or creating new forms of hybridity.
- Tourism has become a major driver of globalisation, and has significant effects on economic, social and cultural development.
- Globalisation has changed our perceptions of the world and can be seen as both good and bad for development.

KEY READING GUIDE

One of the leading texts on economic globalisation and the changing contours of the global economy, now in its seventh edition, is Dicken (2015) *Global Shift*. A useful concise general overview of globalisation is Waters (2001) *Globalization*, and there are a number of extensive tests, notably Held et al (2001) *Global Transformations: Politics, Economics and Culture*, which is supplemented with a reader on globalisation, drawing on a wide range of authors: Held and McGrew (2002) *The Global Transformations Reader*. In addition, Ritzer, who is famous for his book on *The McDonaldization of Society*, has also produced a 500-page text on globalisation: (2015) *Globalization: A Basic Text*. For an overview of globalisation theory, see Axford (2013) *Theories of Globalization*. On the changing nature of globalisation in the 21st century, a good text to consult is Nederveen Pieterse (2018) *Multipolar Globalization*. On tourism and globalisation and its effects on development, a book by Peterson provides a good overview: *Tourism, Development and Globalization* (2018). Another book by Holden examines the relationship between *Tourism, Poverty and Development* (2013).

Part II
Development challenges

6

Population, food and famine: where are we now?

Introduction

> For over 800 million people in the world – men, women, and
> children – hunger is a daily occurrence. (Conway et al, 2019: 33)

A prevailing image of the developing world in the Western media
is that of the starving child. In a number of the poorest countries
in the world hunger and periodic famine appear to be endemic, the
unavoidable consequence of an unhappy coincidence of geography
and demography. When famines hit the headlines in the West they
are commonly seen as resulting from 'natural' disasters such as drought
or flood, with food shortages made worse by the persistent problems
of 'over-population'. How adequate are explanations of this kind?
This chapter will make the point that, at best, they provide only a
partial account of why so many in the developing world go hungry;
at worst, they become enshrined as myths, which serve to disguise
the underlying reasons for world hunger. To understand why famines
occur and why their impact is unevenly felt within a society, this
chapter examines the broader social, economic and political contexts
that determine the ways in which food is produced and distributed.
Hunger is not only present during periods of famine, however, as the
quote at the start of this chapter illustrates, and the United Nations
World Food Programme estimates that more than one in nine of
the world population do not get enough to eat (UN WFP, 2020).

To understand why hunger, undernutrition and malnutrition are still widespread in the world today when there is no global food deficit, it is necessary to consider the wider context of poverty and inequality, and the international dimension – the global politics of food.

This chapter begins by exploring the extent of world hunger and lack of adequate nutrition, and moves on to examine the broader social, economic and political contexts which determine the ways in which food is produced and distributed. This includes a discussion of poverty and inequality and the extent to which they are connected with food shortages and the serious health consequences of undernutrition. Different ways of measuring the nature and extent of hunger and food security will be explored, and the impact of recent crises such as the COVID-19 pandemic will be examined in relation to the possibility of achieving the UN Sustainable Development Goal (SDG 2) of ending hunger and its serious effects on health by 2030. Population is often seen as a key factor in relation to food, famine and hunger, and the chapter will go on to explore the impacts of population on hunger and poverty, and the effects of poverty on population and food insecurity. Economic slowdowns and downturns also play a part in undermining food security, and food shortages and famines are often driven by conflicts and civil wars. Increasingly in the 21st century, climate change, which is a human creation, has had serious impacts on food production and food supply chains. Politics also plays a very significant part in the availability of food, at national, regional and global levels. The chapter concludes by raising the question of whether hunger and food insecurity can ever be resolved without addressing the global politics of food and significantly reducing global inequalities.

Food insecurity and famine

Food insecurity is a major issue facing many countries in the developing world. Six decades on from the United Nations first development decade in the 1960s, the world continues to be haunted by the spectre of mass starvation. Famines killed nearly 75 million people in the 20th century, and hopes that famines would recede into history in the 21st century were cast aside by the onset of severe food deficits and deaths from hunger in countries such as South Sudan, Somalia, Nigeria, Yemen and Haiti. Famines are extreme events in which large populations lack adequate access to food, giving rise to a sharp increase in mortality as a result of acute starvation and related diseases. Famines are often seen as catastrophes caused by 'natural' disasters such as drought, flooding, hurricanes, and crop failures caused by infestations such as the serious locust plague in East Africa in 2020. However, other significant factors also come into play such as poverty, population displacement, civil unrest, conflict and wars which reduce the availability of food and create food insecurity.

Food insecurity and hunger are not only connected to specific events and famines, but can be an ongoing phenomenon, with chronic hunger resulting in sustained nutritional deprivation. Undernutrition and malnutrition have resulted in serious medical conditions in many populations across the world, including wasting and serious stunting in the growth of children. Food security relates to food availability, access and utilisation. Adequate availability and access to enough safe and nutritious food to maintain an active and healthy life is essential to prevent food insecurity and chronic hunger. According to the UN Food and Agricultural Organization (FAO), around two billion people – over a quarter of the global population – suffer from severe or moderate food insecurity with insufficient access to safe, nutritious and sufficient food. Around 750 million people were experiencing severe food insecurity in 2020, or nearly one in ten people in the world, according to the figures provided by the FAO, while those experiencing moderate food insecurity who do not have regular access to sufficient and nutritious food comprise a further 1.25 billion people across the world (UN FAO et al, 2020a: vi). The vast majority suffering from food insecurity live in the Global South. The FAO estimates that by 2030 the number of undernourished people in the world will be more than 840 million (UN FAO et al, 2020a: 3). The world is therefore not on track to achieve the UN Sustainable Development Goal of Zero Hunger by 2030, and the related targets of SDG 2 which include addressing nutritional needs, ending all forms of malnutrition, meeting the internationally agreed targets on reducing stunting and wasting of children under the age of five, and doubling the agricultural productivity and incomes of small-scale food producers and family farmers in developing countries.

The majority of the world's undernourished live in Asia, despite improvements in food security in China, with over 380 million people suffering from undernutrition, while more than 250 million live in Africa where the number of undernourished people is growing faster than in any other region of the world. The overall global percentage of those suffering from undernourishment has not changed very much in recent years, but the absolute numbers have risen in step with the increase in the global population. This has contributed to Africa being the hardest hit region in the world as it has the highest population growth rate of all regions. The percentage of those affected in Africa is over twice the rate in Asia and Latin America and the Caribbean. On the basis of these trends, the FAO estimates that by 2030 Africa will be the region with the highest number of undernourished people, and home to more than half of the world's chronically hungry (UN FAO et al, 2020a: 16).

As with many other areas of development, the COVID-19 pandemic had a dramatic impact on food insecurity, hunger and malnutrition. The pandemic seriously affected food production and distribution, with closed borders, curfews and travel restrictions disrupting food supply chains and people's incomes. Local farming and labour were seriously hit in many countries with famers unable to plant or harvest crops, or access markets to sell their produce and buy the necessary seeds and fertilisers, especially in countries already badly affected by poverty and hunger. It was a crisis that exacerbated existing problems and shortages, pushing millions of the world's poorest people deeper into hunger and poverty, and creating new epicentres of hunger across the globe. In the words of Oxfam International, the pandemic 'added fuel to the fire of an already growing hunger crisis' (Oxfam International, 2020d).

Food insecurity and hunger are clearly a major threat to the overall health of the human population, and one that is exacerbated by other global issues. An important measure of the seriousness of this threat is the Global Hunger Index (GHI) which is produced annually by the international by humanitarian organisations, Welthungerhilfe and Concern Worldwide. The GHI is based on data from the United Nations, including the FAO and UNICEF, and the WHO. The GHI score for each country combines data for the under-five mortality rate, the extent of wasting in children, the prevalence of child stunting, and the proportion of undernourished in the population. The results show that there has been a decline in Global Hunger since the turn of the new millennium, from a GHI score of 29.0 in the year 2000 to 21.0 in 2019, but followed by an increase in 2020/21 as a result of conflict, climate change and the COVID-19 pandemic (Welthungerhilfe and Concern Worldwide, 2021). Child stunting has declined by a third in the 21st century, indicating that there has been a reduction in child malnutrition. However, 45 per cent of deaths among children under the age of five are still linked to undernutrition, and the number of undernourished people of all ages has increased significantly since 2015. According to the Food Security Information Network (FSIN) acute food insecurity, that seriously threatens livelihoods and lives, placed 155 million people in severe crisis at the start of 2021, an increase of 20 million from 2019.

Areas of severe hunger and food insecurity are notably in the regions of South Asia and sub-Saharan Africa where the GHI score of 29.0 persists. There is clearly a great deal that needs to be done to address these problems, and the question that arises is what are the most effective actions that need to be taken. Figure 6.1 illustrates the number of people most affected by the crisis of food insecurity across the world.

The United Nations World Food Programme (WFP) which was founded in the first development decade, in 1961, is the world's largest humanitarian organisation addressing hunger and promoting food security. The WFP provides food and monetary assistance directly to individuals and families most in need. At the same time, it endeavours to assist countries and governments in designing Zero Hunger strategies, and facilitating the exchange of knowledge between countries to advance the humanitarian goal of eliminating hunger. A number of INGOs, notably Action Against Hunger, are also involved in addressing the problems of food security and nutrition

Figure 6.1: Numbers of people in acute food insecurity crisis

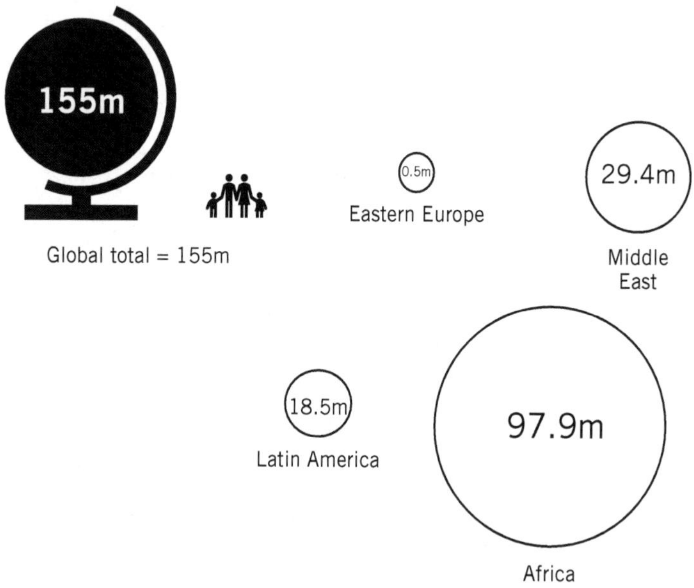

Global total = 155m

Eastern Europe

Middle East

Latin America

Africa

Source: FSIN (2021)

in many countries around the world, and related issues concerning water supplies, sanitation and hygiene. However, aid to support the eradication of hunger, food insecurity and undernutrition can only be effective in the long term if broader issues are also addressed.

The wider context in which hunger and food insecurity can be understood is one in which the main problem is not a global shortage of food, but the lack of access to food and a healthy diet as suffered by many people across the world. While hunger and undernutrition have increased globally, per capita food production has also increased significantly. It is estimated that by the end of the second decade of the 21st century enough food was being produced globally to feed 10 billion people. In other words, there is more than enough food to feed everyone on the planet at a time when so many people are experiencing hunger. The UN Special Rapporteur for the Right to Food has described this as 'suffering from hunger in a world of plenty'

(Elver, 2018). Understanding and addressing issues of food security is therefore more complex than it appears at first sight. As the UN FAO (2002) pointed out: 'Food security [is] a situation that exists when all people, at all times, have physical, social and economic access to sufficient, safe and nutritious food that meets their dietary needs and food preferences for an active and healthy life.'

Reference to physical, social and economic access to food implies that it is necessary to look at broader issues of population, poverty and inequality, and a wide range of human-created causes of hunger, food insecurity and malnutrition, including conflict and war, climate change, displacement and forced migration, and the global politics of food.

Population, poverty and hunger

Rapid population growth is often seen as a major threat to food security and a key factor in exacerbating hunger, famine and poverty. World population has grown rapidly since the start of the modern 'era of development', from 2.5 billion in 1950 to 7.8 billion in 2021, and is predicted to continue to rise to 10 billion in 2060, making the global population four times higher than it was at the start of the development era. Population growth across the world is uneven and there is forecast to be a fall in populations in Europe and Latin America by 2100, with the population in Asia rising until the middle of the 21st century and then falling, while the population in Africa will continue to rise for the rest for the century, with sub-Saharan Africa accounting for more than half of the growth of the world's population, according to the projections of the UN Department of Economic and Social Affairs (UN DESA, 2019a). India is on course to surpass China as the world's most populous country by 2027, and sub-Saharan Africa has by far the strongest predicted population growth, rising to 1.4 billion in 2030 and to 3.77 billion in 2100. By then half of all babies worldwide are expected to be born in Africa (Figure 6.2).

Population is a key factor in relation to food, famine, hunger and poverty. Changes in the size, age structure and location of populations have significant implications for the growth and distribution of

Figure 6.2: World population growth

World population 1950–2020, and predictions for 2020–2100

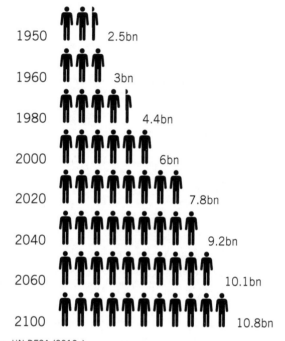

Source: UN DESA (2019a)

economic resources, and hence on poverty and access to nutritional foods. The countries worst affected by food insecurity, in Asia and Africa, are those with the fastest rising populations. India, with its rapidly growing population, is the country with the highest number of people suffering from hunger and is home to a quarter of all undernourished people worldwide. This is despite the fact that the proportion of the population suffering from hunger in India has halved since the 1990s. India has a very low ranking as one of the worst affected countries in the Global Hunger Index, and most of the other poorly ranked countries are those in sub-Saharan Africa. While population growth at a moderate rate can help to stimulate economic growth, rapid population growth can reduce per capita growth, and areas with very high birth rates suffer more poverty. This in turn makes people more vulnerable to food insecurity and less able to cope with events that precipitate famines.

However, population growth is sometimes overplayed as the main factor leading to hunger and famine. While countries with the fastest growing populations and families in poor communities with the largest numbers of young children are often the hardest hit by hunger and famine, many other factors come into play. For example, the uneven distribution of food within countries and across the world has a significant impact to the extent that some communities suffer from a lack of food and undernutrition while others have access to more than sufficient food and enriched diets. The growth of food production globally has exceeded population growth, and there is more than enough food to feed everyone on the planet. The Global Hunger Index shows that hunger and undernutrition, while still a highly serious concern, has generally declined in recent decades despite the continuing growth of the world population. It remains the case that the countries suffering the most from food insecurity and hunger are those with the highest levels of population growth, mainly in sub-Saharan Africa, but poverty is a key related issue.

Poverty is closely associated with chronic hunger, food insecurity and malnutrition, mainly because the people affected cannot afford the cost of safe and healthy diets, and are unable to grow their own safe and nutritious food. People living in poverty often face household food insecurity, and live in unsafe environments with poor access to clean water, sanitation and hygiene, and inadequate access to health services and education – all of which contribute to hunger and malnutrition. In a world of plenty, hunger and poverty are intertwined. In poor countries 60 to 80 per cent of family budgets go towards paying for food, compared with just 10 to 15 per cent in richer countries (Elver, 2018). Poverty and hunger often create a vicious circle which amplifies the risk of, and risks from, malnutrition. People who are poor are more likely to be affected by different forms of malnutrition which are costly to treat, and which also have the effect of reducing productivity and slowing economic growth, which in turn tends to perpetuate a cycle of poverty, hunger and ill-health.

Hunger, inequality and economics

In addition, there is growing evidence that hunger is not only interconnected with poverty but also directly linked to inequality. While much of the data on hunger and undernutrition focuses on comparisons between countries, there are also vast differences between groups within countries. This relates not just to differences in income and wealth, but also to the unequal distribution of social and political power. India is a prime example of a country with a rapidly expanding economy and population, but it is also one of the world's most unequal countries. The number of billionaires in India increased from under ten at the start of the 21st century to over 100 in 2020, while the country's Global Hunger Index ranking has shown that it continues to suffer from a very high level of serious hunger, and is the country with the largest number of people facing hunger in the world. In addition to the considerable economic disparities which have accentuated poverty and hunger, social and political factors also come into play as evidenced by the fact that women, minority ethnic communities and small farmers are at particular risk of hunger. Gender differences, for example, have been acknowledged in many accounts of hunger in developing countries where men are given priority access to the food available in households. Where there are food and water shortages, the power imbalance between men and women means that women suffer the most. The United Nations estimates that women and girls represent 60 per cent of all undernourished people in the world, and women have a much higher chance of being severely food insecure than men (UN FAO et al, 2020a: 24). Babies born to malnourished mothers are much more likely to have low birth weights (LBW), and UNICEF has pointed out that this is one of the strongest predictors of whether a child will die before the age of five, with the vast majority of LBW children, around 75 per cent, born in Southern Asia and Africa (UNICEF/WHO, 2019: 8).

Economic slowdowns and downturns have also played a significant part in undermining food security, mainly because they lead to unemployment, lower wages, income losses and staple food price inflation, all of which have the most serious impacts on the poorest and most marginalised sections of the population, thereby increasing inequality. There has been a significant increase in these economic-related problems in recent years in Africa, and the vulnerability of most African countries is largely due to their dependency on primary commodity exports and their lack of economic diversification. Commodity price falls were viewed by the FAO as the major cause of the economic difficulties that contributed to rising food insecurity and undernourishment in Africa in 2014–18 (UN FAO et al, 2020b). Together with climate shocks and conflicts, economic slowdowns and downturns have been key drivers of rising food insecurity.

Crises, conflicts and political governance

As noted earlier in this chapter, severe food insecurity, hunger and malnutrition can also be caused by specific events such as earthquakes, hurricanes, explosions, and sociopolitical issues such as civil unrest, wars, and political interventions affecting particular countries. Serious food crises and famines have occurred in recent years in affected countries such as Nigeria, South Sudan, Somalia, Yemen, the Democratic Republic of Congo, Afghanistan and Haiti. Many food crises and famines are driven as much by human-induced disasters as by natural ones, such as floods, hurricanes, tornadoes, earthquakes and tsunamis. Significantly, many issues affecting food production in the 21st century are related to climate change which is another human creation, albeit unintended. Another factor which is a key driver of food crises is human conflict, affecting almost 60 per cent of those suffering across the world from acute food insecurity, with economic shocks and weather extremes being the key drivers in only 40 per cent of cases (FSIN, 2020: 3) The UN WFP (2019) has noted that nearly 80 per cent of stunted children – some 122 million out of 155 million children – live in countries affected by conflict. Conflict is clearly a major cause of food emergency, sometimes leading to extreme famine, and often interconnects with other ongoing issues. For example, the effects of climate change can affect food production and limit supplies and access to food, which in turn can lead to armed conflict as people fight for scarce resources in seriously affected environments.

Acute food insecurity and armed conflict can also lead to the outward migration of large numbers of refugees fleeing to other countries which may then experience strains on their food supplies, leaving the displaced communities in dire straits. In South Sudan, over four million people, one in three of the population, were forced to flee their homes as a result of the civil war between 2013 and 2020 with many facing starvation, poor sanitation and lack of access to clean drinking water. There is also evidence that parties to recent conflicts in countries such as Afghanistan, Iraq, South Sudan, Syria and Yemen have deprived civilians of access to food. In many cases the parties in conflicts have used food as a weapon against their adversaries by destroying their crops and blocking food supplies. Conflicts also hamper the ability of farmers to continue working owing to restrictions on their movement and the disruption of food supply chains. The UN Security Council (2018) passed a resolution in 2018 acknowledging the link between hunger and conflict, and pointing out that hunger will never be eliminated without establishing peace in the world.

Political governance can also play a significant role in addressing or failing to address issues that seriously affect food security. One example is the impact of Hurricane Matthew which hit the Caribbean in 2016. Haiti was by far the hardest affected of all countries in the region due to lack of preparation by the government and this had a devastating impact on food and water supplies and the health of the population. Haiti is located in a region which is vulnerable to hurricanes and tropical storms, but poor planning and interventions by the government contributed to the severity of outcomes that the country experienced. By contrast, Cuba was much better prepared for such natural disasters and did not suffer the same consequences as its neighbour. Different forms of political governance can therefore play a significant part in accentuating or reducing the impacts of natural disasters, and governments in different countries may respond very differently to the same crisis.

Global politics of food

Like many other arenas of life, the world of food is a world of politics and power. (Ehrenreich and Lyon, 2011: 1)

At a global level the inequalities between the Global North and the Global South have allowed enterprises from the advanced developed countries to take control of food production and distribution across the world with advanced technologies, and for the rich states of the developed world to set the rules for global trade to their own advantage. Unfair trade patterns have had a significant impact on agriculture and food production in developing countries which has been felt especially by rural communities. Small farmers have been badly affected and a recent study conducted for the World Bank Productivity Project noted that nearly 80 per cent of the world's extreme poor now live in rural areas, with most relying on farming for their livelihoods. While there have been significant increases in world agricultural productivity over the past few decades, undernourishment of the rural poor has risen in recent years, reflecting low productivity in local farming in the poorest areas of the Global South (Fuglie, et al, 2020). The World Bank argues that this needs to be addressed by introducing measures to increase productivity in farming communities in these areas, but it can also be argued that broader measures need to be taken to address global inequalities and the global politics of food and hunger.

The unequal global balance of power has contributed to poverty, food insecurity and hunger in the poorer regions of the world. The growing domination of agricultural production around the world by transnational corporations in the Global North, facilitated by domestic subsidies from their home countries, international monetary policy and 'free trade' agreements, has enabled them to control the agricultural practices in the Global South, leading to the uneven production and distribution of food across the world. Africa, for example, has moved from being a net exporter of food to becoming increasingly reliant on food imports. The increase has been in basic foodstuffs, indicating that food security has become reliant on imports. Africa's import bill for food was approaching $40 billion in 2020, according to the World Bank, and is estimated to continue to rise in the next decade, especially in the wake of the COVID-19 pandemic. There are a number of reasons for increasing reliance on food imports in many developing countries, including population growth and climate change, but, as Carmen González has pointed out, the adoption worldwide of neo-liberal economics and WTO rules has institutionalised inequities in global agricultural trade and enabled highly subsidised agro-exporters in the Global North to undermine the livelihoods of small farmers in the Global South by dumping agricultural commodities in world markets at prices that could not be matched, forcing many small farmers to abandon food production. As a result, many developing countries that were once net food exporters have become net food importers (González, 2011).

To create a more even playing field would require significant changes to the global politics of food, but another line of approach would be to do more at the national and regional level to take back control of food production. While globalisation has undermined national sovereignty in many respects, there may still be room for innovation and change. In *Food for All in Africa* Gordon Conway et al argue that, despite the many challenges they face, it is possible for African farmers to come together and create an agricultural transformation based on the sustainable intensification of farming. The launch of the New Partnership for Africa's Development (NEPAD) with its framework for agricultural development is seen as a positive way forward for a regional partnership to support food production and distribution in Africa (Conway et al, 2019). However, this clearly depends on successfully combatting competition from global agricultural corporations, and developing what has been termed 'food sovereignty' to allow communities control over the way food is produced, traded and consumed. Whether this can be achieved remains to be seen.

Summary and conclusion

This chapter has shown that the issues and circumstances related to population, food and famine are rather more complex that they initially appear to be. Famines, for example, may be precipitated by natural disasters, but their impact is often determined by the levels of poverty experienced by those affected, and other factors such as human conflicts, forced migration and poor governance also come into play and determine the outcomes of events such as droughts, floods and earthquakes. Population growth, as we have seen, is another factor that is often viewed as a key cause of food insecurity and hunger, but food distribution may be a more significant factor given that food production globally has increased at a faster rate than the world's population. The main factors that lead to hunger, famine and food insecurity are illustrated in Figure 6.3.

Food aid by organisations such as the UN World Food Programme, and international monetary assistance from governments in the Global North to tackle poverty and food insecurity in the Global South, go some way towards addressing the key issues of hunger, malnutrition, and the wasting and stunting of young children, but they do not resolve many of the broader related issues that have serious impacts on food security. Taking all of the factors discussed in this chapter into account, it is clear that efforts to address global hunger and malnutrition are unlikely to succeed unless they also address national and global inequalities, enhance the livelihoods of small farmers, allow local food sovereignty, and protect the natural resource base for food production.

Figure 6.3: Hunger, famine and food insecurity

- ◆ Poverty
- ◆ Inequality
- ◆ Conflict
- ◆ Natural disasters
- ◆ Climate change   **The main causes of hunger, famine and food insecurity**
- ◆ Population
- ◆ Poor governance
- ◆ Global politics of food

KEY POINTS SUMMARY

- Population, food insecurity and famine are interconnected, but the issues and circumstances related to them are varied and complex.
- The main problem is not a global shortage of food, but a lack of access to sufficient and nutritious sources of food by many people in the developing world.

- Hunger and undernutrition are closely linked to poverty and high population growth, but also directly linked to inequalities of income, wealth and gender.
- Natural disasters, crises, conflicts, and political failures by nation-states all play a part in seriously accentuating food insecurity and hunger.
- Global politics also plays a very significant role in determining the uneven production and distribution of food across the world, and this has raised the issue of food sovereignty for developing countries.
- Addressing issues such as malnutrition and hunger is not simply a matter of providing food aid and monetary assistance, but requires broader measures that protect local farming and the natural resources, and also help to reduce national and global inequalities.

KEY READING GUIDE

Very few general textbooks on development include a chapter on hunger and famine despite its significant impact in many parts of the developing world. An exception is the Open University text, *Poverty and Development*, which has a chapter titled 'Understanding famine and hunger' (Crow, 2000). More recent works on food insecurity and famine have focused on what needs to be done to address these serious issues. In *Harvesting Prosperity*, Fuglie et al (2020) explore the need to transform the rural economy in developing countries to improve productivity and ensure sufficient food for growing populations. In *Food for All in Africa*, Conway et al (2019) focus on the means to create a sustainable intensification of African farming, including making use of some of the latest digital technologies. Elver (2018) provides a succinct account of the human-created causes of hunger and malnutrition in the article, 'Suffering from hunger in a world of plenty'. The regular reports by the UN FAO and WFP, referenced in this chapter, provide very useful up-to-date information on hunger and food insecurity, and the articles and updates produced by Oxfam International are also helpful and informative.

7

Poverty and inequality: the key challenges for development

Introduction: the relationship of poverty and inequality to development

> As long as poverty, injustice and gross inequality exist in our world, none of us can truly rest. (Nelson Mandela, 2005)

The previous chapter showed that a relationship exists between hunger and undernutrition on the one hand and poverty and inequality on the other. This chapter takes a closer look at poverty and inequality, which have become key issues in the field of international development. It explores the different ways of measuring poverty and inequality, and the impact of recent trends and development programmes in addressing these issues. These will be examined in relation to the possibility of achieving the UN Sustainable Development Goals (SDGs) of eradicating extreme poverty and reducing inequalities by 2030. The chapter will also explore the extent to which poverty and inequality are interconnected, and whether the key to development is tackling poverty or reducing inequality. As the quotation above by Nelson Mandela, the first president of post-apartheid South Africa, clearly states, the world can never rest until these key issues are properly addressed.

Defining and measuring poverty and its impacts

Poverty across the world and its impact on development has mostly been defined and measured in monetary terms. The World Bank has played a leading role in this respect, stating that its goals are to end extreme poverty and promote shared prosperity. How poverty is defined and measured varies across the world, but the main focus has been on wealth and income disparities and the baseline below which people are defined as living in poverty. The national poverty line for a country is typically a monetary threshold below which a person's minimum basic needs cannot be met, and richer countries tend to have higher poverty lines than poorer ones. The national poverty line is a central indicator for SDG 1: ending poverty in all its forms.

Most people in the world, around two thirds of the global population, live in poverty, if we take a basic $10 a day poverty line (Roser and Ortiz-Ospina, 2019). However, this is not the base line that is usually taken, and much lower international poverty lines have been drawn by the World Bank.

Early definitions of poverty, which focused on wealth and income disparities, compared countries around the world, based on gross domestic product (GDP) per capita and gross national income (GNI) per capita. The Brandt Report in 1980 was the first publication to graphically illustrate the global divide as a North-South division, between the rich North and poor South, marked by what became known as the 'Brandt line', as illustrated in Chapter 3. The North-South or developed/underdeveloped dichotomy has been criticised by some as too simplistic (Antunes de Oliveira, 2020), and clearly there have been changes over the last four decades that have seen rapid development in several countries in the South, with increases in GDP and GNI per capita, which would require changes to the Brandt line. However, per capita measurements do not accurately reflect the level of poverty within countries as the figures are based on averages, not the differences among different groups of the population. Poverty lines are different for different countries. National poverty lines are estimates of poverty that are designed to be consistent with each country's specific economic and social circumstances.

To aggregate and compare poverty rates across countries, poverty thresholds that reflect the same real standard of living in each country are used. These are mainly based on income. This was originally set at $1.00 in the late 1980s when economists at the World Bank noticed that a number of developing countries drew their poverty lines at an income of about $370 a year. This reflected the basic amount that a person needed to live annually and worked out at just over $1.00 a day, and became the international poverty line (IPL), adjusted for purchasing power parity (PPP). The PPP exchange rates are constructed to ensure that the same quantity of goods and services are priced equivalently across countries. The IPL was later revised to $1.25 in 2005 to reflect inflation. The most recent adjustment was made in 2015 when $1.90 became the new international poverty line. The IPL reflects the value of national poverty lines in some of the poorest countries, and is now generally referred to as the 'extreme poverty line'. Globally, one in ten of the world's population live below this line.

However, the IPL has been questioned. The World Health Organization (WHO), for example, has pointed out that a healthy diet costs much more than $1.90 a day, and estimated that 3 billion people or more could not afford a healthy diet in 2020. In sub-Saharan Africa and southern Asia, this was the case for 57 per cent of the population (UN FAO, 2020). A further question relates to how far below the poverty line different sections of the poor in the world are located. The IPL is extremely low, and other poverty lines showing less extreme poverty have also been devised. The World Bank has estimated that over half the world's population lives below the poverty line of $5.50 a day, and 84.5 per cent in sub-Saharan Africa (based on data for 2018). Questions have also been raised about the collection of accurate up-to-date data for all parts of the world, and data for some countries may be several years out of date compared with that for other countries. It is therefore evident that 'there is a poverty of data around poverty' (Clarke, 2016: 205).

Poverty measured at the IPL of $1.90 a day is used to track progress toward meeting the World Bank target of reducing the share of people living in extreme poverty to less than 3 per cent by 2030. The UN

SDG target 1.1 is even more ambitious: by 2030, it wants all countries, regions, and groups within countries to achieve zero poverty at the same international poverty line.

What progress is being made? Data based on the poverty lines set by the World Bank shows that 44 per cent of the world population lived below the extreme poverty line in 1981, and since then the share of extremely poor people in the world has rapidly declined, faster than ever before in world history, to the point at which by 2015 only 10 per cent of the world population was living below the international poverty line. However, the rate of decline of extreme poverty has slowed in recent years and, on the basis of current trends, the SDG 1 target of ending extreme poverty by 2030 is unlikely to be achieved, as the United Nations has acknowledged (UN DESA, 2020b). Half a billion people are expected to remain in extreme poverty by 2030 (Roser and Ortiz-Ospina, 2019).

The World Bank (2020b) statistics show that over 700 million people were still living in extreme poverty in 2020, and children were disproportionately affected since they were twice as likely to be in households that live under the global poverty line of $1.90. The consequences of this are evident in many areas of life for the extremely poor. For example, while the under-five mortality rate for children has more than halved since 1990, by the end of the second decade of the 21st century the WHO Global Health Observatory data shows that 39 of every 1,000 children born in the world were still dying before they were five years old. Most under-five deaths are caused by preventable diseases such as malaria, diarrhoea and pneumonia, and the most common contributors to these diseases – malnutrition, contaminated water, poor sanitation and hygiene – are caused by living in extreme poverty.

While at a global level extreme poverty has declined significantly in recent decades, this trend has not occurred evenly across the Global South. The most significant decline has been in the East Asia and Pacific regions where 52 per cent of the world's extremely poor people lived in 1990. By 2015 this had fallen to just 6 per cent. China was the key driver of this change. In South Asia too there was a substantial fall, mainly as a result of economic development and a reduction in the numbers of those suffering from poverty in India. However, while China reduced its extreme poverty rate to 0.7 per cent in 2015, in India over 13 per cent of the population remained below the extreme poverty line at a time when its population was expanding rapidly. Global indicators of poverty therefore need to be looked at in relation to variations in regional and national poverty trends. Regionally, the reductions in extreme poverty in the Asia-Pacific region, where the share of the world's poor has declined in recent decades, contrast sharply with changes in sub-Saharan Africa where the numbers have significantly increased since 1990 when 279 million people in the region were living in extreme poverty. By 2021 the region was home to 490 million extremely poor people. In part this reflects the rapidly growing population in sub-Saharan Africa, but this region also has the slowest rate of poverty reduction of any region in the world.

Reductions in global poverty levels have therefore been mostly a result of just two large and rapidly growing economies that earlier formed part of the poor Global South as depicted by the Brandt line, namely China and India. However, the 'poverty paradox', as Andy Sumner (2016) refers to it, is that most of the world's extreme poor no longer live in the world's poorest countries, but in the new middle-income countries such as India which has the world's second largest population and is set to overtake China by 2024. Back in the 1980s, nine out of ten extremely poor people lived in low-income countries, but by 2015 only four out of ten lived in low-income countries while the rest lived in middle-income countries. This suggests that many countries have the resources to address poverty and inequality but are not doing so.

Many factors play a part in increasing or reducing extreme poverty, as reflected in income levels including changes in national, regional and global economies. For example, greater participation in global value chains, where production of goods and services is distributed across different countries and regions in the developing world, helps to boost employment and incomes. However, at the same time, automation and advancing technologies tend to have a negative impact on developing countries by reducing employment opportunities for manual labourers. Another factor that has played a significant part in offsetting income poverty is the growth of remittances by migrant labourers working in other countries to the families in their home countries. There has been a significant increase in the number of migrant workers and remittances in the 21st century, and most studies show that remittances are a vital source of income in developing countries and play a significant part in reducing poverty. However, there are significant variations in their effectiveness depending on whether the home and host countries have policies which are conducive to remittances being made. In addition, major crises can have a dramatic impact on income and poverty, significantly increasing the number of people below the extreme poverty line. These crises include the deleterious effects of armed conflict and of climate change, which have in recent years slowed poverty reduction in many parts of the developing world. The World Bank estimates that by 2030 two thirds of those living in extreme poverty worldwide will be living in situations of fragility, conflict and violence, which are likely to reverse the progress made towards reducing poverty. A further major crisis combined with these in 2020 to exacerbate the issue of global poverty, namely the coronavirus pandemic. As the World Bank (2020a: 1) noted, 'Poverty reduction has suffered its worst setback in decades, after nearly a quarter century of steady global declines in extreme poverty'.

The impact of COVID-19 has made the attainment of SDG 1 virtually impossible. The pandemic severely affected those living in poverty through job losses and rising prices, and supply chain problems for those reliant on agricultural production. In addition, remittances were hit by the pandemic, mainly due to a fall in the wages and employment of migrant workers. Global remittances declined by as much as 20 per cent in 2020 (World Bank, 2020a: 94). This resulted in the loss of a crucial lifeline for the income of many vulnerable households in the developing world, resulting in significant increases in crisis-level hunger and health-related issues.

So far, this chapter has focused on poverty as defined and measured by IPL. However, this has been questioned on several grounds. First, the adjustments to the IPL from the $1-a-day poverty line of 1990 to the $1.25 line of 2008 and the $1.90 line of 2015, have been criticised for effectively setting purchasing power parity (PPP) in such a way that the changes to the IPL created a sudden modification to the figures and a significant increase in the number of people defined as having been lifted out of extreme poverty. Jason Hickel points out that in 2015 when the new IPL came into effect, it cut the number of extremely poor by 100 million overnight. This helped to promote a good-news narrative about global poverty reduction, but it was 'tenuous in the light of the statistical sleight-of-hand that lies behind it' (Hickel, 2016: 752). The data has also been questioned for failing to recognise what the poverty figures would look like if one country, namely China, was taken out of the equation.

Second, given that $1.90 a day, adjusted for PPP, has been widely recognised as insufficient to buy adequate food to achieve basic nutrition, the IPL is a questionable measure of poverty. In India, for example, children in families living just above the poverty line still have a very serious chance of being malnourished (Chatterjee, 2021). Additional questions have been raised about the extent to which the IPLs truly reflect poverty levels when poverty is about more than just income. Broader definitions of poverty need to move beyond monetary measures to take into account the key areas of life where poverty is experienced, and this is where the concept of 'multidimensional poverty' and a new way of measuring poverty have come into play.

Multidimensional poverty

The goal of SDG 1 is to end poverty in all its forms everywhere, and measuring progress towards this goal means looking not only at the economic dimension of poverty but also its social and cultural dimensions, which include education, health and housing. The UNDP refers to this as **human poverty**; a further dimension is **capability poverty**, which is not so much about material resources as the lack of basic essential human capabilities that enable people to participate freely and effectively in society and have access to genuine opportunities to support and improve their lives. This approach to poverty was first introduced by Amartya Sen (1989) and became known as the **capability approach** to development. A further approach to defining and measuring poverty has focused on what has become known as **participatory poverty assessment**. The idea of a participatory approach to development indicates that communities know better than outsiders the issues they face, and their resources and needs. Therefore, communities are in a better position to identify what their main concerns are in relation to poverty and how they need to be addressed.

What these alternative approaches share in common is a recognition of the need for greater flexibility in the understanding of poverty. A more effective assessment of poverty therefore requires metrics that expand the scope of the income poverty index to make it more multidimensional. The Human Poverty Index (HPI) was the first to move in this direction. Devised by the United Nations Development Programme (UNDP) in 1997, it combined three essential elements of human life: longevity, knowledge and a decent standard of living. In 2010 the HPI was replaced by the Multidimensional Poverty Index (MPI), a more advanced index that directly measures the combination of deprivations that each household experiences. This was devised jointly by the Oxford Poverty and Human Development Initiative (OPHI) and the UNDP. Using ten different indicators it complements monetary-based poverty measures by capturing the acute deprivations that each person experiences at the same time in relation to education, health and living standards. The MPI indicators of the three main dimensions of poverty are illustrated in Figure 7.1.

The MPI assesses poverty at an individual level, and this entails wide-ranging household surveys across over 100 countries. Anyone who is deprived in a third or more of the ten weighted indicators is defined as being 'MPI poor', and the extent and intensity of their poverty is measured by the percentage of deprivations they are experiencing. The global MPI value for each country is calculated on the basis of this data. The MPI showed a decline in poverty in the second decade of 21st century, but in 2020, across 107 developing countries, 1.3 billion people, 22 per cent of the world population, were still living in multidimensional poverty. Nearly half of all MPI poor were aged under 18, with one in three children identified as poor compared

Figure 7.1: Multidimensional Poverty Index (MPI) indicators

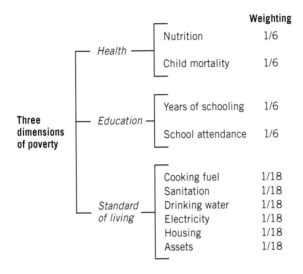

Source: OPHI (2015)

with one in six adults (OPHI/UNDP, 2020: 3). The MPI results
have shown that every indicator makes a difference and has played
a role in reducing poverty. At the same time, the MPI results have
demonstrated that multidimensional poverty trends do not necessarily
match monetary poverty trends, and in the majority of countries the
incidence of multidimensional poverty has fallen faster in absolute
terms than monetary poverty. For example, while both measures show
that sub-Saharan African countries have the highest poverty rates and
some of the worst prognoses, the MPI results also show that some of
the poorest countries in sub-Saharan Africa are among those with
the fastest absolute reduction in multidimensional poverty since 2010,
notably Sierra Leone, Mauritania and Liberia. However, as with food
and famine, population also comes into play. While most sub-Saharan
African countries have reduced their MPI value, the actual number of
poor people has risen as a result of rapid population growth. Progress in
reducing multidimensional poverty has also been seriously affected by
the COVID-19 pandemic. Substantial impacts of the pandemic on two

of the MPI indicators, nutrition and children's school attendance, were particularly noticeable with disruptions to livelihoods and food supply chains, and widespread school closures. The *Global Multidimensional Poverty Index* report for 2020 estimated that COVID-19 would set poverty reduction back by more than five years, with an additional 237 million people falling into multidimensional poverty across 70 countries (OPHI/UNDP, 2020: 15).

The multidimensional approach is clearly an advance on purely monetary assessments of poverty, but additional indicators could be used to identify other important areas that need to be addressed. For example, gender differences in relation to poverty are significant but generally not identified in the MPI, which relies more on household rather than individual data. However, the World's Women 2015 report found that nearly two thirds of the world's illiterate adults were women, mainly due to gender disparities in schooling (UN DESA, 2020b). Another gender-related poverty issue concerns birth rates and population growth. Population, as we have seen, is a key factor in relation to food, famine, hunger and poverty. The countries worst affected, notably in Africa, are those with the fastest rising populations. While population growth at a moderate rate may help to stimulate economic growth, rapid population growth can reduce per capita growth, and areas with very high birth rates suffer more poverty. Families with fewer children are more likely to rise out of poverty. In addition to having fewer mouths to feed, having fewer children to care for make it easier for women to find employment and generate more income. Adolescent motherhood, which is particularly prevalent in poorer developing countries, also causes poverty, whereas birth-spacing of at least three years reduces child malnutrition, and lower fertility creates more income-generating opportunities for women. According to the Population Reference Bureau, birth rates tend to reflect inequalities in wealth and income in poorer countries. In Tanzania, for example, women in the richest one fifth of the population have an average of three children during their lifetimes, while women in the poorest one fifth have an average of between seven and eight children (PRB, 2018). A key driver of this is the availability of contraceptive use among the wealthy, and limited access for the poor. As Karan Singh (1988), a former minister of population in India, famously stated back in the 1980s: 'Development is the best contraceptive.'

This raises the wider question of whether poverty is more about inequality than insufficient resources within countries, and therefore about the distribution rather than the lack of resources, and consequently linked to issues of political economy and governance. Has global poverty also become more about national inequality, and if so, how should it be addressed?

Inequality: global, national and household dimensions

> Inequality can inhibit growth and slow poverty reduction.
> (Birdsall, 2001: 4)

Like poverty, inequality has generally tended to be measured in monetary terms, and this means measuring the differing shares of income and wealth between countries and within a country. Inequality has been given increasing attention in relation to development in recent decades, whereas previously poverty was the main focus of attention. Rising inequality within many countries and between the richest and poorest countries in the world, together with growing global inequality in the world population, has diverted attention from simply addressing poverty as a self-contained problem to looking at the broader context of inequality, which has shaped the nature and extent of poverty. As the quote above from Nancy Birdsall clearly states, inequality must be addressed or poverty reduction will be slowed down. International organisations such as the United Nations have recently shown greater awareness of the need to investigate inequality, as reflected in the title of the Global Multidimensional Poverty report, *Illuminating Inequalities* (OPHI/UNDP, 2019), and the World Social Report: *Inequality in a Rapidly Changing World* (UN DESA, 2020c). The latter report noted that inequality had moved to the forefront of policy debate and for the first time internationally agreed development goals included targets to reduce inequality based on income, as reflected in SDG 10: reduced inequalities.

Income inequalities are particularly striking, and one of the first graphical depictions of such inequality on a world scale appeared in the UNDP 1992 *Human Development Report*; based on the shape of a champagne glass, it has become a classic illustration (Figure 7.2).

The glass is divided into five bands, each representing 20 per cent of the population, and clearly demonstrates the vast gap between the richest and poorest fifths of the world population. To update the layers of inequality shown in the champagne glass model, data for the top 1 per cent and bottom 50 per cent share of global income has been added. This is taken from the *World Social Report 2020* (UN DESA, 2020c: 25). Inequalities in both income and wealth have generally been increasing since the 1980s, following a decline in the earlier

Figure 7.2: Champagne glass model of global income inequality

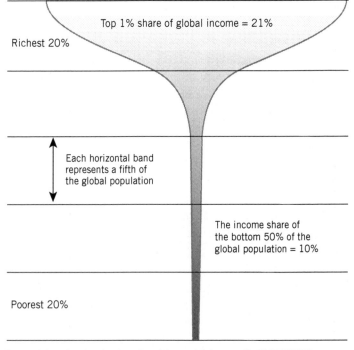

Source: Adapted and updated version of the model presented in UNDP (1992)

post-Second World War development decades. As Jason Hickel (2018: 16) puts it in quite dramatic terms, 'inequality has been exploding'. Looking at the trends more closely, it is clear that while there has been a reduction in inequality among countries in recent years, global inequalities within the world population and within most countries have increased sharply. The reduction among countries has mainly been due to the growth of emerging economies, notably in China and India since 1990, but these countries have also seen increasing internal inequalities. The rise of these middle-income countries has helped to reduce poverty, but at the same time has increased the disparity of incomes among different groups of the population. In India, for example, which is one of the fastest growing economies in the world, 271 million people were lifted out of poverty in ten years between 2006 and 2016, according to the findings of the UN Development Programme (OPHI/UNDP, 2019: 9), but at the same time income inequality has been rising sharply. While the top 1 per cent of the Indian population had an income share of 6 per cent in the early 1980s, that increased to 22 per cent in 2014 (World Inequality Lab, 2018: 123). The level of inequality is such that Oxfam International (2020a) has calculated it would take 941 years for a minimum wage worker in rural India to earn what the top paid executive at a leading Indian garment company earns in one year.

The key indicator used to measure global and national income and wealth inequalities is the Gini index, also known as the Gini coefficient. The index ranges from 0 (or 0 per cent) to 1 (or 100 per cent) with 0 representing perfect equality and 1 representing the most extreme level of inequality in a given country or across the world. The Gini index is often represented graphically with the Lorenz curve, based on a model originally designed by Max O. Lorenz in 1905. The bigger the area between the line of equality and the Lorenz curve, the higher the level of inequality, as illustrated in Figure 7.3 with 50 per cent of the population sharing just 20 per cent of the total income.

The Gini coefficient of international inequality among countries, calculated using population-weighted national incomes per capita, fell by around 15 per cent between 1980 and 2010. However, while inequality among countries has declined in relative terms, the absolute

Figure 7.3: Lorenz curve (example)

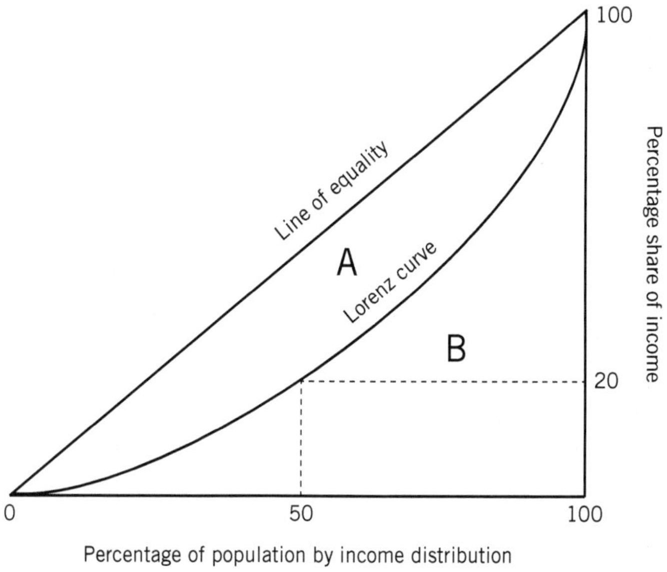

Percentage of population by income distribution

Source: Investopedia (2022)

income differences among countries continue to grow. As for the global level of inequality in the world population as a whole, the income share of the top 1 per cent rose from 16 per cent in 1980 to 20 per cent in 2018, while the share of the bottom 50 per cent of the world population has remained around 9 per cent (World Inequality Lab, 2018: 11). The Gini coefficient has therefore increased and the Lorenz curve has moved further away from the line of equality.

Inequalities of wealth have followed similar trends, with very high levels of wealth inequality both within countries and for the world as a whole. There has been a significant increase in the wealth of the world's top 1 per cent since 1980. Over 70 per cent of the world's population live in countries where the wealth gap is widening (UN DESA, 2020b). According to the Credit Suisse *Global Wealth Report*, the richest 10 per cent of adults in the world possess 82 per cent of global wealth, while the top 1 per cent alone owns over 44 per cent of the world's wealth. Wealth has been rising in all regions of the world, with the fastest rates in India and Latin America, followed by Africa, China and North America, but the bottom 50 per cent of all adults in the world in 2019 had less than a 1 per cent share of total global wealth (Credit Suisse, 2019: 2). Oxfam International has claimed that 'economic inequality is out of control' with the world's 2,153 billionaires in 2019 having more wealth that 4.6 billion people, and the extremity of inequality is also reflected in the astonishing fact that 'The richest 22 men in the world own more wealth than all the women in Africa' (Oxfam International, 2020b: 29).

Inequality of income and wealth is clearly a major issue in relation to development, such that poverty and deprivation are not simply the result of a lack of resources but the maldistribution of resources. This can be seen, for example, in relation to world hunger, as we saw in the previous chapter: more than enough food is produced around the world to feed the global population, but 690 million people were still going hungry in 2020 (Action Against Hunger, 2020). Poverty and deprivation can only be properly addressed by reducing inequalities. Nancy Birdsall points out that the low income of poor people necessarily limits their ability to invest in their own farms, small businesses, and in the health and education of their children, which in turn will tend to condemn their children to poor or limited education and low future income, reducing social mobility and generating 'a self-perpetuating "poverty trap"' (Birdsall, 2001: 14).

Inequality of assets, such as land, housing and human capital play an important part in perpetuating poverty. For rural populations, inequality in land ownership is associated with the concentration of wealth and income in the hands of the agricultural elite; this in turn accentuates the poverty of the poor, which limits human capital accumulation and economic growth for poorer communities. Latin America is a clear example where the highly unequal distribution of land and income has meant that agricultural growth has failed to reduce poverty. Land distribution in Latin America is the most unequal in the world, and women are particularly affected by unequal access to land. Without addressing this inequality, poverty will not be effectively combated. Most studies show that there is inequality not only within rural areas, but also between rural and urban areas in the developing world. This is one of the most conspicuous forms of what is known as **spatial inequality**, and such inequalities within countries are often more striking than those among countries. Four out of every five people living below the IPL reside in rural areas, although the rural population accounts for less than half the global population (World Bank, 2020a: 9). The spatial inequality between rural and urban areas is clearly connected to the economic growth of towns and cities as more and more developing countries have followed the path of urbanisation and industrialisation.

However, there is also increasing inequality within urban areas which tends to be concentrated in specific locations, and this has created another dimension of spatial inequality. The poorest areas suffering from the greatest levels of inequality are slums which are home to more than one billion people worldwide. Known by various names, such as *favelas* in Latin America, these are urban areas characterised by substandard housing, overcrowding, poor sanitation and lack of basic services. Progress has been made in reducing the percentage of people living in slums in the developing world, but the absolute number of slum dwellers has increased over recent decades and reached over a billion in 2020. Mike Davis refers to the continuing rise in the number of slums and slum-dwellers in the title of his book, *Planet of Slums*. He predicts that the number of people living in slums will continue to increase, and by 2035 at the latest the majority of the world's poor will no longer be living in the countryside but in urban slums. The exponential growth of slums is no accident, but a direct result of growing inequality and a massive transfer of wealth from the poor to the rich (Davis, 2017).

Spatial inequality and urbanisation demonstrate that there are many factors related to inequality, which have an effect on the economic inequalities measured by the Gini coefficient. Two thirds of the world's population live in countries where inequality has grown, and other trends which have affected inequality include climate change, technological developments, global pandemics and international migration. Climate change has particularly affected poorer and more vulnerable populations, especially those in rural areas who are highly dependent on agriculture, fishing and other sources of income affected by changes to the ecosystem. It has been estimated that the gap between the income of the richest and poorest 10 per cent of the global population is 25 per cent higher than it would have been without global warming (Diffenbaugh and Burke, 2019).

Technological innovations have also opened up inequalities. Automation, for example, has reduced the number of jobs available for those in routine manual occupations. Low-skilled workers have been particularly affected in developing countries, while the owners of businesses and highly skilled workers have reaped the benefits of the introduction of new technologies. Global pandemics have also contributed to widening inequalities, from the Asian flu outbreak of the 1950s through to COVID-19 that started in 2020. Not only are the poorest sections of the community – that is, those located in crowded and unsanitary living conditions – more likely to be infected by viruses, they are also most likely to suffer from loss of income and access to basic necessities. Lockdown restrictions during the COVID-19 pandemic tended to further widen inequalities between richer and poorer sections of the population as it was possible for the better-off to use technologies to work from home whereas many of the less well-off were unable to continue working and maintaining their incomes.

As the foregoing discussion has shown, inequality exists globally, and also within and among countries. It can be driven by many factors, and it has a number of different dimensions that go beyond the economic inequalities of income and wealth. There are, for example, serious inequalities in access to health services, clean water supplies, sanitation and education. These inequalities may differ significantly among different groups, and not simply between the rich and the poor but among groups differentiated by gender, race and religion. In many developing countries, for example, notably in South Asia and sub-Saharan Africa, the adult literacy rate is much higher for men than for women. Sub-Saharan Africa has the lowest level of female literacy in the world: just 57 per cent in 2019, and in India the rate was 65 per cent (NSO India, 2020). Gender is also a factor in relation to food and health, as exemplified within households. Studies have shown that in the households of many developing countries men and boys are given priority in relation to food over women and girls, and are also more likely to attend school and receive health treatment when suffering from illness.

Household inequalities therefore exist alongside the wider inequalities of wealth and spatial inequalities among regions and countries. This suggests that, like poverty, inequality is also multidimensional. To measure and track gender inequalities, the UNDP has developed the Gender Inequality Index. The index shows some reduction in gender inequality in the 21st century, but continuing sharp differences between developed and developing countries, with those in South Asia and sub-Saharan Africa having the highest inequality ratios (UNDP, 2019: 149). Inequalities of race, ethnicity and religion are also significant, and while they have been addressed in many developing countries, they continue to have a notable impact, with ethnic and religious discrimination resulting in serious disparities in income and occupation. In India, for example, the poverty rates for Muslims are notably higher than for Hindus, Christians and Sikhs. Differences in educational attainment are also very striking, with the illiteracy rate for Muslims being twice as high as for any other religious community in India (NSO India, 2020). These areas of inequality show that while income inequality remains a major driver of inequality, other multidimensional factors also come into play.

Politics also plays a crucial role in relation to inequality, but one which is often overlooked. In Latin America, for example, there are differences in the levels of inequality among countries with similar GNI per capita, and these are related to differences in the nature of their political regimes. Most notably, in the first decade of the 21st century there was a significant shift to the left in many countries in Latin America, resulting in what became known as the 'pink tide' and the rise of radical left-wing governments that were committed to reducing poverty and inequality. In Brazil, one of the most unequal countries in the world, the Gini coefficient fell by six points; this was mainly due to the government's introduction of the Bolsa Família programme, which helped to significantly reduce poverty and inequality by transferring cash to those living in poverty. Known as the largest programme of its kind in the world, it came with conditions: families would have their funds suspended unless they ensured that their children attended school and were vaccinated. This was done to ensure that inequalities of health and education were also addressed, and it clearly demonstrates the importance of politics in addressing inequality. At an international level, politics also comes into play. As Nederveen Pieterse points out, inequality is not simply inherent in the market economy but is a political choice, and while there is an international political consensus on the importance of reducing poverty, there is no consensus and no global perspective on inequality. Inequality remains 'a political and ideological football' (Nederveen Pieterse, 2018: 86).

Summary and conclusion: end extreme inequality to end poverty

Poverty is the worst form of violence. (Mahatma Gandhi, n.d.)[1]

As we have seen in this chapter, poverty and inequality are key challenges for development. Whereas poverty has been the dominant theme for many decades in the development era, inequality has come increasingly to the fore in recent years. There is a growing recognition of the connections between poverty and inequality. However, their interconnectedness is not new. Mahatma Gandhi who led the nationwide campaign to end poverty in India in the 1920s, famously recognised poverty as the worst form of violence, in recognition of the division between the privileged rich and the deprived poor, with the former living at the expense of the latter. Gandhi viewed such inequality as resulting in poverty, hence the famous quotation. Until recently, however, providing aid and support to alleviate poverty has been a guiding principle of development thinking and policy

---

[1] This quotation by Mahatma Gandhi is widely referred to, but there is no written reference, and it is not known in exactly what year or context he said this.

rather than addressing inequality to combat poverty. The fact that poverty has risen most sharply in middle-income rather than lower-income developing countries indicates that it would be possible to end extreme poverty by reducing inequality at a national level.

The growing recognition of the need to address inequality in its various forms at national, regional and global levels, is evident in a number of the more recent annual reports released by leading international bodies and non-governmental organisations. Oxfam International (2020b: 48), for example, in its report, *Time to Care*, focused on a world of extremes in which 'economic inequality is out of control', and its key message was: 'End extreme wealth to end extreme poverty.' The UN DESA World Social Report for 2020, *Inequality in a Rapidly Changing World*, noted that inequality in all its various dimensions had moved to the forefront of policy debate, and that 'highly unequal societies are less effective at reducing poverty than those with low levels of inequality' (UN DESA, 2020c: 4). It is also significant that the United Nations 2030 Agenda for Sustainable Development includes targets to reduce inequality in its various forms, including income inequality. This had never previously been on the international agenda. The World Bank has also turned its attention to inequality and its impact on global poverty, noting that reducing inequality has a bigger effect on reducing extreme poverty than an increase in economic growth does (Lakner et al, 2020).

This chapter has demonstrated the importance for development of tackling both poverty and inequality. They are interconnected and multidimensional, and there is increasing evidence that while measures can be taken to alleviate poverty at both international and national levels, inequality needs to be seriously addressed if poverty is to be properly resolved. There is enough evidence to show that the world has abundant resources to address poverty in all its forms, just as it has sufficient food to combat hunger and undernutrition. Addressing inequality is now moving to the forefront of development agendas.

KEY POINTS SUMMARY

- Poverty has for a long time been a key issue associated with international development and taken up by global organisations such as the United Nations and the World Bank, but until recently less attention has been paid to the need to address national and international inequalities.
- The Brandt line was the first graphical indicator of global poverty, depicting a clear disparity between the rich North and the poor South.
- Various measures of national and global poverty were subsequently set in place, mostly based on income and what became known as the international poverty line.
- More diverse measurements of poverty emerged later in recognition of need to look beyond the economic dimension of poverty to include human poverty and capability poverty. The Multidimensional Poverty Index (MPI) was introduced in 2010.
- The need to address not only poverty but also inequality has become more widely recognised in recent times, although the role that politics can play in relation to inequality is often overlooked.
- Like poverty, inequality is not only about economic disparities but is also multidimensional and can affect different sections of the population, as, for example, in spatial and gender inequalities.
- Both poverty and inequality have to be addressed, and inequality has moved up the international development agenda, as reflected in the recent reports by UN DESA and Oxfam which emphasise the need to reduce inequality to make tackling poverty more viable.

KEY READING GUIDE

Greig et al (2007) provide a good overview of poverty, inequality and development, and the need to address global inequality, as the title of their book indicates: *Challenging Global Inequality: Development Theory and Practice in the 21st Century*. The need to move beyond simply addressing poverty towards resolving global inequality is forcefully argued by Hickel (2018) in his book *The Divide: A Brief Guide to Global Inequality and Its Solutions*. For a shorter account of the impact of inequality on poverty, see Lakner et al (2020) 'How much does reducing inequality matter for global poverty?'. The politics of inequality is particularly well covered by Nederveen Pieterse (2018) *Multipolar Globalization: Emerging Economies and Development*. Informative official reports on poverty and inequality include UN DESA (2020c) *Inequality in a Rapidly Changing World*, and the World Bank (2020a) *Poverty and Shared Prosperity 2020*.

8

Health and education: moving towards healthy human development

Introduction: health, education and human development

Health is not only a vital asset for each individual, it is the very core of human development. (Gro Harlem Brundtland, 1998)

Education is the most powerful weapon which you can use to change the world. (Nelson Mandela, 1990)

Health is now widely seen as one of the vital keys to development, particularly in relation to human development, making a major contribution alongside income growth in addressing poverty and inequality. Human development focuses on improving the lives of people, rather than assuming that economic growth will lead, automatically, to greater opportunities and better lives for all. Education also plays a significant role in development and in many ways is closely linked to health.

The UNDP development reports recognise the vital role played by health and education, together with income, in directly enhancing human life by making possible a long and healthy life, improving levels of knowledge and understanding, and having access to sufficient resources to ensure a decent standard of living. Human development is further advanced by creating conditions that support its advance, including environmental sustainability, human security and rights, gender equality, and widening participation in political and community life. Human development gives people greater opportunities and more choices, enabling men and women to develop their full potential, as illustrated in Figure 8.1. The UNDP's recognition of the importance of both health and education for development is also reflected in the UN Sustainable Development Goals (SDGs) for 2030. In the previous two chapters reference was made to SDGs 1 and 2: no poverty and zero hunger; SDGs 3 and 4 are, respectively: good health and wellbeing, and quality education.

Health and education are closely interconnected, as will be shown in this chapter. It begins by looking at the concept of health, the major issues surrounding health and development, the extent to which progress is being made, and the impacts of globalisation on health, including the global politics of health. The chapter goes on to explore the importance of education for development and the extent to which it has played an important role in making progress towards economic growth, sociopolitical transformations, poverty alleviation and reductions in inequalities. Gro Harlem Brundtland, the director-

Figure 8.1: Human development

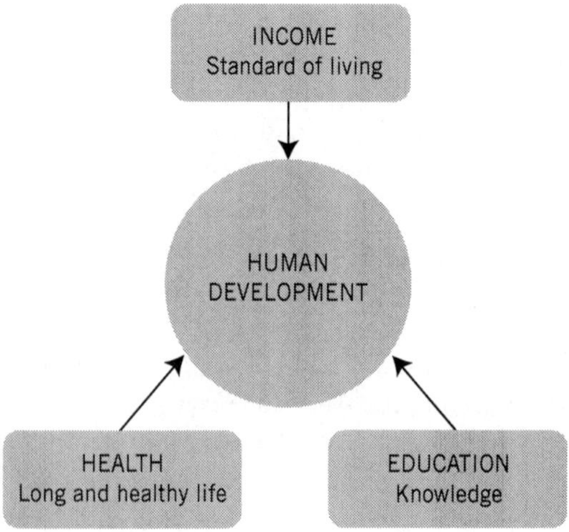

Source: Adapted from UNDP (2022)

general of the World Health Organization (WHO), recognised at the turn of the 21st century that good health was at the heart of human development, and the anti-apartheid revolutionary and later president of South Africa, Nelson Mandela, recognised the vital role played by education, as both quotations at the start of this chapter clearly indicate.

What is health?

Health is usually taken to refer to the absence of disease or infirmity caused by illness or injury. Diseases may be communicable: spread from person to person, or from other species to the human species by various means; or noncommunicable (also known as chronic diseases), such as heart disease, cancer, chronic respiratory diseases and diabetes. The impact of both communicable diseases and noncommunicable diseases can be measured in various ways, including disability-adjusted life years (DALYs) as used by the WHO. One DALY = one lost year of 'healthy' life; DALYs are calculated as the sum of years lost due to premature mortality in the population plus the years lost due to disability, both physical and mental. Injuries may also play a significant part in affecting DALYs. The WHO data shows that the DALYs per 1,000 population have decreased in all regions of the world since 2000 with Africa having the largest decline (44 per cent). However, the African region still had the highest percentage of DALYs, with a much higher proportion due to communicable, maternal, neonatal and nutritional causes compared with other regions of the world.

However, while the prevalence of diseases is often used for measuring the health of a population, the definition of health can go beyond this. As the WHO (1946) stated at the very start of the development era: 'Health is a state of complete physical, mental and social wellbeing and not merely the absence of disease or infirmity.'

The WHO (1986) later went on to add at the first international conference on health promotion in Ottawa that 'health is a positive concept emphasizing social and personal resources, as well as physical capacities'. This means that health is a resource that helps to support an individual's life in society, rather than an end in itself. Health ensures that one can live one's life to the full and play a meaningful role in society. The correlation between health and human development is therefore very close.

Perspectives on health and development

The WHO definition of health is important in that it broadens the understanding of what it means to be healthy. There are differing perspectives on the extent to which this has been achieved and the best ways forward. The two leading theoretical perspectives on development, as discussed in Chapter 4, have contrasting views on health and development.

Modernisation theory offers a positive view in which improvements in health are closely linked to economic development and propelled by advancing towards modernity. As developing countries follow the economic path previously taken by the major advanced economies, this is accompanied by a recapitulation of the demographic and epidemiological transitions associated with modernisation. The demographic transition refers to a process in which there is a shift over time from high birth rates and infant death rates in societies with low levels of economic development, technology and education, to lower birth and death rates as these societies advance towards a modern economy and introduce new technologies and higher levels of educational attainment. Demographic change is accompanied by an epidemiological transition from infectious diseases to degenerative diseases as modernising societies experience improvements in sanitation and hygiene that reduce the risks of infection. Following the epidemiological transition, the main causes of illness and mortality are those primarily due to human behaviour patterns and lifestyles. For example, a longer life-span increases the risk of degenerative disease, and industrialisation has increased risks of air pollution and diseases associated with manufactured products such as tobacco and alcohol. However, the decline in infectious diseases significantly reduces mortality rates, and lower birth rates combined with improved maternal and childcare results in a significant reduction in infant mortality. Modernisation theory therefore takes a generally positive and optimistic perspective on health and development, and adds to this the further benefits that developing countries can gain from the medical advances already made in the developed world. Health interventions, supported by international aid, can further help to improve the health status of developing countries going through the transition to modernity.

Dependency theory, by contrast, offers a far more negative and pessimistic view of health in the countries of the Global South. Economic dependency is seen as having detrimental consequences for health in many respects. In the first place, economic exploitation and unequal exchange in world trading arrangements accentuate poverty and underdevelopment, and poverty is one of the main underlying causes of illness and mortality in the developing world. Developing countries also have fewer resources available to devote to healthcare, and while it is acknowledged that medical aid has been sponsored by Western countries, this has tended to focus on cure, rather than prevention, when much more needs to be spent on providing access to clean water and sanitation to reduce the spread of infectious diseases. Rising external debt in many parts of the developing world is seen as a further issue having an impact on health as this reduces the amount available to spend on advancing healthy living conditions. While the dependency perspective offers a very negative view of health trends in the developing world, it also highlights the need for more far-reaching changes in relation to development to boost improvements in health and wellbeing. Dependency theory points out that the demographic and epidemiological transitions that are seen as beneficial to health have not occurred in the way that modernisation theory predicted. Instead, there is a 'demographic trap' in many developing countries with death rates reducing but birth rates remaining high, and the 'population explosion' has led to reduced living standards and increased poverty. This, in turn, has delayed the epidemiological transition, and infectious diseases continue to be prevalent in the developing world. The following section examines the extent to which progress has been made in addressing health issues in the developing world.

Health indicators: is progress being made towards Health for All?

The need for considerable progress to be made in relation to health was highlighted at the World Health Assembly, the forum of the WHO, in 1979, with the launch of the Global Strategy for Health for All by the Year 2000. This referred to a personal state of health and wellbeing, not just the availability of health services. Some progress was made over the last two decades of the 20th century, but the goal was not achieved. It was, however, taken forward and influenced the Millennium Development Goals (MDGs) for 2015 and the Sustainable Development Goals (SDGs) for 2030. What progress towards Health for All has been made in the current century?

Indicators of health by country and region are important in showing comparisons between the developed and developing world, and whether progress is being made towards global health. Some of the key indicators include: crude death rate, infant mortality rate, life expectancy at birth, and the prevalence of global diseases such as HIV/AIDS. There have been substantial improvements in many of these indicators, including life expectancy, as shown in Table 8.1.

Globally, life expectancy at birth increased from 67.2 years in 2000 to 73.5 in 2019, and there have been significant improvements in some developing countries. For example, in Kenya life expectancy for women rose from 56 in 2010 to 68 in 2020. Healthy life expectancy, the number of years of life spent in good health, increased by more than ten years between 1990 and 2019. Most of these advances are related to changes in the Global South. However, there are still very large discrepancies in life expectancy: in several countries in sub-Saharan Africa average life expectancy is still below 60 years of age, compared with 80 years for countries in Europe and Japan. There have been significant reductions in child mortality and maternal mortality around the world, and the number of deaths of children under five years of age decreased from 9.6 million in 2000 to five million in 2019 (IHME, 2020). Again, however, significant discrepancies exist across the world, and many low-income countries still have infant mortality rates that are ten times higher than those in high-income countries

Table 8.1: Health data for world regions and selected countries, 2020

Country	Population/ millions[1]	Crude death rate per 1,000 per year[2]	Infant mortality rate per 1,000 per year[2]	Life expectancy at birth[3]		HIV prevalence rate[4] % age 15–49	HDI[5] ranking
				Male	Female		
Africa							
Kenya	53.8	5	35	64	68	5.4	147
Mali	20.3	9	63	57	58	1.0	184
Nigeria	206.1	11	59	54	55	2.9	158
South Africa	59.3	9	26	60	67	18.9	113
Zimbabwe	14.9	7	37	59	63	13.5	150
Americas							
Brazil	212.6	6	12	71	78	0.5	79
Cuba	11.3	9	4	75	81	0.4	72
Jamaica	3.0	7	11	73	78	1.7	96
Paraguay	7.1	5	19	72	76	0.5	98
USA	331.0	8	6	76	81	0.3	15

(continued)

Table 8.1: Health data for world regions and selected countries, 2020 (continued)

Country	Population/ millions[1]	Crude death rate per 1,000 per year[2]	Infant mortality rate per 1,000 per year[2]	Life expectancy at birth[3] Male	Life expectancy at birth[3] Female	HIV prevalence rate[4] % age 15–49	HDI[5] ranking
Europe							
Germany	83.8	11	3	78	83	0.1	4
Poland	37.8	10	3	73	81	0.1	32
Portugal	10.2	10	3	77	84	0.5	40
Sweden	10.1	9	2	80	84	0.2	14
UK	67.9	9	4	79	83	0.2	8
Asia							
Bangladesh	164.7	5	25	71	74	0.1	135
China	1,439.3	7	9	75	77	0.09	85
India	1,380.0	7	30	67	70	0.2	129
Japan	126.5	10	2	81	87	0.1	19
Sri Lanka	21.4	6	7	72	78	0.1	71
Russian Federation	145.9	12	5	66	77	1.2	49
World	7,7965	7	28	69	74	0.8	
High-income		10	4				
Low-income		7	42				

Sources: [1] UNFPA (2020); [2] UN DESA (2019b); [3] WHO (2020c); [4] CIA (2020); [5] UNDP (2019)

(see Table 8.1). Communicable diseases that have spread worldwide also show significant differences in rates of infection: for example, the ongoing HIV/AIDS global epidemic has a higher prevalence rate in Latin America compared with North America and Europe, and there are much higher rates in sub-Saharan Africa which has more than two thirds of all people living with HIV globally. Within countries there are also significant differences in infection rates, mortality and healthy life expectancy. This is often due to differences in access to safe drinking water, sanitation and nutritious foods. Significant differences in healthcare access and quality, between rural and urban communities, and between the rich and the poor, also exist in many developing countries.

An assessment and analysis of the burden of diseases and injuries experienced in different countries and regions around the world is clearly very important for health decision making and planning purposes, and this gave rise to the Global Burden of Disease (GBD) project which was initiated in 1990 by the World Bank. Regular GBD reports show the levels of progress and trends in relation to health concerns around the world and the risk factors that cause them. Since 2000, much of the concern of the global health community, including donors, has focused on reducing child deaths, the mortality of mothers, and the burden of illness and death from particular conditions, including tuberculosis, HIV and malaria. These are all health issues that are particularly in need of attention in the developing world, and there is evidence of progress in most areas. GBD studies show that improvements are not only to do with specific health interventions, but also strongly connected to socioeconomic factors such as income, education and the status of women and girls in society. These factors are tracked and incorporated into a sociodemographic index. The close correlation between improvements in the socio-demographic index and progress in health are particularly evident in low-income and lower-middle-income countries, and indicates that health is much more than simply a medical issue and requires a much broader approach. This would include enhancing strategies that stimulate economic growth and reduce poverty, expanding access to primary and secondary schooling, reducing gender inequalities and improving the standing of women. *The Lancet* (2020: 1129) has emphasised the need for such strategies to be a collective priority in addressing the global burden of diseases as it is only by tackling 'deeply embedded structural inequities in society' that we can achieve the goal of Health for All. The link between health and poverty and inequality is very clear; poverty is included in the International Classification of Diseases, as stated in the WHO's (1995) first *World Health Report*: 'The world's biggest killer and the greatest cause of ill health and suffering across the globe is [...] extreme poverty'.

Globalisation and health: trends and perspectives

One of the key questions that arises from recent developments related to health and the global burden of disease is the impact of globalisation. Has globalisation led to improvements in health and healthcare, or has it served to exacerbate health-related problems in certain respects? One of the most notable shifts in global health that is connected with globalisation is the shift in the global burden of disease from communicable diseases to noncommunicable diseases (NCDs). Over half of all diseases in 1990 were communicable, but there has been an ongoing increase in the global proportion of NCDs in the 21st century, from 60 per cent in 2000 to 70 per cent in 2015, and 80 per cent in 2020. The WHO (2018) predicts that this shift will continue over the next decade with the largest increase occurring in Africa. This could be seen as evidence of the epidemiological transition associated with modernisation and a decline in the proportion of communicable diseases. NCDs such as cardiovascular diseases, diabetes, cancer and chronic respiratory diseases have tended to be associated with the lifestyles and consumption habits of people in the more affluent economies of the Global North, but this is changing and NCDs are becoming increasingly prominent in the Global South. NCDs are the leading cause of mortality worldwide, killing 41 million people each year; 75 per cent of NCD deaths occur in low- and middle-income countries (Figure 8.2). However, while NCDs are rising sharply, communicable diseases continue to be most prevalent in developing countries and account for the majority of deaths, as in

Figure 8.2: Global burden of disease

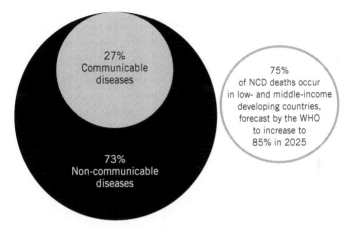

27%
Communicable
diseases

73%
Non-communicable
diseases

75%
of NCD deaths occur
in low- and middle-income
developing countries,
forecast by the WHO
to increase to
85% in 2025

Sources: Figure created using data from IHME (2020) and WHO (2020a)

the case of COVID-19. NCDs are predicted to continue to rise. The WHO (2020a) estimates that by 2030 deaths from NCDs in Africa 'are projected to exceed deaths due to communicable, maternal, perinatal and nutritional diseases combined'.

Developing countries are therefore facing a growing double burden of disease and this is mainly as a result of globalisation. Key factors identified by the WHO as contributing to the rising burden of NCDs globally are tobacco use, physical inactivity, the harmful use of alcohol and unhealthy diets. Globalisation can be seen as having played a crucial role in transferring such lifestyles to the developing world through the roles played by multinational tobacco, alcohol and food industries in expanding their markets globally. Tobacco accounts for over 7.2 million deaths every year, including deaths of smokers and those exposed to smoke, including children. Rising alcohol use has also increased NCDs, including cancer, in developing countries. Meanwhile, unhealthy diets, attributable to the growing number of imported foods that are high in fats, salt and sugar, have resulted in an increase in obesity, heart disease, diabetes and chronic respiratory diseases. Restrictions on tobacco use and advertising that have come into force in the developed countries of the world have been less evident in developing countries. Other factors have also played a significant part in shifting the global burden of NCDs to the developing world. These include rapid and poorly planned urbanisation, increasing exposure to air pollution such as carbon monoxide which in turn accentuates the risk of lung and heart disease, and changes in lifestyle for many moving from rural to expanding urban areas. A more sedentary lifestyle with fewer opportunities for exercise has an impact on health and increases the likelihood of suffering from NCDs.

The globalisation of lifestyles and urbanisation has therefore played a crucial role in the growing burden of disease, and many factors associated with modernisation and development can be seen to have made a significant contribution. For example, the rapidly rising number of motor vehicles in developing countries, often seen as evidence of progress towards modernity, has also had dire consequences as a result of increasing exhaust emissions and road accidents, with more than 90 per cent of road traffic deaths and injuries occurring in low- and middle-income countries. Most deaths and long-term disabilities from road accidents in developing countries happen among the working-age population, and this can seriously reduce a country's productivity. The World Bank (2017b) has estimated that halving deaths and injuries from road traffic crashes would significantly increase per capita GDP by as much as 15 per cent in the two countries with the highest populations, China and India.

Strong links have also been shown to exist between global poverty and vulnerability to NCDs. These links have led to diseases sometimes being referred to as 'diseases of poverty' (Parker and Wilson, 2000: 75). For example, under-nutrition during pregnancy and low birth weight, which are particularly prevalent among low-income populations in developing countries, have been found to increase the subsequent risk of cardiovascular disease and diabetes. The costs of healthcare in treating such diseases also increases poverty; moreover, NCDs during adulthood may prevent people from working, thereby reducing family income. NCDs have been linked not only to poverty but also to other social determinants, notably education. In China, for example, lower educational levels have been strongly associated with an increased risk of diabetes, and the findings of a study in India showed that tobacco use, hypertension and physical inactivity were significantly more prevalent in less educated groups of the population. In Vietnam, deaths from cardiovascular diseases were found to be much lower among the more educated and much higher among those without formal education (WHO, 2010: 34). Global and national inequalities have a significant impact on vulnerability to NCDs. On the other hand, globalisation has helped the dissemination across the world of information relating to the causes of NCDs and their treatment via new communication technologies, and medications that were previously only available in the more developed parts of the world have become more widely available in developing regions. However, the high cost of many new medications has meant that poorer sections of the population have often not been able to access them.

A further impact of globalisation on NCDs in the developing world has been the spread of communicable diseases through viruses. NCDs have been shown to increase susceptibility to global infectious diseases, including the COVID-19 pandemic in 2020 where people with pre-existing NCDs were more vulnerable to becoming severely ill or dying from the virus. To take another example, where diabetes has not been effectively controlled in developing countries, it has increased the risk and severity of infectious diseases such as the dengue fever, a viral infection spread by tropical mosquitos. Where developing countries have been able to treat NCDs more effectively, such infections have had less impact. For example, in Brazil where the mosquito-borne Zika virus broke out in 2015, it had far less impact than in other countries where NCDs were less under control. Another problem created by infectious epidemics in the 21st century, such as SARS (severe acute respiratory syndrome), avian influenza (bird flu), Ebola virus disease and HIV/AIDS, is that addressing these serious outbreaks has disrupted existing healthcare services for NCDs and diverted attention and resources to the new emergencies. The WHO (2020b: 11) has recognised the significant impact of the COVID-19 pandemic on NCD resources and services in developing countries, with large parts of the population having no access to essential health services during the crisis due to the lack of available health workers, especially in rural and remote areas.

The global spread of communicable diseases in recent decades raises the question of why this has happened, given increasing awareness and advanced medical understanding of bacterial and viral infections. Again, key aspects of globalisation have played a major part in spreading epidemics and creating pandemics across the world. The rise of international travel and tourism has been momentous since the start of the development era. The number of international tourists increased from just 25 million in 1950 to 1.5 billion in 2019 (UNWTO, 2020). Such developments have inevitably played a significant role in the transmission of infections across the world. At the same time, the impact of increasing travel on the environment and climate change has also been profound, and this in turn has raised health risks, particularly in parts of the developing world where droughts, floods and other extreme weather-related conditions have had serious consequences for the health of their populations. Modernisation and globalisation have therefore created what Ulrich Beck describes as a 'world risk society' (Beck, 2009). Clearly, the consequences for health have been profound, and the impact of the coronavirus pandemic is a striking example of what it can mean to live in a world risk society as it reduced global life expectancy by around one year by 2021.

HIV (human immunodeficiency virus) which can lead to AIDS (acquired immune deficiency syndrome) is a striking example of a long-standing global disease which was first recognised as an epidemic in the early 1980s. It is widely believed that HIV originated in the Democratic Republic of Congo as early as 1920 when HIV crossed species from chimpanzees to humans. Since the 1980s it has spread across the world, with 37.7 million people living with the virus in 2020. More women than men are infected, and 1.8 million children under the age of 14 were estimated to be living with the virus. The global spread of the disease and its continuing prevalence has resulted in it being defined by the WHO as a global epidemic. The virus is mostly transmitted sexually but also from mothers to babies before and during birth. Globalisation has increased the spread of HIV across countries. At the same time, global awareness and medical interventions have helped to curb the rate of increase in the number of cases globally, with a decline in the annual rate of new infections since 2010. However, sub-Saharan Africa remains by far the worst affected region of the world (Figure 8.3), and HIV/AIDS is also the leading cause of morbidity and mortality, causing 75 per cent of deaths in this region.

These trends demonstrate that the global patterns of inequality and poverty that were outlined in the previous chapter are as closely connected to communicable diseases (such as HIV/AIDS) as they are to NCDs. Poverty and income inequalities affect the transmission of diseases as a result of poorer members of the population having less access to health services and being unaware of their infectivity status through testing; they are therefore more likely to pass infections such as HIV on to others. Studies have also shown that people are more biologically vulnerable to infection when they are malnourished or suffer from parasitic infections, which are particularly prevalent in many developing countries in tropical and subtropical regions. Parasitic infections such as hookworm and Guinea worm weaken the immune system, and are associated with such factors as poor sanitation, contaminated food and water, and inadequate toilet facilities. Intestinal parasitic infections are among the most common infections in developing countries. While over 200 million people are infected each year with malaria spread by mosquitos, the WHO (2020d) estimates that 1.5 billion people suffer from intestinal parasitic conditions caused by soil-transmitted worm infections, with the

Figure 8.3: Global HIV

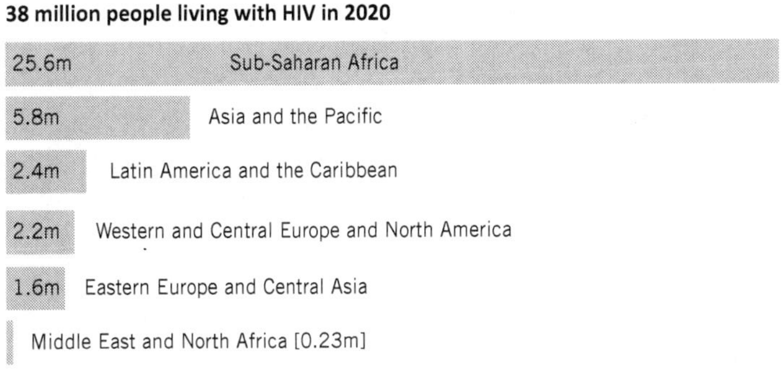

38 million people living with HIV in 2020

25.6m	Sub-Saharan Africa
5.8m	Asia and the Pacific
2.4m	Latin America and the Caribbean
2.2m	Western and Central Europe and North America
1.6m	Eastern Europe and Central Asia
	Middle East and North Africa [0.23m]

Source: UNAIDS (2021)

greatest numbers occurring in sub-Saharan Africa, China and East Asia, and Latin America.

A further factor associated with the prevalence of HIV among poor communities in the Global South is education. The proportion of infected people is higher among the least educated sections of the population. One reason for this is that educated people are generally better informed about prevention measures. The number of years of education that children experience can also have an impact on HIV prevalence by delaying the age of onset of sexual activity, but in poorer communities girls are often sent into marriage at a very early age as poor families see this as an economic survival strategy: pushing a girl into marriage means one less child to feed or educate. Girls who marry at a very young age are susceptible to many health risks, are more vulnerable to HIV infection and passing this on to their offspring. Adolescent girls and young women account for a disproportionate number of new HIV infections, and in sub-Saharan Africa women and girls accounted for 63 per cent of all new HIV infections in 2020 (UNAIDS, 2021: 3).

The devastating impact of HIV/AIDS in the Global South is clearly related to many other issues associated with globalisation and unequal patterns of development. Together with poverty and inequality, politics also plays a significant role in determining whether health concerns are properly addressed. Interventions by governments can make a big difference, as demonstrated by the introduction of the Bolsa Familia programme in Brazil in 2003 which was subsequently found to have contributed to a significant reduction in mortality in children, especially in relation to poverty-related causes such as diarrhoea and malnutrition, and improved educational levels were also found to have a beneficial effect on health. Cuba provides another example of where government intervention in promoting and controlling health programmes has played a significant role. The Cuban government has focused on addressing poverty and providing free community-based healthcare to its population since the revolution of 1959, and while it continues to be a moderately poor developing country in Latin America, it has made remarkable achievements in providing public healthcare. Cubans enjoy longer life expectancy than others in most of

Latin America, and on a par with the US in 2021 at 79 years of age. In relation to HIV/AIDS, Cuba's health programme has been one of the most successful in the world. The programme has involved strict government measures, including quarantining all people found to be HIV infected and providing an intensive educational and preventative programme for all HIV-positive individuals consigned to sanitoriums. Cuba also produces its own generic anti-retroviral drugs to treat all the country's AIDS patients, and all pregnant women have to undergo an HIV test to prevent transmission to new-borns. While it would be difficult for other countries with very different political regimes to implement such policies, Cuba stands out as an example of what can be achieved in successfully addressing serious health issues in developing countries.

Health, security and global health governance

In a broader context, health has been linked to both human security and national security. National security refers to the ability of a state to cater for the protection and defence of its citizenry. Armed conflict and cross-border migration can create health problems that have an impact on national security, and life-threatening epidemics can become serious matters of political concern. At the first meeting in the new millennium of the UN Security Council in January 2000, the prime topic was the 'impact of AIDS on peace and security'. On the other hand, national security is enhanced when the growing provision of healthcare indicates progress, security and stability in a country, and this can be reflected at a global level too.

The importance of health in addressing human, national and global security has resulted in what has become known as global health governance. The WHO is the most prominent intergovernmental organisation that addresses global health concerns. However, the WHO is not the only organisation responsible for global health governance, which has over the years come to embrace a variety of inter-governmental and non-governmental organisations. These include the World Bank, which has no formal mandate to address health issues but is now the biggest financier of global health programmes. Other global health organisations have also been created in response to specific health issues, notably the United Nations' formation of UNAIDS to address the ongoing HIV/AIDS global epidemic. Private actors have also played a significant role in global health governance by setting up their own international philanthropic health foundations. Notable examples include the Clinton Foundation, established in 1997 by former US president Bill Clinton, which focuses mainly on HIV/AIDS, and the Gates Foundation, set up by Bill and Melinda Gates in 2000. Civil society organisations have also played an active and important role in addressing global public health concerns. Well-known examples include Rotary International, which has more than one million members worldwide and has taken the lead in global campaigns to eradicate polio; and Oxfam International, which works in around one hundred countries worldwide and is renowned for its Health and Education for All campaign, and has drawn attention to global inequalities and the need to address poverty and the structural factors that undermine access to health services. Global health governance is therefore quite complex with many different and important players. What is clear, however, is that while particular health issues, epidemics and global pandemics require specific interventions, there has been an increasing awareness of the need to address broader health concerns, strengthen health systems, and reduce poverty and inequality. Global health governance has widened its scope.

Primary healthcare

One of the key directions associated with global health governance has been the emphasis on primary healthcare (PHC). It first became an internationally agreed approach to health in 1978 with the Alma-Ata Declaration, which stated that health is a fundamental human right and that inequalities in the health status of people in the developed and developing worlds had to be addressed. PHC was defined as the essential means of achieving this goal by making healthcare 'universally accessible to individuals and families in the community through their full participation and at a cost that the community and country can afford' (WHO, 1978: 3). The Alma-Ata Declaration also stated that the promotion and protection of health was essential to sustained social and economic development, and would contribute towards both a better quality of life and world peace. PHC was designed to address the main health issues in communities, providing promotive, preventive and curative services, including health education, promotion of food supply and nutrition, access to safe water and sanitation, maternal and child healthcare, as well as appropriate treatment for common diseases and injuries. Community participation through appropriate education and training was also seen as essential to PHC provision, and all countries were advised to cooperate in a spirit of partnership to advance PHC throughout the world. Some 40 years later, in 2018, a global conference on primary healthcare held in Astana reaffirmed the Alma-Ata commitments (WHO/UNICEF, 2018). The Astana Declaration stressed that strengthening PHC was the most inclusive, effective and efficient way to enhance people's health and wellbeing. It also underlined the importance of health for peace, security and socioeconomic development, and confirmed the need to build sustainable PHC in line with the SDGs. Universal health coverage is at the centre of SDG 3: good health and wellbeing. The new declaration also recognises the increasing importance of NCDs and the health impacts of climate change.

PHC and community participation have had clear benefits in countries where they have been most effectively implemented. Examples include Chile and Cuba in Latin America, and Sri Lanka and Nepal in South Asia. PHC has also increased global awareness of health issues in the developing world and has prompted interventions by NGOs and individuals to address particular concerns that have previously been ignored. One example is the treatment of poor eyesight due to refractive error, such as myopia. Many people suffer from this condition, estimated at around 2.5 billion in 2020, and it is a particular problem for people in developing countries who do not have access to optical services. It is ranked highly in the Global Burden of Disease project: more than one billion people live with vision impairment because they do not receive the eye care they need. Not only is it a health issue that affects people's quality of life but also one that has significant impacts on employment and productivity. The WHO (2019: 16) has estimated that poor eyesight results in a loss of $270 billion per year as a result of loss of productivity, with low- and middle-income countries in the developing regions of the world being the most severely affected by far. The WHO has become much more concerned with addressing eye conditions, including eye care as an essential component of PHC and making it part of the SDG 3 goal of universal health coverage. The WHO refers to this as integrated people-centred eye care. This goes beyond medical interventions to include 'eye health literacy', which is designed to raise people's awareness of the issues surrounding common eye conditions, and the availability of vision rehabilitation. Once again, education plays an important role in addressing health concerns, and primary healthcare is brought to the fore.

Wider role of education in development

While health and education are closely linked, education also plays a wider role in development as it equips people with necessary life skills and provides them with better opportunities in life, including employment and active participation in their local communities. In return, a well-educated population can have a profound impact on the nature and extent of a country's social and economic development, resulting in more effective democratic participation in local and national politics, and higher levels of economic growth. Education also plays a role in addressing wider global issues, such as climate change and environmental pollution, as awareness of these issues is closely associated with literacy and educational understanding. Studies have shown that well-educated people are much better informed about their surrounding environment. The impressive and rapid rise in the economic growth of a number of countries in east and south-east Asia, such as South Korea, Singapore, Hong Kong and Taiwan, which became known as the Four Asian Tigers, was facilitated by having a strong focus on investment in education at primary, secondary and tertiary levels. Many developing countries, for example in sub-Saharan Africa, have not been able to invest in education to the same extent, but even the provision of basic education can play a vital role in reducing poverty, improving health, and generally contributing to a country's development. Good basic education increases employment opportunities, helps to break down the barriers of inequality, and provides the tools for greater engagement in politics and civil society. UNESCO (2017: 12) estimates that each year of schooling raises earnings by around 10 per cent; the increase is significantly higher for women than for men as uneducated women generally suffer greater income inequalities.

Education has also been shown to improve social attitudes regarding gender differences and to empower women in such a way that they have more control over their lives, including when they marry and how many children they have. There is a strong correlation between high levels of child mortality and low levels of maternal education. Education generally contributes to lower fertility rates for women and healthier lives for the fewer children to whom they give birth. Addressing gender inequalities in education therefore plays a significant role in promoting health and development. The more educated women are, the more power they have over their lives, such that if all girls in sub-Saharan Africa completed secondary education, child marriages would drop by an estimated 64 per cent (Oxfam International, 2019: 6). Clearly, education can play a very important role in addressing inequalities in the developing world, but in the third decade of the 21st century there is still a long way to go. Inequalities seriously affect the poorest fifth of children in the world: as many as 44 per cent of girls and 34 per cent of boys from the poorest quintile have never attended school or have dropped out of primary education (UNICEF, 2020).

The SDGs have set a target for quality education by 2030, including universal literacy and numeracy, but in some parts of the developing world a great deal remains to be done. Progress has been impeded by epidemics such as SARS, HIV and Ebola, and by the COVID-19 pandemic, which have reduced government expenditure on education, led to school closures, and in the case of poorer families have led to lower household incomes and support for the education of their children.

Clearly, education is a public good and can change the world, as the quotation from Nelson Mandela at the start of this chapter indicates, but there is still a very long way to go (Figures 8.4 and 8.5). UNESCO has estimated that extreme poverty would be halved if primary and secondary education were made universally available to the world's children. There is evidence of progress being made in improving levels of education across many parts of the Global South, notably in children's access to primary and secondary schooling. The development of information and communications technologies (ICTs) in recent times has also helped in promoting digital access to education. Globalisation itself has facilitated the spread of ICTs to less developed parts of the world, as demonstrated by China's Belt and Road Initiative and the expansion of new digital technologies across the continent of Africa. However, while access to education and the average levels of schooling have increased across developing countries over the decades, the disparity between developed and developing countries continues to persist, as shown in Figure 8.5.

Figure 8.4: Illiteracy rate for adults (over 15 years) by world region

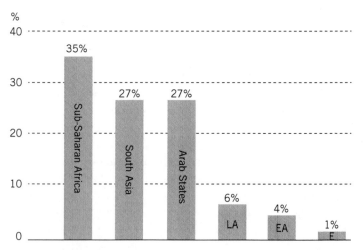

Note: LA = Latin America and the Caribbean; EA = East Asia and the Pacific; E = Europe and Central Asia

Source: World Bank (2019)

Figure 8.5: Average years of schooling by education level

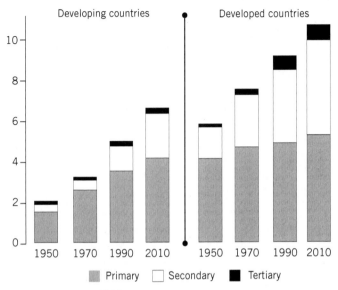

Source: Barro and Lee (2010)

Globalisation, however, may offer new opportunities for educational development by encouraging greater national and international commitment to improving educational facilities for people across the world. A rapidly changing global world is one which requires greater knowledge and understanding, and education becomes an increasingly important and necessary component of development in responding to globalisation and achieving economic growth and social development. To engage and integrate with the global economy is becoming ever more important for developing countries, and this can only be properly achieved if their populations are equipped with the new skills and knowledge that are needed to be successful in an increasingly interconnected world. Global connections can assist in the sharing of knowledge and intellectual assets, and may also promote international understanding and collaboration. Education is crucial to living and working in the age of globalisation, and for a nation it is a vital component of its social and economic standing in the world.

China is a key example of a country where the education system has played a crucial role in creating a literate and informed workforce and allowing for the training of more skilled workers and professionals to meet the changing requirements of the global economy. This has served to elevate China's status as a nation and its position in the global economy. With the largest population of all countries in the world, the Chinese education sector is the largest in the world.

Further evidence of the increasing impact of globalisation on education is the growing number of tertiary-level students from developing countries studying at universities and colleges overseas. China again leads the world in the number of students studying abroad with around 1.5 million enrolled on overseas courses at the start of 2020. The majority of Chinese students enrol on courses in the US and UK, which are the two most popular destinations for international students as a whole, followed by Australia. This in part reflects the extent to which English has become a global language and how this is indicated in the number of schools around the world teaching the English language. Alongside the growth in numbers of students from developing countries studying overseas, there has also been an expansion of what has become known as transnational education. This refers to various forms of international education in which educational programmes are delivered by one country in another country. A number of countries in the developed world have created such programmes which can include distance/online learning, franchised programmes, international branch campuses and other forms of partnership arrangements. The UK is a world leader in delivering transnational education, and the vast majority of UK universities now deliver it, with Asia hosting the largest proportion, around 50 per cent, followed by Africa and the Middle East (UUKi, 2020: 20).

Summary and conclusion

Health and education are both crucial components of development and can help to accelerate progress in many areas. While the quotation from Brundtland at the start of this chapter claims that health is the 'core of development', the same can be said about education too. The quotation from Mandela recognises the key role played by education in transforming the world. Both are essential to the advance of development in many different areas of society, economics, politics and culture. The crucial roles of health and education have been recognised in the SDGs, where good health and wellbeing and quality education are recognised as vital to the future of a developing and sustainable world.

Global crises and pandemics such as COVID-19 can seriously disrupt progress towards health and education for all, and thereby affect many other positive aspects of development, including promoting economic growth, tackling inequalities, and supporting the growth of civil society, democracy and political stability. UN DESA (2021) noted that COVID-19 had effectively wiped out 20 years of education gains. The pandemic has also played a significant role in setting back progress towards the SDG goals for health by 2030. Many other factors come into play too, and have an impact on progress towards better health and education for all, including poverty and inequality, environmental issues and climate change, conflict and insecurity, and various aspects of globalisation. As we have seen in this chapter, there is evidence of both progression and regression in relation to health and education and their role in the broader processes of social and economic development. It is clear that advances in health and education are both crucial for development, while at the same time many other aspects of development play a significant role in assisting their progress and their ability to strengthen human development on a global scale.

KEY POINTS SUMMARY

- Education and health are closely interconnected as crucial components of development, and the UNDP has acknowledged their importance in advancing human development.
- Definitions of health vary, but the WHO definition makes clear that health is not simply about the absence of disease or infirmity, but refers to a state of complete physical, mental and social wellbeing.

- Primary healthcare and community participation are vital in making progress towards health for all and meeting the SDG target of good health and wellbeing by 2030.
- Education plays a vital role in all areas of development, including economic growth, reducing poverty and inequality, improving health and wellbeing, and supporting civil society engagement and political participation.
- Health pandemics can have serious negative consequences for education in developing countries, as evidenced by the coronavirus outbreak in 2020.
- Education improves awareness of risks to health and vulnerability to environmental issues, and helps to address inequalities in dealing with these issues.
- Literacy and education play a significant part in addressing a range of inequalities, not only between the rich and the poor, but also between men and women, and between urban and rural communities.
- Globalisation has become a major issue in relation to health and development, as reflected in the inequalities of the global burden of disease connected with communicable and non-communicable diseases.
- Health is also linked to the issues of human, national and international security, which raises serious questions about the nature of global health governance.

KEY READING GUIDE

Health as a topic is not given priority in most general texts on development. Useful overviews are provided in some texts, however: for example, a chapter on 'Health, Education and Population' in the book by Hopper (2018) *Understanding Development*. Most of the more comprehensive accounts of health and development can be found in texts on globalisation and health. These include Hanefeld (2015) *Globalization and Health*; Davies (2010) *Global Politics of Health*; and Youde (2012) which focuses on *Global Health Governance*. A more specific focus in relation HIV and AIDS is presented in the book edited by Poku et al (2010) *AIDS and Governance*. Regular reports by the WHO provide updated accounts of different health concerns, measurements of progress in addressing health issues, and regional and country profiles. Global Health Watch has produced a number of alternative reports which challenge the WHO reports and argue for a more people-centred approach that highlights social justice and calls for careful monitoring of global health institutions (GHW, 2017).

In a similar way to health, education does not feature as one of the main topics in many of the general texts on development. However, as noted above, a useful overview is provided in Hopper's *Understanding Development* (2018). A number of insightful articles are also included in the 'Health and Education' section of Desai and Potter (2014) *The Companion to Development Studies*. In relation to specific countries where education has been advanced but in different ways, a good example is the book by Tilak (2018) *Education and Development in India*. International organisations such as UNESCO and UNICEF have produced a number of important reports in recent years, including UNESCO (2020) *Inclusion and Education*, and UNICEF (2020) *Addressing the Learning Crisis*. Oxfam International have also addressed some of the key issues in relation to education and development; for example, in their 2019 publication, *The Power of Education to Fight Inequality*.

9

Looking to the future: digital technology, a green environment and gender equality

Introduction: global development issues in the 21st century

We will never stop fighting for the living planet and for our future. (Greta Thunberg, 2019: 105)

Addressing issues of poverty and inequality, and providing health and education for all, together with assessing the impact of growing areas of the global economy, such as tourism, are all crucial to finding the best ways forward for development, as we have seen in the previous chapters. Increasingly in the 21st century, however, certain areas related to development have become highly prominent in development thinking, partly as a result of globalisation and growing awareness of issues and patterns of change that affect the world as a whole. Three key areas are the expansion of global digital technologies and their role in the future, concerns over the impact of economic growth and modernisation on the environment, and the need to address gender inequalities in order to advance development across the world. These have all received some attention in the preceding chapters, but in this chapter the focus is specifically on these three areas, which will have a crucial impact on development in the 21st century. Looking to the future, successful attention to these areas could lead to the advance of digital technology for the benefit of all, the development of a green environment that secures the future of people and the planet, and a full-scale transition to gender equality that will facilitate progressive development. The following sections will examine each of these three areas of development, the problems that need to be addressed, the practices that are being implemented, and the extent to which progress is being made. All three areas are interconnected in various ways, and this means that issues surrounding technology, the environment and gender need to be simultaneously addressed.

Advance of digital technology

In an increasingly interconnected world, digital technologies have come to the fore in relation to the links between technology and development. However, many other technologies that have been invented and rapidly expanded during the development era have also played a major role in addressing important issues and providing a new way forward. Solar power is a good example of an advanced technology that can provide renewable and cost-effective energy for developing countries by allowing them to gain energy independence and reduce or eliminate dependence on imported sources of energy.

It is particularly appropriate and beneficial for the developing world because most regions in the Global South have enormous solar power potential due to the prevalence of strong sunlight. Where sunshine is abundant, but electricity supplies are unreliable, solar energy provides the way forward for development. The use of solar power has grown most strongly in Asia – in Bangladesh, China and India – where projects have been supported by governments and by international organisations such as the World Bank. Solar home energy systems have become widely used, and not only provide cheaper energy sources, but also benefit local communities and households by reducing reliance on kerosene lamps and candles for their lighting, which emit pollutants that can have serious health consequences. Small solar set-ups, known as 'pico solar systems', are becoming especially popular in some African countries such as Kenya and Tanzania. Rural populations of sub-Saharan Africa stand to benefit greatly from increased access to solar energy, given that most of the people in the world without access to electricity live in this region. Access to solar energy has the potential to reduce poverty by leading to improvements in agricultural productivity, health, education and communications. A number of projects are in place to promote solar projects in Africa, including the Lighting Africa programme, sponsored by the World Bank, which has provided over 32 million people with access to electricity via solar power. However, there is still a long way to go, and in 2020 more than half a billion people in sub-Saharan Africa were living without any access to electricity. The environmental benefits of using solar power are also considerable, and the potential for future use is enormous as it is estimated that Earth gets more solar energy in one hour than the entire world uses in a year (Nussey, 2019).

One of the many advantages of solar energy is that it can be used to power digital devices and thereby facilitate access to the advancing communication systems of the 21st century. The growth of digital technology and its global expansion is most notably associated with the rise of the internet, and has really taken off in the 21st century, spreading well beyond the more advanced countries of the world. As digital technology has advanced, we have moved into what Jonathan Crary (2013: 29) has described as a '24/7 world' in which the world can be constantly connected, regardless of different time zones. Modern smartphones, which combine cellular phone communication with camera facilities and access to the internet, took off in the 21st century. As in other areas of development, the economically and technologically advanced countries of the world led the way. By 2021, around 48 per cent of the world's population owned a smartphone. Developing countries are catching up, but progress is much quicker in some countries than in others. China, for example, has come to play a leading role in the production of smartphones and in digital communication networks, but many developing countries lag far behind with smartphones accounting for only 50 per cent of all mobile phones in the Global South by 2020. The potential advantages of advancing communication technologies have increasingly come to be seen as paramount for development in a global age, and the abbreviation ICT4D, which stands for information and communications technology for development, has become a central theme of much development thinking.

While progress is being made in developing countries, there are significant variations between and within countries. Digital connectivity is growing rapidly in some emerging economies, notably among some of the BRICS: Brazil, China and South Africa. Smartphone ownership was as high as 60 per cent in these countries in 2019, but in one of the other BRICS, India, ownership was as low as 25 per cent (Statista, 2021). Internet use is also rising across the Global South, but again there are significant variations between countries. Within countries, there are differences connected with education, income and gender. More educated and higher-income groups are more likely to be digitally connected. While smartphone ownership has tended to increase across both genders in recent years, there is still a tendency for more men to possess smartphones than women and to have greater access to social media sites. The differences have been found to be notable in countries in Africa and Asia such as Kenya, Nigeria and India. While 34 per cent of men in India were found to own smartphones in 2018, only 15 per cent of women owned one, and while around half of men in Kenya were using social media in 2018, only around a third of women were doing so (Taylor and Silver, 2019).

The digital divide between the Global South and Global North is reducing over time, but is still significant, and in addition to differences in the extent of access to the latest information and communication technologies, there is a considerable divide in relation to the control of global digital platforms such as Microsoft. Here, the US is way ahead of the rest of the world, but China is also ahead too. This results in what has been referred to as the geography of the digital economy being highly concentrated in just two countries, with the US and China having 90 per cent of the market capitalisation value of the world's largest digital platforms. The vast differences in digital platforms between the five regions of the world are clearly illustrated in Figure 9.1.

The rise of China in the expanding digital economy indicates that, in the multipolar world of the 21st century, the global economy is no longer driven solely by the Western powers of the Global North. At the same time, there is much evidence that digital technologies

Figure 9.1: Geography of the global digital platforms

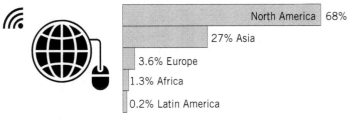

Source: UNCTAD (2019)

bring a number of advantages to developing countries that will play an increasing role in addressing many important issues in the coming decades.

Information and communication technologies (ICTs) are increasingly integral to how people now live in many parts of the world, and are serving to transform societies and economies. The role that they can play in advancing development has become ever more apparent, and therefore it is of crucial importance that developing countries no longer lag behind in their ICT capacities. We have already seen in earlier chapters how ICTs can play a very important role in addressing health and education issues in developing countries by providing access to online health services and e-learning. More generally, increasing access to information and knowledge via ICT networks can help to empower people in developing countries, particularly in more remote rural locations, and generate a greater degree of inclusiveness and equality for individuals and local communities. At a national state level, essential infrastructures and services can also be greatly improved by ICTs. In addition to health and education services, these include government services, financial services, water and power supplies, food distribution chains, transport and navigation systems, industrial processes and supply chains, and so on. ICTs have also helped to generate employment in a number of developing countries by enabling the growth of industries in the service sector. India is the most remarkable example of a country that has successfully expanded its service sector to the point at which it was contributing over 60 per cent to the country's gross domestic product (GDP) in 2020 and employing around 25 per cent of the national labour force. The World Bank acknowledges that the benefits of digital technologies filter through the economy and boost development, but also recognises that there is still a long way to go before digital technologies are more widely available to the global population: 'Making the internet universally accessible and affordable should be a global priority' (World Bank, 2016: 4).

Environmental sustainability is another field of development where digital technologies can provide a positive way forward. Having access to environmental data and what needs to be done to protect and manage the environment is clearly of increasing importance in the 21st century, particularly in relation to growing concern about the effects of climate change. Many developing countries have been seriously affected, and environmental information on the best practices to address weather and climate extremes, air quality and pollution is vital for sustainable future development. Having instant access to information on pending natural disasters such as hurricanes, droughts and flooding can also be very helpful in enabling local communities to take as many precautionary measures as possible. In addition to making environmental information more readily available to all developing countries, and especially to those in more isolated rural communities, the use of ICTs can help to reduce CO_2 emissions and their effects on global warming and air pollution. Energy-efficient ICTs replace physical goods and services with virtual, digital means of communication that are far less energy-intensive. Moving digital data is much less detrimental to the environment than the movement of people and goods, and ICTs can help to raise awareness of environmental issues. For example, in Zambia they have helped to engage local communities in rural areas and increase family usage of more carbon-efficient cookstoves (Heeks, 2018: 291). ICTs can also help, through the use of smart applications, to improve the utilisation of advanced technologies such as solar power and other renewable energy sources. There is a growing awareness of the role of digital technologies in achieving sustainable forms of development, and this is particularly evident as we move towards 2030 and the Sustainable

Development Goals targets set for that year. The 2019 World Summit on the Information Society (WSIS), co-organised by several UN organisations, stated that, 'Information and communication technologies (ICTs) are now integral to how we approach sustainable development' (WSIS, 2019: 3-4).

The advance of digital technology clearly provides a positive way forward for development in many different areas, from poverty and inequality to health, education and the environment, but there is still a long way for ICT4D to go. Digital divides need to be addressed, as too do concerns over the geography of the digital economy and the control of digital platforms by major corporations. Fears have been expressed that this is creating a new global digital divide based on 'data colonialism'. Digital development therefore holds both hopes and challenges for the future of the developing world.

The environment in the age of the Anthropocene

> If modernity is a runaway train, what can the passengers do?
> (David Goldblatt, 1996: 194)

Digital technologies can play an important role in addressing environmental issues, but the continuing rapid growth of the global economy and world population raises the question of what can be done to ensure sustainable development if modernity advances so rapidly that it becomes 'a runaway train'. The international development literature has shifted towards a growing concern with the future of the planet. This is reflected in the concept of the Anthropocene, a new geological epoch marked by the impact of the human species on the environment in which history and geology have become interwoven. The origins of the Anthropocene go back a long way, but it is particularly associated with the industrial age and the acceleration of modernity post-1945, which was also the start of the development era. It is a time which has seen the rapidly increasing effects of economic and industrial growth on nature with new forms of atmospheric and ocean pollution, destruction of wildlife habitats and global climate change. Humanity has created the Anthropocene.

The Anthropocene has become increasingly central to much development thinking, and the vital need to move towards a green environment is evident in much of the recent literature, including the UN development reports. Many of the environmental issues have arisen in the era of development, driven by the primary focus on the acceleration of economic development at the expense of the environment, and an alternative concept, the 'Developmentocene' has been invented to signify this (Figueiredo et al, 2020). Looking to the future with a growing awareness of the need for action in relation to the human impact on the planet, especially as global population continues to grow, is a positive sign that development will move in the right direction, no longer based essentially on economic growth. It has also led to calls for 'intergenerational justice' to make the planet a safer place for future generations. Significantly, at least seven of the 17 UN Sustainable Development Goals (SDGs) relate directly to environmental concerns and goals for 2030 (Figure 9.2).

Environmental issues may have local, transborder or global consequences, and there is growing evidence that countries in the Global South are experiencing more environmental concerns than countries in the Global North. High rates of population growth in many developing countries also increase their impact on the environment, and it is predicted that the continuing growth of the world population in the 21st century will be mainly in the developing world, notably in sub-Saharan Africa and Southern Asia (UN DESA, 2019a). The three main environmental challenges facing the world

Figure 9.2: Key environmental SDGs

today are climate change and pollution, resource depletion and loss of biodiversity.

Climate change and pollution

The significant rise in global warming and ozone depletion in recent decades has seen the issue of climate change rise to the top of the environmental agenda. The effects of climate change have been most intense in the countries of the Global South, which have experienced a wide range of extreme weather conditions from heatwaves and wildfires to droughts and tropical cyclones, the latter causing hurricanes and typhoons that lead to storm surges and flooding. The Himalayan glaciers on the Tibetan Plateau, for example, have been severely affected by global warming. This is very serious as they provide more than half of the drinking water for 40 per cent of the world's population. As a result of the impact of global warming, David Wallace-Wells (2019) has warned of the potential danger of our planet becoming 'the uninhabitable Earth'. Naomi Klein (2014: 28) has gone so far as to claim that 'climate change changes everything', and that it must be the catalyst for people across the world to come together and address the crisis to make the world a safe place. The extent to which the developed world is responsible for climate change that is most severely felt in the developing world is very evident from the quantity of greenhouse gas emissions in the Global North. The transfer of manufacturing to parts of the developing world has further increased greenhouse gas (particularly CO_2) emissions, which contribute both to global warming and to air pollution. Asian countries, notably India and China, are now by a very large margin the greatest producers of CO_2 emissions, but in relation to their population ratios North America and Europe are the worst contributors to global warming, as can be seen graphically in Figure 9.3.

Motor vehicles are a major source of air pollution through their exhaust emissions and also contribute to the quantity of CO_2 in the atmosphere. The number of vehicles, especially cars, has grown considerably in the 21st century and continues to do so, doubling over two decades (Figure 9.4) with 1.4 billion cars on the world's roads in

Figure 9.3: Global share of carbon dioxide (CO_2) emissions and population by region

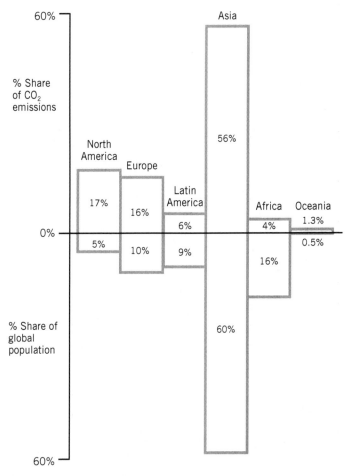

Source: Ritchie and Roser (2020)

2020 and projected to double again by 2050. Expanding car ownership in the Global South is often seen as evidence of successful development and catching up with the Global North, but the environmental and health-related issues associated with vehicle production and driving have serious negative implications for sustainable development.

Figure 9.4: Number of cars on the world's roads

Source: Live-counter.com (2022)

The introduction of electric cars has been seen by many in the developed world as leading to a more environmentally sustainable form of transport, something that has been questioned by critics. They point out the environmental risks associated with the increased production of cars and electricity, together with the rising number of injuries and deaths from road traffic accidents as the number of vehicles increases in the developing world, which has a much higher accident and mortality rate than the developed world. Over 90 per cent of the world's fatalities on the roads occur in low- and middle-income countries, which have only approximately 60 per cent of the world's vehicles. Road traffic injuries and deaths are highest in the African region (WHO, 2020e). Motor vehicle production has continued to grow rapidly in the 21st century with by far the biggest increases seen in the Global South. This is very clearly illustrated in Figure 9.5, with the most significant increase in Asia/Oceania.

Figure 9.5: Motor vehicle production statistics, 2000–19

	2000	2019
Europe	20.2m	21.3m
North America	17.8m	16.8m
South America	2.0m	3.3m
Asia/Oceania	17.9m	49.2m
Africa	0.3m	1.1m
World =	**58.2m**	**91.7m**

Source: www.oica.net/production-statistics

The transfer of much of the car industry together with other areas of manufacturing to the developing world has had a significant impact on CO_2 emissions and pollution of the environment, and the continuing growth of such industries is a huge drain on Earth's non-renewable resources. The rich world's responsibility for greenhouse gas emissions and climate change, and the fact that wealthy nations are using vastly more than their fair share of the Earth's resources, has led to the concept of 'climate debt'. Climate change is inextricably linked to economic inequality, and the people most vulnerable to the effects of climate change are the poorer populations living in low- and middle-income developing countries. As Ulrich Beck (2010: 175) points out, climate change 'exacerbates existing inequalities of poor and rich, centre and periphery'. Oxfam International notes that those most at risk in the world are the poorest half of the global population who have the lowest carbon footprint and are responsible for only around 7 per cent of the total emissions from individual consumption (Oxfam International (2020e). The vast numbers of people who die each year from air pollution are predominantly from this half of the global population and located in the developing countries of the Global South (Figure 9.6). Inequality, poverty and the environment are therefore closely interconnected.

Resource depletion

Resource depletion refers to a situation where the consumption of natural resources is faster than it can be replenished. This is a growing concern for developing countries that are affected by increasing levels of extractivism – the extraction of natural resources, mainly for export to the developed world and often implemented by transnational corporations. The environmental impact of extractivism through mining, drilling and cutting down forests, is of growing concern in relation to key issues such as climate change, soil depletion, freshwater contamination and deforestation. It is an issue which has been particularly evident in Latin America and the Caribbean where natural resources such as oil, gas, gold, silver, iron, copper, tin and other materials have been exploited on a large scale for export purposes

Figure 9.6: Air pollution: the silent killer

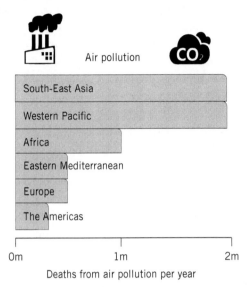

Source: UNWHO (2020)

with insufficient regard to the impacts of such practices and the need to ensure sustainable forms of development. Over the years, extractive practices have expanded significantly, and in addition to their serious environmental and social consequences – the contamination of ecosystems, pollution and health problems for local populations – they have also displaced traditional communities and their access to essential resources. The most seriously affected groups have been indigenous populations, rural communities and women. Extractivism has often resulted in local communities no longer having sufficient access to safe essential resources such as water supplies and farming land.

Loss of biodiversity

Increasing population and global trade is putting unsustainable pressure on renewable natural resources, which is exacerbating long-term poverty and biodiversity loss. Habitat destruction, particularly in tropical forests, is one of the most important factors affecting the fate of biodiversity on Earth and the vast numbers of animal and plant species. The destruction and degradation of many parts of the Amazon rainforest, for example, threatens not only the regulation of the world's CO_2 emissions, but also much of the diversity of wildlife by eradicating plant species and threatening the survival of the animals that depend on them. The loss of biodiversity in developing countries is caused both by the increasing extraction of natural resources and by the transformation of the environment to grow crops for the global market: for example, soya cultivation for export has been a major driver of deforestation in the Amazon basin where more than half the world's tropical forests are located. In addition to the loss of biodiversity caused by the growing demands of the global market and the power of transnational corporations, poverty also plays a part in the degradation of local environments. Poor living conditions lead to the organic pollution of land and water. Poor people without appropriate resources, skills and land tenure are often forced into short-term survival strategies that damage the environment, and may have no alternative but to access land in protected areas where conversion to agriculture results in a loss of biodiversity.

Continuing population growth and the movement of more people across the natural world also plays an important role in diminishing biodiversity. In many parts of the developing world, the huge increase in the number of vehicles accompanied by the vast expansion of road building has had a significant impact on the ecosystem. Estimates indicate that between 15 and 25 million kilometres of new roads will be built by 2050, with 90 per cent of these in developing countries. Many of these roads are being built in regions which have very high levels of biodiversity and vital ecosystems, and some of the largest road works are happening in some of the world's most important wilderness regions, such as the Amazon, the Congo Basin and New Guinea (Meijer et al, 2018). Road building in such areas often causes habitat loss and fragmentation, forest fires and other environmental degradations which have irreversible impacts on ecosystems. The modernisation of travel and infrastructure, seen by many as advancing development, has seriously negative consequences for the environment, and therefore reflects what Jeffrey Alexander (2013) has termed, 'the dark side of modernity'.

The impact of biodiversity loss on human life has been evident in many areas, and the spread of many global infections has been linked to environmental disruptions and ecological changes caused by unrestrained economic and industrial development. Human pressure on biodiversity increases the risk of infectious disease; changes to the land and nature resulting from agricultural expansion, logging, infrastructure development and other human activities has become a key driver of the emergence of infectious diseases. The coronavirus pandemic brought this to the fore with its dramatic effect on the human population, and demonstrated the links between new viral infections of this kind and changes to the environment and biodiversity loss. The European Commission president, Ursula von der Leyen, pointed out that COVID-19 'brought into sharper focus the planetary fragility that we see every day through melting glaciers, burning forests, and now through global pandemics' (von der Leyen, 2020). Not surprisingly, COVID-19 came to be described as 'the disease of the Anthropocene' (O'Callaghan-Gordo and Antó, 2020).

Towards a green future?

On a more positive note, growing awareness of environmental concerns in the 21st century has stimulated moves towards making development more sustainable and creating a green future, as the quotation from Greta Thunberg at the start of this chapter illustrates. The global spread of COVID-19, for example, has demonstrated that the pandemic and climate change are both caused by factors related to the Anthropocene, and this may help to raise further awareness of the need to seriously address climate change and other environmental issues to preserve the planet and humanity. As Thomas Heyd (2020: 10) puts it, the pandemic has alerted the world to the need to take action 'if we care for a liveable Anthropocene for present and future generations'.

One of earliest and most profound moves to address environmental issues and save planetary life was the formation of the Club of Rome in 1968, which brought together a group of scientists, economists, business leaders and a number of heads of state from around the world. Its most famous report, *The Limits to Growth* (Meadows et al, 1972), highlighted the potential impact of continuing economic growth on the environment. It stated that if the world's population growth and consumption patterns continued at the same high rates as at the time, Earth would reach its limits within a century. The report did not initially have a great impact in bringing about changes, but growing international awareness and concern regarding climate change and planetary sustainability began to gather pace towards the end of the 20th century as globalisation advanced and shared concerns over the environment moved up the global agenda. There was also a growing recognition that low-income countries were at greater environmental risk, and the poorest were often the worst affected by environmental hazards. A number of international agencies have been set up to deal with environmental issues, such as the BioCarbon Fund Initiative for Sustainable Forest Landscapes, with the aim of cutting greenhouse gas emissions from the land sector by reducing deforestation and land degradation in developing countries and promoting more sustainable agriculture.

Awareness of global environmental issues, combined with the need to help poorer regions develop without damaging ecosystems, was also reflected in the rise of NGOs and social movements calling for a green economy during the 1970s. One of the best-known examples was the idea of enhancing development by introducing 'intermediate technology' that would benefit local communities in developing countries without causing the environmental damage and resource depletion which the introduction of advanced high-technology equipment had already done in many parts of the Global South. Intermediate technology would also be in the hands of local populations rather than controlled by large companies and transnational corporations, and could therefore be used more effectively to meet local needs and maintain their environments. This approach was first developed by E.F. Schumacher (1973) and described in the title of his pioneering book as *Small is Beautiful*. The Intermediate Technology Development Group was founded in the UK. It later changed its name to Practical Action, reinforcing its focus on pragmatic, holistic and systemic approaches to tackling poverty and creating environmentally friendly forms of development. Many other international NGOs have also been formed to press for development based on local participation and decision making that avoids the environmental pitfalls of conventional global economic development. A growing number of green movements have also taken off in the 21st century, displaying different shades of green as environmentalists and ecologists, depending on the extent and depth of their proposals for a sustainable planet. Individual environmental activists have also made a mark, including notably Greta Thunberg, the adolescent Swedish environmental activist, who has become internationally well known for challenging world leaders and organisations to take strong and immediate action against climate change. As she tweeted in a New Year's Day message in 2021: 'Let's all continue the never-ending fight for a living planet'.

Concerns have been expressed about some of the pledges made by governments and international organisations to combat climate change and promote a green environment. For example, the reductions in carbon emissions and waste products that governments in the Global North claim to have made have actually been achieved by offshoring emissions to developing countries with the transfer of manufacturing plants, and by exporting much of their post-consumer plastic waste to poorer countries. The movement of hazardous waste from the Global North to the Global South has been termed 'toxic waste colonialism' (Pratt, 2011). A further area where progress has been disputed is in relation to claims of moving towards a more environmentally sustainable economy. Many governments have adopted policies of 'green growth'; in 2009 the OECD countries signed the Green Growth Declaration, which was designed to address environmental issues from climate change and ecosystem protection to resource saving, water conservation and natural disaster prevention.

However, questions have been raised about whether green growth is a contradiction in terms since economic growth inevitably has an impact in some way on the environment. The idea behind green growth is to introduce more environmentally friendly measures and to use fewer natural resources, while at the same time allowing the economy to grow in a sustainable fashion. This involves decoupling environmental pressures from GDP growth. However, this may have rebound effects given that efficiency improvements are often compensated for by a reallocation of the saved resources and money into further production and consumption. Many industries that claim to be addressing environmental issues, are accused of 'greenwashing'. For example, the production of electric cars may appear to be a move in a green direction away from the use of fossil fuels, but their construction puts pressure on lithium, copper and cobalt resources, and the production of biofuel raises concerns about land use and natural resources (EEB, 2019). It is therefore highly questionable whether green growth can really work, and critics have pointed to the need to create limits to growth, induce population control, promote green consumerism, and to recognise the wider impact of local actions – as embraced in the expression 'act local, think global'. Some critics have pointed out that, although economic growth is necessary in developing countries, there are many environmental dangers that need to be addressed in order to avoid 'self-devouring growth' (Livingstone, 2019). The consequences of this are being particularly felt in parts of Africa as population and consumption grow, while crucial water sources run dry, pollution escalates, and biodiversity is lost.

One of the alternatives to green growth that has gathered momentum in the 21st century is 'degrowth'. This goes beyond the limits to the growth or zero growth approach of the Club of Rome, and is associated with writers such as Serge Latouche and the equivalent French concept of *décroissance*. It does not mean negative growth, according to Latouche, but is 'primarily designed to make it perfectly clear that we must abandon the goal of exponential growth' and build an alternative society 'in which we can live better lives while working less and consuming less' (Latouche, 2009: 8). It therefore follows Schumacher's principle of maximising wellbeing while minimising consumption and preserving the environment. Degrowth makes it possible to divert money from consumption to building green infrastructure, and many proponents of the concept have argued that it is the only way to prevent climate catastrophe and disastrous impacts on global ecosystems. In addition to the increasing focus on the need to address global warming, there are growing concerns about the pollution of the oceans as a result of the expanding maritime industry and increasing plastic waste disposal which finds its way into the oceans; this has led to calls to abandon 'blue growth' and replace it with 'blue degrowth' (Ertör and Hadjimichael, 2020). A number of countries in the South have adopted approaches to development that support the principles of degrowth. A notable example is *buen vivir* in Latin America, which translates as 'the good life' or collective wellbeing, prioritising harmony with nature and the environment over economic development, and respecting different cultures and indigenous peoples. *Buen vivir* was enshrined in law in the Andean countries of Ecuador and Bolivia in the first decade of the 21st century. A similar concept to *buen vivir* that emerged in parts of sub-Saharan Africa is *ubuntu*, a concept which translates as 'humanness'. This is an expression of the interconnectedness between people and the biophysical world of nature.

Debates have continued regarding the setting of green agendas and the best way forward. For example, a distinction has been drawn between long-term threats to the world's ecosystems and the more immediate environmental concerns faced by affected populations. This has been seen as creating two environmental agendas: a green agenda for global issues such as climate change and resource depletion, and a brown agenda for more immediate concerns in impoverished areas of developing countries, such as inadequate access to basic water supplies, poor sanitation and housing, and local sources of pollution that particularly affect households living in poverty. Some critics of the tendency for the global media and intergovernmental organisations to focus on global warming and climate change, have argued that much more attention should be given to the issues that are currently facing poorer populations, including reducing poverty and protecting their local environments, as this will create a better chance of eventually halting the long-term environmental dangers faced by the whole world. Bjorn Lomborg (2007: 227) argues that to address global warming we must 'cool the rhetoric' by dealing with the more immediate problems that will help to resolve the broader issues facing the planet.

The Sustainable Development Goals go well beyond the environmental issues of climate change and global warming. SDG 13 focuses on climate action, but SDGs 6 and 7 address the more immediate concerns of clean water and sanitation, and affordable and clean energy. A number of the other SDGs address issues facing the natural world, such as biodiversity loss and the decline of forest areas, plastic pollution of the oceans which threatens sea life, and so on. The SDGs also call for more responsible consumption and production, and the need to make cities and communities more sustainable with reductions in air pollution and the number of people confined to living in unhealthy slums. The SDGs reflect a significant shift in development theory from seeing poverty and underdevelopment as separate from environmental issues, to recognising they are in fact closely connected. The SDGs are therefore a clear indication of the extent to which environmental issues have moved up the global agenda, and they offer a positive scenario by looking to the future and setting dates for the achievement of these goals. The 2019 UN Climate Change report, *The Heat is On*, points out that action to address climate change is inseparable from delivering the SDGs to eradicate poverty and hunger and reduce inequality (UNDP/UNFCCC, 2019: 22).

The SDG 8 target is for 3 per cent annual global GDP growth and for the least developed countries (LDCs) to increase their annual GDP growth much further and maintain it at a minimum of 7 per cent per year. Jason Hickel questions whether this is attainable for the LDCs, while meeting the SDG's environmental sustainability objectives at the same time. He points out that while it may be acceptable to call for significant GDP growth in the poorest nations, to avoid violating the sustainability objectives it would be necessary for the rich developed nations to follow degrowth strategies. Shifting a portion of global income from the richer to the poorer countries would be the best way forward to achieve sustainability: 'Reducing global income inequality becomes the only reasonable method by which the SDGs can accomplish the human development objectives without violating the sustainability objectives' (Hickel, 2019: 881).

This confirms the point made in an earlier chapter, that global inequality is a key barrier to development, but not only human development as it is also an impediment to sustainable development. Environmental issues have come to the fore in the 21st century and addressing them is clearly very important for both developed and developing countries, but the interrelationship of these issues with other areas of development must become a priority in both the theory and practice of international development.

Gender equality: a prerequisite for development

Another area of inequality that needs to be addressed, not only to advance human development but also to assist in progress towards sustainable development, is gender inequality. Gender equality also features as one of the SDGs, and has moved on from how it was defined in the earlier Millennium Development Goals to include not only equality in relation to education, health, political representation and access to income, but also domestic equality in the sharing of tasks at home and freedom from male violence.

While much of the focus on overcoming gender inequalities has tended to be on developing 'women's empowerment', there has been a growing recognition that men's behaviour and positions in society, and how they are socially constructed, also need to be addressed. As Katie Willis (2021: 177) points out, this is reflected in the move from **women in development** (WID) to **gender and development** (GAD) approaches. International organisations have become increasingly aware of how gender and development are linked, and as a result have changed some of the ways in which development is measured to make it more gender-sensitive. The UNDP's *Human Development Report* (2010) introduced the Gender Inequality Index (GII), and the World Economic Forum (WEF, 2006) introduced a Global Gender Gap Index (GGGI), which measures and combines four dimensions of gender inequality: educational attainment, economic participation and opportunity, health and survival, and political empowerment. The global gender gap varies by world region, as illustrated in Figure 9.7, with the worst affected areas in the Global South.

Gender inequalities in education, health, nutrition, and employment and income have been noted in the previous chapters,

Figure 9.7: Global gender gap by world region

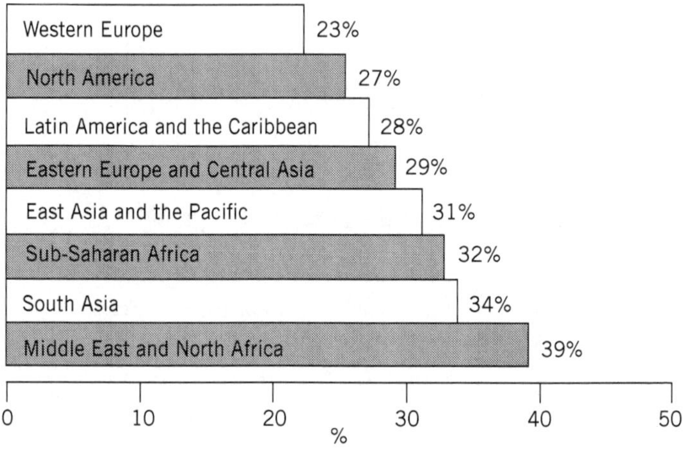

Source: WEF (2020)

but alongside these are a number of gender-related issues to which women and girls are especially prone in developing countries. These include forced child marriage of young girls, female genital mutilation and domestic violence. UNICEF has estimated that every year around 12 million girls are married before reaching adulthood, and up to 40 per cent of all girls in the least developed countries experience child marriage, with the highest rates in sub-Saharan Africa and Bangladesh (UNICEF, 2014). There is a strong link between poverty and child marriage as struggling families seek to reduce their living costs by marrying off their daughters. Unlike boys, girls are less likely to be seen as potential wage-earners and are therefore viewed as financial burdens to their families. Gender bias in favour of sons over daughters is also evident in gender-biased sex selection and the termination of female pregnancies. A number of developing countries also have excess infant mortality rates for girls under five years of age compared with boys, which is largely attributable to neglect and other forms of postnatal sex selection. One in nine deaths of girls under five years old in India may be attributed to postnatal sex selection (UNFPA, 2020: 47).

Women also suffer from higher levels of poverty than men, and have less access to paid work in most developing countries. Globally, only 47 per cent of women of working age participated in the labour market in 2020, compared with 74 per cent of men, and in Southern Asia and Northern Africa women's participation was particularly low, at below 30 per cent. The gender gap has only improved marginally in the 21st century. Across the whole world, women spend many more hours on unpaid domestic work than men, and this is particularly pronounced in parts of the developing world, notably Africa and Asia, where women spend more than seven times as many hours on unpaid domestic labour than men, including taking care of children, cooking, cleaning and general housework (UN DESA, 2020a). Where women are employed in the labour market in the developing regions of the world, they tend to be in the lowest-paid work and often without formal employment contracts and legal rights. Oxfam International has pointed out that women are often not paid enough to escape poverty. Gender inequality is 'a key driver of poverty' and 'a fundamental denial of women's rights' (Oxfam International, 2020c). Addressing women's poverty and gender income inequality would give a significant boost to development, as evidence from several regions and countries shows that closing the gender gap leads to a reduction in poverty. In Latin America and the Caribbean, for example, an increase in the number of women in paid work between 2000 and 2010 resulted in a 30 per cent reduction in poverty and income inequality. Clearly, addressing gender inequality correlates with advancing development for the benefit of those most in need, and in Latin America the reductions in female poverty and gender inequality were also reflected in higher school enrolment rates for children and gains in life expectancy and reductions in mortality rates. Recognition of the many benefits of gender equality for development has increased the attention given to women's empowerment and reducing gender inequalities. As Janet Momsen (2020: 11) succinctly states, 'gender equality enhances development'.

Empowering women has been given greater attention in the 21st century and has been broadly addressed in the field of international development. Access to new technologies has been shown to be beneficial in giving women greater opportunities to develop their capacities for engagement in social and economic domains from which they were previously excluded. The rise of mobile telephony generally has increased women's access to information relating to health, education and the environment, and the continuing expansion of ICTs is seen as bringing many advantages both now and into the future. One of the targets of SDG 5 is to enhance the use of ICTs to promote the empowerment of women. However, the empowerment discourse for women has been criticised for focusing on what women can do to improve their lives and positions in society, rather than giving sufficient attention to the broader arrangements and social structures that create gender inequalities.

The so-called girl effect, based on the idea that investing in the skills and labour of young girls is the key to generating economic growth and reducing poverty in the developing world, became part of the development strategy of many of the leading intergovernmental agencies in the 21st century. Jason Hickel is one of the main critics of this approach, claiming that it makes women and girls 'bear the responsibility for bootstrapping themselves out of poverty that is caused in part by the very institutions that purport to save them' (Hickel, 2014: 1356). As a result, initiatives that are designed to empower women and girls by encouraging their entry into the labour market often result in their being placed in subservient roles with unfair wages and unsafe working conditions. Empowering women, therefore, needs to genuinely emancipate them and to be accompanied by broader changes in society to address gender inequality. This appears to have been recognised to some extent by the United Nations in its formulation of SDG 5 which calls for far-reaching political and economic changes to achieve gender equality, including reforms to give women equal rights to economic resources, and equal opportunities for leadership at all levels of decision making in political, economic and public life.

Gender equality is clearly a prerequisite for development, and many different areas of gender inequality need to be addressed. In many of these areas there is evidence of both progress and continuing inequality. For example, while the increasing use of ICTs is seen as particularly beneficial for women in developing countries, gender inequalities in relation to literacy, employment and income have impaired women's access to the new digital technologies. Where women do gain access to ICTs, inequalities can be reduced. Access to the internet can provide a wide range of opportunities for women in developing countries to open up avenues for learning, communication and engagement with online movements, and to find ways of generating income and developing business interests. Women in rural locations who play a crucial role in food production and consumption can gain a great deal from learning online about price and product information, supply chain options, and so on. As Amy Antonio and David Tuffley (2014: 682) point out, 'Women's use of ICTs could, potentially, play a part in sustainable poverty reduction,' and a number of digital literacy programmes have been set up to address gender inequalities regarding access to the internet, such as the Easy Steps programme in the Asia Pacific region and the She Will Connect programme in Africa which set the goal of reaching five million women and reducing the gender gap by 50 per cent.

The advance of digital technology and the prospect of greater gender equality provide a positive view in looking to the future. The interconnections between the environment and gender are also important for future development as this is another area where there is clear evidence of gender inequalities. In many developing countries women in rural areas are closely tied to nature with a considerable proportion of their daily lives spent growing and harvesting food, and collecting water and natural sources of fuel and energy. In Africa, women produce 70 per cent of the country's food, and as much as 80 per cent in parts of sub-Saharan Africa, but have very few rights over the land they work on (Abass, 2018). Similarly, in India, over two thirds of the farmers are women, but very few actually own the land. According to the UN FAO, less than 10 per cent of land in developing countries is owned by women. Vandana Shiva, a leading Indian environmentalist, was one of the first to argue that women's close connection with nature means that they are disproportionately disadvantaged by environmental degradation. The violation of nature is linked with the exploitation and marginalisation of women as part of the process of development based on conventional economic modernisation (Shiva, 2002: xvi).

Where key components of the ecosystem – energy, land and water – are degraded as a result of industrialisation and overuse of resources, the impacts on rural communities and women in particular are very pronounced. The local impacts of major global issues such as climate change and ozone depletion, which can result in desertification and deforestation, are particularly evident in regions of the Global South where they have exacerbated land degradation, water scarcity and a reduction in fuelwood supplies. The consequences for women are that they have to work harder to compensate for the soil erosion and loss of natural resources in the production of food, and they have to walk further and spend more of their time collecting water and fuelwood. As 'protectors of the environment', women's work burden has increased (Nunan, 2015: 99). The gendered environmental effects of damage to the ecosystem have been further compounded by deliberate deforestation and loss of land, often by large corporations seeking to produce crops for export or to extract natural resources from the earth.

Women in developing countries have also been disproportionately affected by natural disasters such as cyclones and tsunamis. For example, 70 per cent of the 250,000 fatalities of the 2004 Indian Ocean tsunami were women. In Bangladesh frequent tropical cyclones have caused immense harm to lives, property, forestry and agriculture, and women and children have been the hardest hit. A study by the Bangladesh Institute of Social Research found that women and adolescent girls were the most vulnerable in natural disasters and account for 75 per cent of displaced persons (Alam and Rahman, 2014). Many other environmental issues also predominantly affect women. For example, standing water can pose a significant health risk by transferring water-borne diseases such as typhoid fever and cholera, and vector-borne diseases such as malaria and dengue fever. These environmental health risks are much greater for women in rural locations, as they are far more exposed to areas of standing water because of their assigned roles for collecting drinking water, preparing food and looking after livestock (Aguilar et al, 2015: 33).

Gender inequalities need to be addressed both in the interests of women and the environment, and society as a whole. Gender, the environment and development have often been treated as separate categories rather than as crucially interconnected areas. A report by a leading climate research organisation has estimated that increasing women's access to education, family planning and birth control could reduce carbon emissions by as much as 85 gigatons by 2050 (Project Drawdown, 2020). The report shows that with this access, women have fewer children and are less likely to become pregnant during adolescence. This results in slower population growth which in turn relieves the stress on ecosystems. It also helps to reduce poverty and enables more sustainable development which can particularly benefit women who have tended to bear the brunt of environmental crises.

However, addressing major environmental issues and preserving ecosystems requires more than women's empowerment. Many environmental movements have been set up, calling for major changes to be made, and a number of these have been led by women, recognising the need for both gender equality and environmental sustainability. Sometimes referred to as 'ecofeminism', the movements led by women have emphasised the need to understand the nature and significance of the relationship between women and nature, and to recognise the connection between the exploitation and degradation of the natural world and the subordination and oppression of women.

This has become particularly important in the 21st century as climate change and environmental degradation continues to exacerbate women's vulnerability in the developing world and makes it more difficult to reduce the gender gap. Addressing the causes of environmental decay and inequity, ecofeminist movements have called for policies that include the halting of resource extraction and depletion by multinational corporations, transitioning to safe and renewable energy, dramatic reduction in production and consumption patterns especially in the developed world, and ensuring gender equality and human rights in all climate actions. The Women's Global Call for Climate Justice was launched in 2015 to bring feminist organisations together to campaign on these key issues. Saving the planet and humanity has become associated with leading environmental feminist voices such as Jane Goodall who began her activities in sub-Saharan Africa, Vandana Shiva who began defending biodiversity in India, Marina Silva who campaigned to protect the Amazon Rainforest in Brazil, and most recently Greta Thunberg who has become very well known for her activism concerning the global climate crisis. In addressing the issues surrounding the environment and humanity, women have become the 'voices of liberation and transformation' (Shiva, 2002: 47).

Women's movements have clearly had some success in moving intergovernmental organisations in a direction more favourable to interconnected environmental and gender issues. The UN's Sustainable Development Goals have notably moved on from the earlier Millennium Development Goals, as reflected in their title, and the 2030 Agenda includes reference to a number of the key concerns addressed in ecofeminist thinking, including the essential idea that the goals relating to different aspects of development are interconnected and 'leave no one behind'. The notion of equality is clearly built into the SDGs, and the United Nations Entity for Gender Equality and the Empowerment of Women, also known as UN Women, has published a number of reports showing how women are affected by each of the SDGs, including those related to the conservation of the environment and preservation of terrestrial ecosystems (UN Women, 2016). This marks a significant step forward at the international level, but, as in other areas of development, much depends on the involvement of nation states and the role of politics in carrying these objectives forward. Looking to the future, gender equality is an essential component of sustainable development, along with a genuinely green environment, and appropriate digital technologies that can positively assist in bringing people and ideas together in the global age of the 21st century.

Summary and conclusion

This chapter has focused on three highly significant and interconnected areas of development that have grown in importance over recent decades. There is evidence, as we have seen, that the key issues related to these areas are becoming more evident and attempts are being made to seriously address them. Social movements and international organisations have played a major role in bringing these issues to the attention of policy makers, nation-states and intergovernmental bodies. While there is evidence that progress is being made and relevant goals have been set, notably by the United Nations SDGs, there is still a very long way to go, and, as in most areas of international development, much will depend on the actions taken by governments and transnational corporations in the Global North. The political economy of development in an increasingly globalised world is crucial to the success or failure of tackling issues such as climate change and global warming. At the level of individual nations in the developing world, local politics also plays an important role. In many developing countries, however, deep digital divides continue to exist between the rich and the poor, and also between men and women. Gender inequalities have generally reduced over recent decades with more girls going to school, fewer girls forced into adolescent marriages, and more women entering politics and leadership positions in many countries. However, much remains to be done, as this chapter has shown. In addition, unexpected events such as the outbreak of COVID-19 – the 'disease of the Anthropocene' – can have deleterious effects on progress made in areas such as gender equality. As we have seen in this and previous chapters, the coronavirus outbreak exacerbated inequalities for women and girls in many different areas, from health and education, to security and social protection.

Greater awareness of the challenges to sustainable development in the 21st century provides grounds for hope, provided appropriate actions are taken. The problem is in achieving the goal of collective responsibility for addressing environmental concerns and issues such as those surrounding gender inequalities and access to digital technologies. Bringing various interests together, including international organisations, nation-states, private corporations and social movements, to collaborate and develop common solutions is highly problematic and makes it difficult to find a universally agreed way forward. However, increasing recognition that the future survival of humanity and the planet depends on addressing issues such as climate change and creating sustainable development, may help to bring the world together to find common solutions to the most pressing issues of the 21st century.

KEY POINTS SUMMARY

- Looking to the future in the 21st century, three key issues in global development have come to the fore, and they are all interrelated: digital technology, a green environment and gender equality.
- ICT4D can play a crucial role in advancing sustainable social and economic development and reducing the digital divide between the Global South and the Global North, but much still remains to be done.
- Digital technologies can play an important role in addressing local and global environmental issues, which are of particular concern for countries in the Global South.
- The three main environmental challenges facing the world in the advancing age of the Anthropocene are climate change and pollution, resource depletion, and loss of biodiversity.
- The Global North is primarily responsible for the global environmental issues that threaten the sustainability of the planet, but the Global South has a disproportionate share of the burden.
- Many routes towards a green future have been set out, but some are more effective than others, and debate continues over the best way forward, from 'green growth' to 'degrowth'.
- Gender equality has moved up the development agenda, and is important both as a goal in itself and as a way of more effectively addressing other crucial issues, notably environmental concerns.
- Gender equality is not only about the empowerment of women, but also about the need to reduce inequalities between men and women in many areas of development, including income and employment, education, health and the environment.
- Politics plays a crucial role, at local, national and international levels, in addressing issues related to technology, the environment and gender, and it is necessary to bring together international

organisations, nation-states, private corporations and popular social movements, in order to advance sustainable development.

KEY READING GUIDE

Of the many books on information and communications technologies, one of the few which focuses on ICT4D is Heeks (2018) *Information and Communication Technology for Development (ICT4D)*. Most general texts on development do not include a chapter on technology and development, but Haslam et al (2017) is an exception with a useful discussion by Alampay on information technologies and development. International organisations, such as UNCTAD (2019), the World Bank (2016), and WSIS (2019), have produced various reports on digital technologies, the digital economy and digital divide, and their implications for developing countries. On the environment and its relation to the North-South divide, a key text is Calvert and Calvert (1999) *The South, the North and the Environment*. General texts on development mostly include a chapter on the environment, and a good example is 'Environment and development', chapter 10 of Kingsbury et al (2016). Strongly argued accounts of the need to address environmental concerns and related social and economic issues can be found in Klein (2014) *This Changes Everything*, and Wallace-Wells (2019) *The Uninhabitable Earth*. A study which makes a very strong case for degrowth is Livingstone (2019) *Self-Devouring Growth*. The relationship of poverty and the environment is examined in detail in Nunan (2015) *Understanding Poverty and the Environment*. A key text on gender and development issues is Momsen (2020) *Gender and Development*. In relation to gender and the environment, there are a number of books and articles that raise key issues and discuss future solutions, including Aguilar et al (2015) *Roots for the Future*, and Shiva (2002) *Staying Alive*. On the gender digital divide, a good overview is available by Antonio and Tuffley (2014) 'The gender digital divide in developing countries'.

10

Conclusion: making international development sustainable

Sustainable development is development that meets the needs of the present without compromising the ability of future generations to meet their own needs. (WCED, 1987: 41)

This short guide to international development has demonstrated that there are many different topics associated with the broad concept of development, which encompasses economic, social, political and environmental themes that are viewed from a variety of contrasting perspectives. It is an area of academic interest and practical concern that requires detailed understanding and careful analysis in order to fully comprehend what is happening and to take appropriate action. The preceding chapters have also shown that international development is not just about the here and now. We also need to understand the changes that have taken place over time and how new issues have emerged on the development agenda: for example, as a result of the growth of globalisation. There are key development issues that need to be prioritised and addressed now, but at the same time it is important to look beyond the present and to take into account the impact of current actions on future generations, including in the increasingly important area of environmental change. Development has to be sustainable, and that means addressing the needs not only of the present but also of future generations, as the quotation at the start of this chapter clearly indicates.

Just as the issues associated with development have changed over time, so too has the concept itself. Development is not a static or uncontested concept, and earlier definitions which delineated development as depicted by the modernised Western world have been called into question by its critics, as discussed in Chapter 4. This is perhaps not surprising given that it is now over 70 years since the start of the so-called era of development. Many earlier academic titles that were given to the study of development such as 'third world studies' were later replaced with 'international development' and 'global development', as the Third World became a rather obsolete concept following the end of the Cold War in 1991 and the dissolving of the division between the First and Second Worlds. Some of the earlier journals, such as *Third World Quarterly*, founded in 1979, have nevertheless retained their titles, while others have subsequently changed: for example, the *Journal of Third World Studies* changed its name to the *Journal of Global South Studies* in 2016. The *Journal of International Development* was founded in 1989 and has retained its title. The concept of international development retains its validity.

As an academic discipline the central focus of international development on the developing countries of the world distinguishes it from international relations, but in many ways it is also concerned with the relations among and between different countries and regions of the world and the consequences for development, which have their impacts at national and sub-national levels. The developing countries comprise over 80 per cent of the world population, and international development focuses on the need to address a wide range of issues that affect these countries and their citizens. As the various chapters of this book have illustrated, it is an interdisciplinary subject, drawing on economics, history, sociology and geography, and follows theoretical, empirical and policy-oriented approaches to development.

The relationship of developed and developing countries or regions is central to international development, and this, as we have seen, means that what happens in one part of the world can have a significant impact on the rest of the world – as is the case with global climate change. Mutual vulnerabilities have become increasingly recognised: for example, in relation to environmental and health concerns, international terrorism and global security. The use of the concept of global development reflects the increasing interconnectedness of the world, but international development also recognises what is happening at a global level while at the same time focusing on different aspects of development driven by international relations among specific countries and regions: for example, China's increasing involvement in parts of Asia and Africa as a result of its Belt and Road Initiative, and the growing diplomatic and economic ties between China and parts of Latin America, as discussed in Chapter 5. The concept and academic subject title of 'international development' has therefore retained its relevance.

Theories of development have evolved over time, both in relation to the changing nature of the world and changing trends in social science theory. An increasing focus on sustainable development reflects a growing concern with environmental issues and recognition that economic growth has to be carefully controlled and constrained. Development theory has also been influenced by the emergence of new theoretical viewpoints in the social sciences, such as theories of post-modernity which influenced post-development thinking. Contrasting theories have helped to open up different views on development and have also inspired different strategies for the best way forward.

One of the key concepts associated with the changing nature of international development and the academic writings on international development, is globalisation. As Chapter 5 indicated, we live in a shrinking world but one where a multidimensional approach to globalisation is necessary as there are several different areas of globalisation: techno-economic, sociopolitical and cultural-civilizational, and there are a number of different perspectives on where globalisation is heading. Theoretical interpretations of globalisation include the positive hyperglobalist, the sceptical internationalist, and the more nuanced transformationalist viewpoint, which offers a more open-ended perspective on the relationship between globalisation and development. What is clear, however, is that globalisation and development have become more closely connected over time, and perspectives on development have changed as a result. International development as a field of study has moved forward in recognising significant changes in the world of development as globalisation has advanced, and this had led to some new concepts being introduced into the academic vocabulary. For example, as was outlined in Chapter 5, the emergence in the 21st century of new concepts such as 'multipolar globalisation' is in recognition of an historic shift from a simple division of the world along North-South or developed-underdeveloped lines, towards a more multicentric world in which some of the strongly emerging countries of the Global South are becoming increasingly important drivers of the world economy. This has led to what has been described as 'a new development era'.

Development in the 21st century has shown signs of progress in addressing key issues such as poverty, education and health. A number of other issues have also been given closer attention during this period; notably, environmental concerns, gender inequality, and the need to extend new, especially digital, technologies to the developing world. There is some evidence of positive global trends as outlined in the preceding chapters. However, development also shows considerable variation across the countries and regions of the Global South. Sub-Saharan Africa has generally fared badly compared with parts of Asia and Latin America where more significant progress has been made. Trends at a global level, such as reductions in extreme poverty, may be positive, and certainly demonstrate a significant reduction in the proportion of the world's population living below the international poverty line (IPL) in recent decades, but the share of the global poor living in sub-Saharan Africa is forecast to rise to around 87 per cent by 2030 (World Bank, 2018: 4). While nearly nine out of ten of the poorest people in the world will be living in this region of Africa, the United Nations Foundation has focused on individual countries and has predicted that nearly 40 per cent of world's extreme poor will be living in just two countries in sub-Saharan Africa by 2030: Nigeria and the Democratic Republic of Congo (Figure 10.1).

It is therefore important for international development to have a clear and comprehensive picture of what is happening across the world and in different parts of the Global South, as it can be misleading if some data is given prominence and other facts and figures are sidelined.

Figure 10.1: Share of the world's extreme poor, 2020

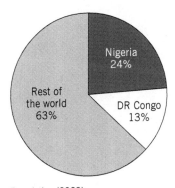

Source: United Nations Foundation (2020)

Positive trends in poverty reduction have tended to be highlighted, despite evidence to the contrary in some parts of the Global South. The data is often presented in the form of infographics, such as those produced online by Our World In Data, which is heavily funded by the Bill and Melissa Gates Foundation. The global data on poverty reduction overlooks the fact that the majority of gains have come from five countries in one region of the world, East Asia: China and the Four Asian Tigers – South Korea, Taiwan, Singapore and Hong Kong. It also uses a very low-income IPL, set by the World Bank in 2015 at $1.90 per day to measure extreme poverty. Focusing on poverty often ignores global wealth inequality which, as we have seen in Chapter 7, has been increasing to the point at which, as Oxfam International has pointed out, the richest 1 per cent has more of the world's wealth that the whole of the rest of the human population. It is therefore very important to be aware of the limitations of much of the data which is now widely available on the internet. In relation to poverty, the development of new indicators, such as the Multidimensional Poverty Index, offer more nuanced depictions of the nature and extent of poverty than the much-publicised data and infographics based on the questionable IPLs that have been set by the World Bank.

Data relating to environmental issues has also been questioned, particularly in relation to the extent to which individual countries and regions are responsible for concerns that have arisen over carbon emissions and pollution from waste disposal. As we have seen in Chapter 9, many companies in the Global North have offshored some of their most environmentally damaging manufacturing activities to countries in the Global South, and much hazardous waste has also been exported to poorer developing countries. Imports of raw materials from the Global South, the extraction of which may cause deforestation, mining pollution and CO_2 emissions, similarly help to reduce environmental impacts in the countries of the Global North, but serve to raise the negative environmental consequences for the affected developing countries. This has all resulted in more favourable environmental ratings for the Global North which makes the data misleading. To address this issue in relation to the Sustainable Development Goals (SDG) Index, an additional set of indicators has been introduced by the Sustainable Development Solutions Network, which measures the environmental transboundary impacts generated by one country on others. This is known as the Spillover Index Score, which ranks countries according to the environmental and social impacts embodied into trade and consumption, such as biodiversity loss, CO_2 emissions and accidents at work. The 2020 *Sustainable Development Report* reveals a striking difference in rankings for the SDG and the Spillover indexes. For example, of the 166 countries listed, the UK is ranked 13th on the SDG Index and 157th on the Spillover Index. By contrast, the North African country Sudan is ranked 159th on the SDG Index and 3rd on the Spillover Index (SDSN, 2020: 93).

Awareness of the benefits and drawbacks of living in an increasingly interconnected world is crucial to understanding the best ways forward for international development. As we have seen in relation to both economic and environmental issues, it is not just about introducing positive changes to the developing world, but also about the need for global transformations that address the Global North as well as the Global South. Chapter 5, for example, questioned the widely held view that the expansion of the tourist sector in the Global South is necessarily beneficial for development. It can bring economic, social and environmental benefits to developing countries, but it can also have negative effects on the local economy and society, and cause damage to the native and global environments. Similarly, technological innovations which are seen as particularly advantageous for developing countries, such as solar energy and ICTs, may actually have drawbacks. They come at a cost and this can sometimes serve to perpetuate or even accentuate existing inequalities. One of the latest technologies is the development of satellite internet and this would be particularly beneficial to the more remote areas of Africa where it has not been possible to install fibre broadband. However, again, the costs of accessing the internet via these new systems may accentuate inequalities between the poor and the better off, and gender inequalities may be amplified too. We cannot predict all the new technologies and innovations that the future will hold, but it is very likely that these will also affect development in various ways, both positively and negatively.

Politics plays a very important role in advancing development and in determining its direction. As we have seen, politics at local, national and international levels can help to advance development agendas, but can also impede particular development projects. International efforts to sustain the Amazon Rainforest, for example, have been undermined in recent years by the priority given to economic growth and deforestation by the Brazilian government. The governments of the rich nations of the Global North agreed in 1970 to a target of 0.7 per cent of their gross national income to be donated to foreign aid, but few countries have actually met the target and most have fallen well short. Beyond the role played by national governments, the emergence of new international organisations, NGOs and intergovernmental organisations has also been influential in raising issues on the international agenda, and offering positive scenarios for the future by setting clear goals. Notable examples are the United Nations MDGs and SDGs which have been discussed throughout the course of this book. The SDGs replaced the MDGs in 2015 and set key targets for 2030, which pulled together a number of different themes, defined as the 'five Ps' – partnership, peace, people, prosperity and the planet – which have to be brought together in a sustainable fashion to meet the overarching goal of sustainable development (Figure 10.2). As an international organisation the UN has defined

Figure 10.2: The five Ps of sustainable development

Source: Adapted from UN DESA (2015)

the best ways forward to reach this goal for its member states to follow. Under the 2030 Agenda, a series of 17 global SDGs have been agreed that call for universal action to bring people together to end poverty, protect the planet and improve the lives and prospects of everyone, everywhere.

Under the Paris Agreement of 2016 countries are required to submit a 'nationally determined contribution', which outlines their specific policy commitments to reduce greenhouse gas emissions and strengthen resilience to climate change. The SDGs do not legally bind national governments, but they are expected to set up national frameworks to achieve the goals. This means that there are differences between states in the strength of their frameworks, and governments may choose to withdraw from global agreements, as the US did in 2020 when it became the first and only country to withdraw from the Paris Agreement. This raises questions about the effectiveness of international agreements. Decision making remains with the sovereign states. As Susan Park (2018: 217) has pointed out, while states may agree to certain goals and principles, 'enacting them is another matter altogether'. Whether it is possible to move towards a more centralised form of global governance, to monitor and ensure that agreed goals are met, remains to be seen.

Looking to the future, there are grounds for both hope and concern. Globalisation in its various forms continues to have an enormous impact on development with both positive and negative consequences. Climate change and global pandemics are unfortunate and potentially catastrophic consequences of globalisation, which have become more prominent as industrialisation and travel have increased massively during the era of development; but globalisation has also assisted development in parts of the Global South, especially with the shift towards a more multipolar world. At the same time, growing awareness of the interconnectedness of the planet and the need to address issues such as global warming and COVID-19 – 'the disease of the Anthropocene' – may help to bring people and nations closer together to resolve the challenges that face humanity and the planet, and possibly to recognise the need to address inequalities across the world. Reducing global inequalities, both among and within regions and countries of the Global North and South, is vital to development, and this does appear to be more widely recognised now than in the earlier decades of the development era. Inequalities are evident in all areas of development, which means addressing not only income and wealth inequalities, but environmental and gender inequalities too.

Addressing inequality in its various forms has risen to the top of the agenda for a number of international non-governmental organisations, such as Oxfam International (2020b: 19), which has recognised the need to 'end extreme wealth to end extreme poverty'. Reducing inequality within and among countries is also one of the SDGs. Inequality and exploitation of the developing world undermines development, even if programmes are put in place to divert some resources to poor people. Whereas, previously, the focus of much development thinking was mainly about finding ways of providing support and aid for developing countries and those in poverty, now there is a growing recognition of the need to create a more equal world, one where one half of the world does not economically exploit and inflict environmental damage on the other half. Development can therefore be seen to be about creating a fairer and more just world, and recognising what James Galbraith (2019) has described as 'the unsustainability of inequality'. Understanding and reducing inequality is an imperative for sustainable development in the key areas of socioeconomics, ecology and politics.

International development, as a field of study and practice, has helped to create greater awareness and reflection on how we live in the developed world and how it is affecting the rest of the world. How viable are the lifestyles of the developed world? Is it just as important to address the challenges of over-development in the Global North as it is to address under-development in the Global South? Development can no longer be simply about helping the poorer countries of the world to develop in the same way as the richer countries, but requires rethinking about how we all live on a single planet and how we can make development sustainable as we move into the future.

The SDGs have helped to adjust the focus on international development, and the SDG Index provides a guide to how far the goals are being met by different countries. However, other ways of compiling data and constructing indexes that rank countries very differently, have also been produced by independent organisations such as the New Economics Foundation, a UK-registered charity and think tank, which has produced the Happy Planet Index (Figure 10.3). Based on four key indicators – wellbeing, life expectancy, inequality

Figure 10.3: Happy Planet Index

HPI = Wellbeing × Life expectancy × Inequality of outcomes

Ecological footprint

Source: Adapted from NEF (2019)

of outcomes and ecological footprint – the Happy Planet Index draws on data from a variety of international sources, including the UN, the World Bank and the Gallup World Poll, and is designed to show how well nations are doing in relation to achieving long, happy, sustainable lives for all.

According to the results of the Happy Planet Index , the wealthier countries of the Global North generally do not rank as highly as a number of countries in Latin America and the Asia Pacific region. Costa Rica topped the Happy Planet Index rankings for the third time in 2016, showing that their population has higher wellbeing than the residents of many rich nations, including the UK and the US, and longer life expectancy than people in North America. Costa Rica's ecological footprint per person is calculated as being just one third of that in the US, and nearly all electricity used in Costa Rica comes from renewable sources. However, income inequality was found to be high in the country, so it still has some way to go to be completely sustainable. Some Latin American countries, such as Bolivia and Paraguay, are much lower in the rankings, and sub-Saharan African countries are nearly all in the bottom third. There is also considerable diversity in the rankings of rich Western countries, with Norway and Switzerland in the top 20, the UK ranked 34th and the US ranked 108th in the list of 140 countries. The Happy Planet Index provides an interesting alternative framework for assessing sustainable development and the issues that need to be addressed in different countries. It is included here in the concluding chapter to demonstrate the diversity of materials that are available and can provide interesting new perspectives on development. International development as a field of academic study and practice can never stand still, but must always consider the changing nature of the world and new ways of measuring and assessing the transformations that occur over time.

International development is a distinctive area of study which addresses the most serious issues facing the world and those most affected. Its focus, as we have seen, is on the countries of the developing world, but in the context of the whole world and the relationships of the Global South with the Global North. It is interdisciplinary in nature because any clear understanding of development requires insights from a number of different academic disciplines, and it includes a wide range of studies which examine what is happening at local, regional, national, international and global levels. Theoretical, empirical and policy-oriented aspects of international development all play a vital role in understanding development and formulating the best ways forward. Ultimately, as is now increasingly recognised, development has to be sustainable, and the challenges faced by the developing world require us to reflect on how we live in the developed world and the changes that need to be made if we are all to live together on a happy planet.

References

Abass, J. (2018) 'Women grow 70% of Africa's food. But have few rights over the land they tend', World Economic Forum, 21 March, www.weforum.org/agenda/2018/03/women-farmers-food-production-land-rights

Action Against Hunger (2020) *World Hunger: Key Facts and Statistics 2020*, www.actionagainsthunger.org/world-hunger-facts-statistics

Aguilar, L., Granat, M. and Owren, C. (2015) *Roots for the Future: The Landscape and Way Forward on Gender and Climate Change*, Washington, DC: IUCN/GGCA, www.iucn.org/content/roots-future

Alam, K. and Rahman, Md. H. (2014) 'Women in natural disasters: a case study from southern coastal region of Bangladesh', *International Journal of Disaster Risk Reduction*, 8: 68–82

Alexander, J.C. (2013) *The Dark Side of Modernity*, Cambridge/Malden, MA: Polity

Antonio, A. and Tuffley, D. (2014) 'The gender digital divide in developing countries', *Future Internet*, 6(4): 673–87, www.mdpi.com/1999-5903/6/4/673

Antunes de Oliveira, F. (2020) 'Development for whom? Beyond the developed/underdeveloped dichotomy', *Journal of International Relations and Development*, 23: 924–46, https://doi.org/10.1057/s41268-019-00173-9

Axford, B. (2013) *Theories of Globalization*, Cambridge/Malden, MA: Polity

Barber, B.R. (2003) *Jihad vs. McWorld*, London: Corgi Books

Barro, R.J. and Lee, J-W. (2010) 'A new data set of educational attainment in the world, 1950–2010,' NBER Working Paper Series, Cambridge, MA: National Bureau of Economic Research, www.nber.org/system/files/working_papers/w15902/w15902.pdf

Beck, U. (2009) *World at Risk*, Cambridge: Polity

Beck, U. (2010) 'Remapping social inequalities in an age of climate change: for a cosmopolitan renewal of sociology', *Global Networks*, 10(2): 165–81

Becker, D. (1987) *Postimperialism: International Capitalism and Development in the Late Twentieth Century*, Boulder, CO: Lynne Rienner Publishers

Bendix, R. (1964) *Nation-Building and Citizenship: Studies of Our Changing Social Order*, New York: Wiley

Bessis, S. (2003) *Western Supremacy: The Triumph of an Idea?*, London/ New York: Zed Books

Birdsall, N. (2001) 'Why Inequality Matters: Some Economic Issues', *Ethics and International Affairs*, 15(2): 3–28

Bisley, N. (2007) *Rethinking Globalization*, Basingstoke/New York: Palgrave Macmillan

Bond, P. and Garcia, A. (eds) (2017) *BRICS: An Anti-Capitalist Critique*, London: Pluto Press

Brandt, W. (1980) *North–South: A Program for Survival: Report of the International Commission on International Development Issues*, London/ Sydney: Pan Books

Brenner, R. (1977) 'The origins of capitalist development: a critique of neo-Smithian Marxism', *New Left Review*, 1/104, (July–Aug): 25–92

Brohman, J. (1996) *Popular Development: Rethinking the Theory and Practice of Development*, Oxford: Blackwell

Brundtland Commission (1987) *Our Common Future: Report of the World Commission on Environment and Development* ['the Brundtland Report'], Oxford: Oxford University Press

Brundtland, G.H. (1998) Statement to the Regional Committee for the Western Pacific Region, 14 September, Manila: Philippines

Calvert, S. and Calvert, P. (1999) *The South, the North and the Environment*, London/New York: Pinter

Cardoso, F.H. (1972) 'Dependent capitalist development in Latin America', *New Left Review*, 1/74, July–Aug: 83–95

Cardoso, F.H. and Faletto, E. (1979) *Dependency and Development in Latin America*, Trans. by M.M. Urquidi, Berkeley, CA: University of California Press

Chambers, R. (1997) 'Responsible well-being: a personal agenda for development', *World Development*, 25(11): 1743–54

Chatterjee, P. (2021) 'India's child malnutrition story worsens', *The Lancet*, 5(5), May 01: 319–20

CIA (2020) The World Factbook: HIV/AIDS – adult prevalence rate, www.cia.gov/the-world-factbook/field/hiv-aids-adult-prevalence-rate/country-comparison

Clarke, M. (2016) 'Defining and measuring poverty', in D. Kingsbury, J. McKay, J. Hunt, M. McGillivray and M. Clarke, *International Development: Issues and Challenges*, London/New York: Palgrave

Conway, G., Badiane, D. and Glatzel, K. (2019) *Food for All in Africa: Sustainable Intensification for African Farmers*, New York: Cornell University Press

Corbridge, S. (2007) 'The (im)possibility of development studies', *Economy and Society*, 36(2): 179–211

Crary, J. (2013) *24/7: Late Capitalism and the Ends of Sleep*, London/New York: Verso

Credit Suisse (2019) *Global Wealth Report 2019*, www.credit-suisse.com/about-us/en/reports-research/global-wealth-report.html

Crow, B. (2000) 'Understanding famine and hunger', in T. Allen and A. Thomas (eds) *Poverty and Development: Into the 21st Century*, Oxford: Oxford University Press

Crush, J. (1995) *Power of Development*, London/New York: Routledge

Davies, S.E. (2010) *Global Politics of Health*, Cambridge/Malden, MA: Polity

Davis, M. (2017) *Planet of Slums*, London/New York: Verso

Desai, V. and Potter, R.B. (2014) *The Companion to Development Studies*, 3rd edn, London/New York: Routledge

Dicken, P. (2015) *Global Shift: Mapping the Changing Contours of the World Economy*, 7th edn, London/New Delhi/Singapore/Thousand Oaks, CA: Sage

Diffenbaugh, N. and Burke, M. (2019) 'Global warming has increased global inequality', *Proceedings of the National Academy of Sciences (PNAS)*, 116(20): 9808–13

The Economist (2020) 'Has COVID-19 killed globalisation?' [editorial leader], 16 May

Edmond, C. (2017) 'The number of displaced people in the world just hit a record high', World Economic Forum, 20 June, www.weforum.org/agenda/2017/06/there-are-now-more-refugees-than-the-entire-population-of-the-uk

EEB (European Environmental Bureau) (2019) *Decoupling Debunked: Evidence and Arguments against Green Growth as a Sole Strategy for Sustainability*, Brussels: EEB, https://eeb.org/decoupling-debunked1

Ehrenreich, N. and Lyon, B. (2011) 'The global politics of food: a critical overview', *University of Miami Inter-American Law Review*, 43(1): 1–43, http://repository.law.miami.edu/umialr/vol43/iss1/3

Eisenstadt, S.N. (1992) 'A reappraisal of theories of social change and modernization', in H. Haferkamp and N.J. Smelser (eds) *Social Change and Modernity*, Berkeley, CA: University of California Press, 412–31

Elver, H. (2018) 'Suffering from hunger in a world of plenty', *Middle East Report*, 286 (Spring), https://merip.org/2018/10/suffering-from-hunger-in-a-world-of-plenty

Ertör, I. and Hadjimichael, M. (2020) 'Blue degrowth and the politics of the sea: rethinking the blue economy', *Sustainability Science*, 15: 1–10, https://degrowth.org/2020/01/30/new-special-issue-blue-degrowth-and-the-politics-of-the-sea-rethinking-the-blue-economy

Escobar, A. (1995) *Encountering Development: The Making and Unmaking of the Third World*, Princeton, NJ: Princeton University Press

Escobar, A. (2018) *Designs for the Pluriverse: Radical Independence, Autonomy and the Making of Worlds*, London/Durham, NC: Duke University Press

Esteva, G. (1985) 'Development: metaphor, myth, threat', *Seeds of Change*, 3: pp 78–9

Esteva, G. and Prakash, M.S. (1998) 'Beyond development, what?', *Development in Practice*, 8(3): 280–96

Farrell, H. and Newman, A. (2020) 'Chained to globalization: why it's too late to decouple', *Foreign Affairs*: January/February

Figueiredo, M.D., Marquesan, F.F.S. and Imas, J.M. (2020) 'Anthropocene and "development": intertwined trajectories since the beginning of the great acceleration', *Journal of Contemporary Administration*, 24(5): 400–13, www.scielo.br/j/rac/a/nQC4dJbWRZfx6NF4W56cJWF/?format=pdf&lang=en

Frank, A.G. (1966) 'The development of underdevelopment', *Monthly Review*, 18(4), September: 17–31

Frank, A.G. (1967a) 'Sociology of development and underdevelopment of sociology', *Catalyst*, 3: 20–73

Frank, A.G. (1967b) *Capitalism and Underdevelopment in Latin America: Historical Studies of Chile and Brazil*, New York/London: Monthly Review Press

Frank, A.G. (1969) *Latin America: Underdevelopment or Revolution*, New York/London: Monthly Review Press

Frank, A.G. (1972) *Lumpenbourgeoisie: Lumpendevelopment*, New York/London: Monthly Review Press

Friedman, T.L. (2007) *The World Is Flat: The Globalized World in the Twenty-First Century*, London/New York: Penguin

FSIN (Food Security Information Network) (2020) *Global Report on Food Crises 2020*, www.fsinplatform.org/global-report-food-crises-2020

FSIN (2021) *Global Report on Food Crises 2021*, www.wfp.org/publications/global-report-food-crises-2021

Fuglie, K., Gautam, M., Goyal, A. and Maloney, W.F. (2020) *Harvesting Prosperity: Technology and Productivity Growth in Agriculture*, IBRD/World Bank: Washington

Fukuyama, F. (1992) *The End of History and the Last Man*, New York: The Free Press, Macmillan

Galbraith, J.K. (2019) 'The unsustainability of inequality', *Project Syndicate*, August, New York, www.project-syndicate.org/onpoint/the-unsustainability-of-inequality-by-james-k--galbraith-2019-08

George, S. (2015) *Shadow Sovereigns: How Global Corporations Are Seizing Power*, Cambridge/Malden, MA: Polity

GHW (Global Health Watch) (2017) *Global Health Watch 5: An Alternative World Health Report*, London/New York: Zed Books

Goldblatt, D. (1996) *Social Theory and the Environment*, Cambridge/Malden, MA: Polity

González, C.G. (2011) 'The global politics of food: sustainability and subordination', *University of Miami Inter-American Law Review*, 43(1): 77–87

Gray, K. and Gills, B.K. (2016) 'South–South cooperation and the rise of the Global South', *Third World Quarterly*, 37(4), April: 557–74

Greig, A., Hulme, D. and Turner, M. (2007) *Challenging Global Inequality*, Basingstoke/New York: Palgrave Macmillan

Handelman, H. (2013) *The Challenge of Third World Development*, 7th edn, Boston: Pearson

Hanefeld, J. (ed.) (2015) *Globalization and Health*, Maidenhead/New York: McGraw-Hill/Open University Press

Hannerz, U. (2001) *Transnational Connections: Culture, People, Places*, London/New York: Routledge

Hardt, M. and Negri, A. (2019) 'Empire, twenty years on', *New Left Review*, 120, Nov/Dec: 67-92

Harrison, D. (1988) *The Sociology of Modernization and Development*, London, Winchester, Sydney/Wellington: Unwin Hyman

Harvey, D. (1989) *The Condition of Postmodernity*, Oxford/Cambridge, MA: Blackwell

Haslam, P.A., Schafer, J. and Beaudet, P. (eds) (2017) *Introduction to International Development: Approaches, Actors, Issues, and Practice*, 3rd edn, Oxford: Oxford University Press

Held, D. and McGrew, A. (eds) (2002) *The Global Transformations Reader*, 2nd edn, Cambridge: Polity

Held, D., McGrew, A. and Perraton, J. (2001) *Global Transformations: Politics, Economics and Culture*, Cambridge: Polity

Heeks, R. (2018) *Information and Communication Technology for Development (ICT4D)*, Abingdon/New York: Routledge

Hertz, N. (2001) *The Silent Takeover: Global Capitalism and the Death of Democracy*, London: William Heinemann

Heyd, T. (2020) 'COVID-19 and climate change in the times of the Anthropocene', *The Anthropocene Review*, September, https://journals.sagepub.com/doi/10.1177/2053019620961799

Hickel, J. (2014) 'The "girl effect": liberalism, empowerment and the contradictions of development', *Third World Quarterly*, 35(8): 1355–73, www.tandfonline.com/doi/abs/10.1080/01436597.2014.946250

Hickel, J. (2016) 'The true extent of global poverty and hunger: questioning the good news narrative of the Millennium Development Goals', *Third World Quarterly*, 37(5): 749–67

Hickel, J. (2018) *The Divide: A Brief Guide to Global Inequality and Its Solutions*, London: Windmill Books

Hickel, J. (2019) 'The contradiction of the sustainable development goals: growth versus ecology on a finite planet', *Sustainable Development*, 27(5): 873–84, https://doi.org/10.1002/sd.1947

Hirst, P., Thompson, G. and Bromley, S. (2009) *Globalization in Question*, 3rd edn, Cambridge/Malden, MA: Polity

Holden, A. (2013) *Tourism, Poverty and Development*, London/New York: Routledge

Hollington, A., Salverda, T., Schwarz, T. and Tappe, O. (2015) 'Concepts of the Global South: voices from around the world', Global South Studies Center, University of Cologne, http://kups.ub.uni-koeln.de/6399

Hopper, P. (2018) *Understanding Development*, 2nd edn, Cambridge/Malden, MA: Polity

Huntington, S.P. (2002) *The Clash of Civilizations and the Remaking of the World Order*, New York: Simon & Schuster

IHME (Institute for Health Metrics and Evaluation) (2020) *Financing Global Health 2019: Tracking Health Spending in a Time of Crisis*, Seattle, WA, IHME, www.healthdata.org/policy-report/financing-global-health-2019-tracking-health-spending-time-crisis

IMF (International Monetary Fund) (2018) *World Economic Outlook, April 2018: Cyclical Upswing, Structural Change*, www.imf.org/en/Publications/WEO

Inkeles, A. and Smith, D.H. (1974) *Becoming Modern: Individual Change in Six Developing Countries*, Cambridge, MA: Harvard University Press

Investopedia (2022) Lorenz curve example, www.investopedia.com/terms/l/lorenz-curve.asp

Kingsbury, D., McKay, J., Hunt, J., McGillivray, M. and Clarke, M. (2016) *International Development: Issues and Challenges*, 3rd edn, London/New York: Palgrave

Klein, N. (2014) *This Changes Everything: Capitalism vs. the Climate*, London/New York: Penguin Books

Korten, D.C. (1995) *When Corporations Rule the World*, San Francisco, CA: Berrett-Koehler

Kothari, A., Salleh, A., Escobar, A., Demaria, F. and Acosta, A. (eds) (2019) *Pluriverse: A Post-Development Dictionary*, New Delhi: Tulika Books

Kroll, C. (2015) *Sustainable Development Goals: Are the Rich Countries Ready?*, SDG Index Report 2015, Bertelsmann Stiftung: Gütersloh, www.sdgindex.org/reports/sdg-index-report-2015

Laclau, E. (1971) 'Feudalism and capitalism in Latin America', *New Left Review*, 1/67, May–June: 19–38

Lakner, C., Gerszon Mahler, D., Negre, M. and Prydz, E.B. (2020) 'How much does reducing inequality matter for global poverty?', World Bank eLibrary, https://elibrary.worldbank.org/doi/pdf/10.1596/33902

Lancet (2020) 'Global health: time for radical change?', Editorial, *The Lancet*, 396(10258): 1129, www.thelancet.com/journals/lancet/article/PIIS0140-6736(20)32131-0/fulltext?dgcid=raven_jbs_etoc_email

Latouche, S. (1996) *The Westernization of the World: The Significance, Scope and Limits of the Drive Towards Global Uniformity*, Cambridge: Polity

Latouche, S. (2009) *Farewell to Growth*, Cambridge/Malden, MA: Polity

Lerner, D. (1964) *The Passing of Traditional Society: Modernizing the Middle East*, New York: The Free Press

Live-counter.com (2022) Cars worldwide: How many cars are in the world?, www.live-counter.com/number-of-cars

Livingstone, J. (2019) *Self-Devouring Growth: A Planetary Parable as Told from Southern Africa*, London/Durham, NC: Duke University Press

Lomborg, B. (2007) *Cool It: The Skeptical Environmentalist's Guide to Global Warming*, London: Cyan/Marshall Cavendish

Lundestad, G. (2010) *East, West, North, South: Major Developments in International Politics since 1945*, 6th edn, London/New Delhi/Singapore/Thousand Oaks, CA: Sage

Mandela, N. (1990) Speech, Madison Park High School, Boston, 23 June

Mandela, N. (2005) 'Make poverty history', Speech, Trafalgar Square, London, 3 February

Manuel, G. (1974) *The Fourth World: An Indian Reality*, Cambridge, Ontario: Collier-Macmillan

Martinelli, A. (2005) *Global Modernization: Rethinking the Project of Modernity*, London/New Delhi/Thousand Oaks, CA: Sage

McClelland, D.C. (1961) *The Achieving Society*, Princeton, NJ: Van Nostrand

McLuhan, M. (1962) *The Gutenberg Galaxy: The Making of Typographic Man*, Toronto/Buffalo/London: University of Toronto Press

McMichael, P. (2016) *Development and Social Change: A Global Perspective*, London/New Delhi/Singapore/Thousand Oaks, CA: Sage

Meadows, D.H., Meadows, D.L., Randers, J. and Behrens III, W.W. (1972) *The Limits to Growth: A Report for the Club of Rome's Project on the Predicament of Mankind*, New York: Universe Books

Meijer, J.R., Huijbregts, M.A.J., Schotten, K.C.G.J. and Schipper, A.M. (2018) 'Global patterns of current and future road infrastructure', *Environmental Research Letters*, 13(6): 1–10, https://iopscience.iop.org/article/10.1088/1748-9326/aabd42

Momsen, J. (2020) *Gender and Development*, 3rd edn, Abingdon/New York: Routledge

Moore, B. Jr (1966) *Social Origins of Dictatorship and Democracy: Lord and Peasant in the Making of the Modern World*, Boston, MA: Beacon Press

Nederveen Pieterse, J. (2000) 'After post-development', *Third World Quarterly*, 21(2): 175–91

Nederveen Pieterse, J.N. (2009) 'Postdevelopment', in R. Kitchin and N. Thrift (eds) *International Encyclopedia of Human Geography*, Vol. 8: 339–43

Nederveen Pieterse, J. (2010) *Development Theory*, 2nd edn, London/New Delhi/Singapore/Thousand Oaks, CA: Sage

Nederveen Pieterse, J. (2012) 'Twenty-first century globalization: a new development era', *Forum for Development Studies*, 39(3): 367–85, www.tandfonline.com/toc/sfds20/39/3

Nederveen Pieterse, J. (2018) *Multipolar Globalization: Emerging Economies and Development*, Abingdon/New York: Routledge

NEF (New Economics Foundation) (2019) Happy Planet Index: how happy is the planet?, https://happyplanetindex.org

NSO India (2020) *Annual Report 2020: Periodic Labour Force Survey*, New Delhi: Government of India National Statistical Office

Nunan, F. (2015) *Understanding Poverty and the Environment: Analytical Frameworks and Approaches*, London/New York: Routledge

Nussey, B. (2019) 'The Earth gets more solar energy in one hour than the entire world uses in a year', Freeing Energy, 7 July, www.freeingenergy.com/the-earth-gets-more-solar-energy-in-one-hour-than-the-entire-world-uses-in-a-year

Nyerere, J. (1979) 'Third world negotiating strategy', *Third World Quarterly*, 1(2): 20–3

O'Callaghan-Gordo, C. and Antó, J.M. (2020) 'COVID-19: the disease of the Anthropocene', *Environmental Research*, 187 (May), doi.org/10.1016/j.envres.2020.109683

Ohmae, K. (2005) *The Next Global Stage: Challenges and Opportunities in Our Borderless World*, New Jersey: Wharton School Publishing

OPHI (Oxford Poverty and Human Development Initiative) (2015) Global Multidimensional Poverty Index 2015, www.ophi.org.uk/wp-content/uploads/Global-MPI-8-pager_10_15.pdf

OPHI/UNDP (Oxford Poverty and Human Development Initiative/United Nations Development Programme) (2019) *Global Multidimensional Poverty Index 2019: Illuminating Inequalities*, https://ophi.org.uk/global-multidimensional-poverty-index-2019-illuminating-inequalities

OPHI/UNDP (2020) *Global Multidimensional Poverty Index 2020: Charting Pathways out of Multidimensional Poverty: Achieving the SDGs*, https://ophi.org.uk/global-mpi-report-2020

Oxfam International (2019) *The Power of Education to Fight Inequality*, Oxford: Oxfam, www.oxfam.org/en/research/power-education-fight-inequality

Oxfam International (2020a) *India: Extreme Inequality in Numbers*, Oxford, www.oxfam.org/en/india-extreme-inequality-numbers

Oxfam International (2020b) *Time to Care*, Oxford, www.oxfam.org/en/research/time-care

Oxfam International (2020c) *Gender Justice and Women's Rights*, Oxfam International, www.oxfam.org/en/what-we-do/issues/gender-justice-and-womens-rights

Oxfam International (2020d) 'The hunger virus: how COVID-19 is fuelling hunger in a hungry world', www.oxfam.org/en/research/hunger-virus-how-covid-19-fuelling-hunger-hungry-world

Oxfam International (2020e) 'Confronting carbon inequality', Oxfam media briefing, 21 September, www.oxfam.org/en/research/confronting-carbon-inequality

Pagel, H., Ranke, K. and Köhler, J. (2014) 'The use of the concept "global south" in social science and humanities', presented at Globaler Süden/Global South: Kritische Perspektiven, Symposium, Humboldt University, Berlin, 11 July

Park, S. (2018) *International Organisations and Global Problems: Theories and Explanations*, Cambridge: Cambridge University Press

Parker, M. and Wilson, G. (2000) 'Diseases of poverty', in T. Allen and A. Thomas (eds) *Poverty and Development: Into the 21st Century*, pp 75–98, Oxford: Oxford University Press

Peet, R. and Hartwick, E. (2015) *Theories of Development*, 3rd edn, New York: The Guilford Press

Peterson, D. (2018) *Tourism, Development and Globalization*, New York: Clanrye International

Pilger, J. (2002) *The New Rulers of the World*, London/New York: Verso

Pleyers, G. (2011) *Alter-Globalization: Becoming Actors in the Global Age*, Cambridge/Malden, MA: Polity

Poku, N.K., Whiteside, A. and Sandkjaer, B. (eds) (2010) *AIDS and Governance*, Aldershot: Ashgate

Pratt, L.A. (2011) 'Decreasing dirty dumping? A re-evaluation of toxic waste colonialism and the global management of transboundary hazardous waste', *William & Mary Environmental Law and Policy Review*, 35(2), https://scholarship.law.wm.edu/wmelpr/vol35/iss2/5

PRB (Population Reference Bureau) (2018) '2018 World population data sheet with focus on changing age structures', www.prb.org/resources/2018-world-population-data-sheet-with-focus-on-changing-age-structures

Project Drawdown (2020) 'Improve society: health and education', Solution summary, www.drawdown.org/solutions/health-and-education

Rinaldi, A. and Salerno, I. (2020) 'The tourism gender gap and its potential impact on the development of the emerging countries', *Qual Quant*, 54: 1465–77, https://doi.org/10.1007/s11135-019-00881-x

Rist, G. (2014) *The History of Development: From Western Origins to Global Faith*, 4th edn, London/New York: Zed Books

Ritchie, H. and Roser, M. (2020) 'CO_2 and greenhouse gas emissions', Our World In Data , https://ourworldindata.org/co2-and-other-greenhouse-gas-emissions

Ritzer, G. (2015) *Globalization: A Basic Text*, 2nd edn, Chichester, Oxford/Malden, MA: Wiley-Blackwell

Ritzer, G. (2019) *The McDonaldization of Society: Into the Digital Age*, 9th edn, London/New Delhi/Singapore/Thousand Oaks, CA: Sage

Rodrik, D. (2016) 'Premature deindustrialization', *Journal of Economic Growth*, 21(1): 1–33

Roser, M. (2019) 'Future population growth', Our World In Data, November https://ourworldindata.org/future-population-growth#citation

Roser, M. and Ortiz-Ospina, E. (2019) 'Global extreme poverty', Our World In Data, November, https://ourworldindata.org/extreme-poverty

Roser, M., Ortiz-Ospina, E. and Ritchie, H. (2019a) 'Life expectancy', Our World In Data, October, https://ourworldindata.org/life-expectancy

Roser, M., Ritchie, H. and Dadonaite, B. (2019b) 'Child and infant mortality', Our World In Data, November, https://ourworldindata.org/child-mortality

Rostow, W.W. ([1960] 1990) *The Stages of Economic Growth: A Non-Communist Manifesto*, 3rd edn, Cambridge: Cambridge University Press

Sachs, W. (ed.) (1992) *The Development Dictionary: A Guide to Knowledge as Power*, London: Zed Books

Sachs, W. (ed.) (2019) *The Development Dictionary: A Guide to Knowledge and Power*, revised edn, London: Zed Books

Sauvy, A. (1952) 'Trois mondes, une planète', *L'Observateur*, no. 118, 14 August

Scholte, J.A. (2005) *Globalization: A Critical Introduction*, 2nd edn, Basingstoke/New York: Palgrave Macmillan

Schumacher, E.F. (1973) *Small is Beautiful: A Study of Economics as if People Mattered*, London: Blond & Briggs

SDSN (2020) *Sustainable Development Report 2020*, Cambridge: Cambridge University Press, https://sdgindex.org/reports/sustainable-development-report-2020

Sen, A. (1989) 'Development as capability expansion', *Journal of Development Planning*, 19(1): 41–58

Sen, A. (1999) *Development as Freedom*, Oxford: Oxford University Press

Shiva, V. (2002) *Staying Alive: Women, Ecology and Survival in India*, New Delhi, London/New Delhi: Zed Books

Singh, K. (1988) 'Development is the best contraceptive', *Interdisciplinary Science Reviews*, 13(4): 301–2

Skocpol, T. (1977) 'Wallerstein's world capitalist system: a theoretical and historical critique', *American Journal of Sociology*, 82(5): 1075–90

Statista (2021) *Smartphone Ownership Rate by Country*, www.statista.com/statistics/539395/smartphone-penetration-worldwide-by-country

Stiglitz, J. (2017) *Globalization and Its Discontents Revisited: Anti-Globalization in the Era of Trump*, London/New York: Penguin

STWR (Share the World's Resources) (2006) *The Brandt Report: A Summary*, 31 January, www.sharing.org/information-centre/reports/brandt-report-summary

Sumner, A. (2016) *Global Poverty: Deprivation, Distribution and Development since the Cold War*, Oxford: OUP

Sumner, A. and Tribe, M. (2008) *International Development Studies: Theories and Methods in Research and Practice*, London/New Delhi/Thousand Oaks, CA: Sage

Taylor, K. and Silver, S. (2019) *Smartphone Ownership Is Growing Rapidly around the World, but Not Always Equally*, Washington, DC: Pew Research Centre, www.pewresearch.org/search/smartphone+ownership

Thomas, A. (2000) 'Meanings and views of development', in T. Allen and A. Thomas (eds) *Poverty and Development into the 21st Century*, Oxford: Oxford University Press, pp 23–48

Thunberg, G. (2019) *No One Is Too Small to Make a Difference*, London/New York: Penguin Books

Tilak, J.B.G. (2018) *Education and Development in India: Critical Issues in Public Policy and Development*, London/New York: Palgrave Macmillan

Tribe, M., Nixson, F. and Sumner, A. (2010) *Economics and Development Studies*, Abingdon/New York: Routledge

Truman, H.S. (1949) Inaugural address, 20 January, *Documents on American Foreign Relations*, Princeton, NJ: Princeton University Press

UN (United Nations) (1992) 'Rio Declaration on Environment and Development 1992', *Report of The United Nations Conference on Environment and Development*, Annex 1, Rio de Janeiro, 3–14 June, www.un.org/documents/ga/conf151/aconf15126-1annex1.htm

UNAIDS (2021) *Global HIV & AIDS statistics*, www.unaids.org/en/resources/fact-sheet

UNCTAD (United Nations Conference on Trade and Development) (2017) *Economic Development in Africa: Tourism for Transformative and Inclusive Growth*, UN Conference on Trade and Development, Report: New York/Geneva, https://unctad.org/webflyer/economic-development-africa-report-2017

UNCTAD (2019) *Digital Economy Report 2019. Value Creation and Capture: Implications for Developing Countries*, New York: UN Publications, https://unctad.org/webflyer/digital-economy-report-2019

UN DESA (United Nations Department of Economic and Social Affairs) (2015) Transforming our world: the 2030 Agenda for Sustainable Development, https://sdgs.un.org/2030agenda

UN DESA (2017) *Policy Brief #53: Reflection on Development Policy in the 1970s and 1980s*, www.un.org/development/desa/dpad/category/publications-general/wess

UN DESA (2019a) *World Population Prospects 2019: Highlights*, New York: UNDESA, https://population.un.org/wpp

UN DESA (2019b) *World Mortality 2019: Data Booklet*, www.un.org/en/development/desa/population/publications/index.asp

UN DESA (2020a) *Least Developed Countries (LDCs)*, www.un.org/development/desa/dpad/least-developed-country-category.html

UN DESA (2020b) *The Sustainable Development Goals Report 2020*, https://unstats.un.org/sdgs/report/2020

UN DESA (2020c) *World Social Report 2020: Inequality in a Rapidly Changing World*, www.un.org/development/desa/dspd/world-social-report/2020-2.html

UN DESA (2021) *World Social Report 2021: Reconsidering Rural Development*, www.un.org/development/desa/dspd/world-social-report/2021-2.html

UNDP (United Nations Development Programme) (1990) *Human Development Report 1994: Concept and Measurement of Human Development*, New York/Oxford: Oxford University Press, https://hdr.undp.org/en/reports/global/hdr1990

UNDP (1992) *Human Development Report 1992: Global Dimensions of Human Development*, https://hdr.undp.org/en/reports/global/hdr1992

UNDP (1994) *Human Development Report 1994: New Dimensions of Human Security*, http://hdr.undp.org/en/content/human-development-report-1994

UNDP (1997) *Human Development Report 1997: Human Development to Eradicate Poverty*, http://hdr.undp.org/en/content/human-development-report-1997

UNDP (2010) *Human Development Report 2010: The Real Wealth of Nations: Pathways to Human Development*, https://hdr.undp.org/en/content/human-development-report-2010

UNDP (2015) *Sustainable Development Goals*, www.undp.org/publications/sustainable-development-goals-booklet

UNDP (2019) *Human Development Report 2019. Beyond Income, Beyond Averages, Beyond Today: Inequalities in Human Development in the 21st Century*, http://hdr.undp.org/en/2019-report

UNDP (2020) *Human Development Report 2020. The Next Frontier: Human Development and the Anthropocene*, New York: UNDP, http://hdr.undp.org/en/2020-report

UNDP (2022) What is human development?, Human Development Reports, https://hdr.undp.org/en/content/what-human-development

UNDP/UNFCCC (2019) *The Heat is On: Taking Stock of Global Climate Ambition*, New York/Bonn: UNDP/UNFCCC, https://outlook.ndcs.undp.org

UNESCO (United Nations Educational, Scientific and Cultural Organization) (2017) *Reducing Global Poverty through Universal Primary and Secondary Education*, https://en.unesco.org/gem-report/publications

UNESCO (2020) *Inclusion and Education: All Means All*, Paris: UNESCO, https://en.unesco.org/gem-report/report/2020/inclusion

UN FAO (2002) *The State of Food Insecurity in the World 2001*, Rome, www.fao.org/3/y1500e/y1500e00.htm

UN FAO (2020) *The State of Food Security and Nutrition in the World, 2020*, Rome, www.fao.org/documents/card/en/c/ca9692en

UN FAO, IFAD, UNICEF, UN WFP and WHO (2020a) *The State of Food Security and Nutrition in the World 2020: Transforming Food Systems for Affordable Healthy Diets*, Rome, https://doi.org/10.4060/ca9692en

UN FAO, ECA and AUC (2020b) *Africa: Regional Overview of Food Security and Nutrition 2019*, Accra, www.fao.org/documents/card/en/c/ca7343en

United Nations Foundation (2020) *Emerging Issues 2020*, https://unfoundation.org/what-we-do/issues/emerging-issues

UNFPA (2020) *Against My Will: Defying the Practices that Harm Women and Girls and Undermine Equality*, State of the World Population 2020, New York: UNFPA, www.unfpa.org/swop

UN General Assembly Resolution (1961) Resolution 1710 (XVI). United Nations Development Decade: A programme for international economic co-operation (I), https://digitallibrary.un.org/record/204609?ln=en

UNHCR (2020) *Global Trends: Forced Displacement in 2019*, www.unhcr.org/search?comid=56b079c44&&cid=49aea93aba&tags=globaltrends

UNICEF (2014) *Ending Child Marriage: Progress and Prospects*, New York: UNICEF, https://data.unicef.org/resources/ending-child-marriage-progress-and-prospects

UNICEF (2020) *Addressing the Learning Crisis: An Urgent Need to Better Finance Education for the Poorest Children*, www.unicef.org/reports/addressing-learning-crisis-2020

UNICEF/WHO (2019) *Low Birthweight Estimates: Levels and trends 2000–2015*, www.unicef.org/reports/UNICEF-WHO-low-birthweight-estimates-2019

UN News (2020) Waiting to declare famine 'will be too late for Yemenis on brink of starvation', https://news.un.org/en/story/2020/07/1068101

UN Security Council (2018) Resolution 2417, 24 May, http://undocs.org/S/RES/2417(2018)

UN WFP (2019) *Fact Sheet: Hunger & Conflict*, www.wfp.org/publications/2019-hunger-and-conflict-factsheet

UN WFP (2020) *Hunger Map 2020*, www.wfp.org/publications/hunger-map-2020

UN Women (2016) *Women and Sustainable Development Goals*, UNDESA, https://sustainabledevelopment.un.org/index.php?page=view&type=400&nr=2322&menu=1515

UNWHO (2020) Air pollution – the silent killer, Infographic, www.euro.who.int/en/health-topics/environment-and-health/air-quality/news/news/2018/5/over-half-a-million-premature-deaths-annually-in-the-european-region-attributable-to-household-and-ambient-air-pollution/infographic-air-pollution-the-silent-killer

UNWTO (UN World Tourism Organization) (2019a) *International Tourism Highlights 2019 Edition*, Madrid, www.unwto.org/publication/international-tourism-highlights-2019-edition

UNWTO (2019b) *Global Report on Women in Tourism – Second Edition*, Madrid, https://doi.org/10.18111/9789284420384

UNWTO (2020) *International Tourism Highlights 2020 Edition*, Madrid, www.e-unwto.org/doi/book/10.18111/9789284422456

UNWTO (2022) UNWTO tourism data dashboard, www.unwto. org/unwto-tourism-dashboard

UUKi (2020) *International Facts and Figures 2020*, London: Universities UK International, www.universitiesuk.ac.uk/policy-and-analysis/ reports

von der Leyen, U. (2020) State of the Union Address by President von der Leyen, European Parliament Plenary, Brussels, 16 September, https://ec.europa.eu/commission/presscorner/detail/en/SPEECH_ 20_1655

Wallace-Wells, D. (2019) *The Uninhabitable Earth: A Story of the Future*, London/New York: Penguin Books

Wallerstein, I. (1974) *The Modern World System: Capitalist Agriculture and the Origins of the European World Economy in the Sixteenth Century*, New York: Academic Press

Wallerstein, I. (1979) *The Capitalist World-Economy*, Cambridge: Cambridge University Press

Waters, M. (2001) *Globalization*, 2nd edn, London/New York: Routledge

WCED (World Commission on Environment and Development) (1987) *Our Common Future*, Brundtland Report, Geneva: WCED

Weatherby, J.N., Arceneaux, C., Leithner, A., Reed, I., Timms, B.F. and Zhang, S.N. (2018) *The Other World*, 10th edn, London/New York: Routledge

WEF (World Economic Forum) (2006) *The Global Gender Gap Report 2006*, Geneva: WEF, www3.weforum.org/docs/WEF_GenderGap_ Report_2006.pdf

WEF (2020) *Global Gender Gap Index 2020*, https://reports.weforum. org/global-gender-gap-report-2020/the-global-gender-gap- index-2020/results-and-analysis/

Welthungerhilfe and Concern Worldwide (2021) *Global Hunger Index 2021*, Bonn/Dublin, www.globalhungerindex.org/download/all. html

WHO (World Health Organization) (1946) *Constitution of the World Health Organization*, New York: WHO, www.who.int/about/who- we-are/constitution

WHO (1978) *Alma-Ata 1978: Primary Health Care*, Geneva: WHO, www.unicef.org/about/history/files/Alma_Ata_conference_1978_report.pdf

WHO (1986) The 1st International Conference on Health Promotion, Ottawa, 1986, www.who.int/teams/health-promotion/enhanced-wellbeing/first-global-conference

WHO (1995) *The World Health Report: Bridging the Gaps*, Geneva: WHO, https://pubmed.ncbi.nlm.nih.gov/8534341

WHO (2010) *Global status report on noncommunicable diseases*, Geneva: WHO, www.who.int/chp/ncd_global_status_report/en

WHO (2018) *Noncommunicable Diseases: Country Profiles 2018*, Geneva: WHO, www.who.int/nmh/publications/ncd-profiles-2018/en

WHO (2019) *World Report on Vision*, Geneva: WHO, www.who.int/publications/i/item/9789241516570

WHO (2020a) *Noncommunicable Diseases*, Geneva: WHO, www.afro.who.int/health-topics/noncommunicable-diseases

WHO (2020b) *The Impact of the COVID-19 Pandemic on Noncommunicable Disease Resources and Services*, Geneva: WHO, https://apps.who.int/iris/handle/10665/334136

WHO (2020c) *World Health Statistics 2020*, www.who.int/data/gho/publications

WHO (2020d) Soil-transmitted helminth infections, Geneva: WHO, www.who.int/news-room/fact-sheets/detail/soil-transmitted-helminth-infections

WHO (2020e) *Road Traffic Injuries*, Geneva: WHO, www.who.int/news-room/fact-sheets/detail/road-traffic-injuries

WHO/UNICEF (2018) *Declaration of Astana*, www.who.int/teams/primary-health-care/conference/declaration

Willis, K. (2021) *Theories and Practices of Development*, 3rd edn, Abingdon/New York: Routledge

World Atlas (2020) *The Poorest Countries in the World*, www.worldatlas.com/articles/the-poorest-countries-in-the-world.html

World Bank (1991) *World Development Report 1991: The Challenge of Development*, New York: Oxford University Press, https://openknowledge.worldbank.org/handle/10986/5974

World Bank (1994) *Infrastructure for Development*, World Development Report 1994, Washington, DC: World Bank Group, https://openknowledge.worldbank.org/handle/10986/5977

World Bank (2010) *Development and Climate Change*, World Development Report 2010, Washington, DC: World Bank Group, https://openknowledge.worldbank.org/handle/10986/4387

World Bank (2016*) Digital Dividends*, World Development Report 2016, Washington, DC: World Bank Group, www.worldbank.org/en/publication/wdr2016

World Bank (2017a) *Forcibly Displaced: Toward a Development Approach Supporting Refugees, the Internally Displaced, and Their Hosts*, Washington, DC: World Bank, https://openknowledge.worldbank.org/handle/10986/25016

World Bank (2017b) *The High Toll of Traffic Injuries: Unacceptable and Preventable*, Washington DC: World Bank, https://openknowledge.worldbank.org/handle/10986/29129

World Bank (2018) *Poverty and Shared Prosperity 2018: Piecing Together the Poverty Puzzle*, New York: IBRD/World Bank, www.worldbank.org/en/publication/poverty-and-shared-prosperity-2018

World Bank (2019) Open Data, https://data.worldbank.org

World Bank (2020a) *Poverty and Shared Prosperity 2020: Reversals of Fortune*, Washington, DC: IBRD/World Bank, www.worldbank.org/en/publication/poverty-and-shared-prosperity

World Bank (2020b) *Global Estimate of Children in Monetary Poverty: An Update*, Poverty and Equity discussion paper, Washington, DC: World Bank Group, http://documents.worldbank.org/curated/en/966791603123453576/Global-Estimate-of-Children-in-Monetary-Poverty-An-Update

World Bank (2020c) *Atlas of Sustainable Development Goals 2020: From World Development Indicators*, Washington, DC: World Bank Group, https://datatopics.worldbank.org/sdgatlas

World Bank (2021a) *From Crisis to Green, Resilient and Inclusive Recovery*, World Development Report 2021, Washington, DC: World Bank Group, https://openknowledge.worldbank.org/handle/10986/36067

World Bank (2021b) World Development Indicators, Gross domestic product 2020, PPP, https://databank.worldbank.org/data/download/GDP_PPP.pdf

World Inequality Lab (2018) *World Inequality Report 2018*, https://wir2018.wid.world

WSIS (World Summit on the Information Society) (2019) *WSIS Forum 2019: WSIS Action Lines Contributing towards Empowering People and Ensuring Inclusiveness and Equality*, Geneva: WSIS, www.itu.int/net4/wsis/forum/2019/Home/Outcomes#documents

Youde, J. (2012) *Global Health Governance*, Cambridge/Malden, MA: Polity

Ziai, A. (2015) 'Post-development: premature burials and haunting ghosts', *Development and Change*, 46(4): 833–54

Ziai, A. (2017a) 'Post-development 25 years after *The Development Dictionary*', *Third World Quarterly*, 38(12): 2547–58

Ziai, A. (2017b) 'I am not a post-developmentalist, but …': the influence of post-development on development studies', *Third World Quarterly*, 38(12): 2719–34

Index

References to figures are in *italics*; references to tables are in **bold**